JESUS

the One and Only

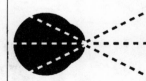

JESUS
the One and Only

BETH MOORE

Walker Large Print • Waterville, Maine

Published in 2006 by arrangement with Broadman & Holman Publishers.

The text of this Large Print edition is unabridged. Other aspects of the book may vary from the original edition.

Set in 16 pt. Plantin by Christina S. Huff.

Printed in the United States on permanent paper.

Library of Congress Cataloging-in-Publication Data

Moore, Beth, 1957–
    Jesus, the one and only / by Beth Moore. — Large print ed.
      p. cm.
    Includes bibliographical references.
    ISBN 1-59415-146-6 (lg. print : sc : alk. paper)
    1. Jesus Christ.   2. Large type books.   I. Title.
BT203.M66 2006
   232—dc22   2006008969

Dedication

To Marge Caldwell,
my mother and teacher in ministry.
You were the first person whose passionate
love for Jesus took my breath away.
I will never comprehend how I have been so
blessed by God to know you,
love you, and learn from you.
God has so tightly knitted the threads of our
ministries together that I'm not sure where
one ends and the other begins.
Something of you is lived out in me every
single good day. You taught me
countless things like how to be not only a
woman in ministry but also a lady.
Your love for Jesus the One and Only
is wildly contagious.
I am only one of many
who caught it feverishly.
How will I ever thank you
for all you have invested in me?
I love you dearly.

Contents

Acknowledgments   13

Introduction   17

Part 1   The Word Made Flesh   21

    Chapter 1   Unexpected Company   23

    Chapter 2   Give Him the Name
                  Jesus   32

    Chapter 3   Kindred Hearts   42

    Chapter 4   His Name Is John   51

    Chapter 5   A Savior Is Born   57

    Chapter 6   In the Stable with
                  Mary   67

Part 2   The Son of God   75

    Chapter 7   The Lord's Christ   77

Chapter 8   The Child Jesus   87

Chapter 9   Picturing Jesus   97

Chapter 10   Waist Deep in Jordan   108

Chapter 11   Wilderness Welcome
                  to Ministry   122

Chapter 12   The Preacher   130

Part 3   The Way and Life   141

Chapter 13   "What Is This
                  Teaching?"   143

Chapter 14   A House Call   152

Chapter 15   A Catch in Deep
                  Waters   161

Chapter 16   If You Are Willing   171

Chapter 17   The Lord of the
                  Sabbath   180

Part 4   The Esteem of Man   189

Chapter 18   Amazing Faith   191

Chapter 19   Compassion without
                      Restraint   199

Chapter 20   A Bout with Doubt   208

Chapter 21   Loving Much   216

Chapter 22   His True Brothers
                      and Sisters   228

Part 5   The Christ of God   239

Chapter 23   The Other Side   241

Chapter 24   Interwoven Wonders 247

Chapter 25   Extended Authority   254

Chapter 26   Baskets of Blessing   261

Chapter 27   Confessions of the
                      Heart   268

Part 6   The Necessity   279

Chapter 28   Who Is This Man?   281

Chapter 29   Everything Is
                      Possible   293

Chapter 30   The Road to
              Greatness   303

Chapter 31   The Seventy-two   312

Chapter 32   The Heart of a
              Neighbor   320

Chapter 33   A True Tale of Two
              Sisters   326

Part 7   The Infinite Treasure   337

Chapter 34   Someone Stronger   339

Chapter 35   His Treasure,
              Your Treasure   348

Chapter 36   Keep Your Lamps
              Burning   356

Chapter 37   How Often Have I
              Longed?   361

Chapter 38   When God Runs   369

Part 8   The Answer   379

Chapter 39   Causing Others
              to Sin   381

Chapter 40   Where Are the Nine?   389

Chapter 41   Lacking One Thing   399

Chapter 42   A Wee Little Man   410

Chapter 43   Signs of His Coming   422

Part 9   The Lamb of God   431

Chapter 44   An Available
                     Conspirator   433

Chapter 45   The Last Supper   441

Chapter 46   Sifted like Wheat   451

Chapter 47   The Kiss of Betrayal   461

Chapter 48   A Serious Case
                     of Denial   471

Part 10   The Risen Hope   483

Chapter 49   The Ultimate Mock
                     Court   485

Chapter 50   To the Cross   496

Chapter 51   He Has Risen!   508

Chapter 52   A Burning Heart   518

Chapter 53   Jesus Himself   528

Endnotes   542

Acknowledgments

I really struggled with the overwhelming task of writing a book on the life of Christ. First of all, others far brighter and more knowledgeable already filled the shelves of libraries. Second, I feared that human commentary might accomplish little more than a detraction from what the Gospels have already divinely stated. I found the task extremely intimidating from beginning to end. I distinctly recall my chief request of God when I began this book: "Just don't let me embarrass You!" Though God no doubt watches over every word of commentary voiced over Scripture, I can't help but think He's even more particular when the subject matter is His one and only Son.

That Son of His is the dearest thing in my whole life. I don't have pens or paper enough to express my gratitude for the privilege to know Him and love Him. The little I know is so transforming and revolutionary to me that I yearn to know more. My chief request of God is that He will supernaturally flood my life with an unending, ever-increasing desire for His Son. Jesus is not only my delight; He is my safety. Loving Him with absolute abandon is no doubt in my own best interest. As one who has been delivered from a life of defeat and hidden self-destruction, I have found the psalmist's words to be my greatest reality: His love is indeed better than life. My deepest desire for every man, woman, youth, and child is to find that love.

My Dear Redeemer and Love of my life, I am so grateful for your measureless grace. Thank You, Lord Jesus, for loving me when I was so unlovely and for making my life — as we would say it back home — mean more than a hill of beans.

I also wish to thank my dear friend and editor, Dale McCleskey, for once again re-formatting a work that was originally in Bible study form so that it might be more easily read. I can pay you no higher compliment than to tell you that I trust your work. This trade book version would not exist without you.

Thank you, Broadman & Holman, for allowing me the privilege of partnering with you in ministry. You have been so gracious to me. And, by the way, this is one of the most beautiful covers I've ever seen. We

14

could never have captured the beauty of Christ's exquisite face, but one day we will see Him! May we stand before Him having done everything possible to invite others to see Him too.

My Father in heaven, I ask one thing for this book above all others. May each reader love Your precious Son more lavishly on the last page than the first.

May God be glorified, Christ magnified, and His bride edified.

Introduction

My romance with Jesus Christ began in a tiny circle of baby-bear chairs in a Sunday school class of a small town church. My teachers were not biblical scholars. They were moms and homemakers. I'm not sure they ever delved into the depths of Scripture or researched a single Greek word. They simply taught what they knew. I don't know any other way to explain what happened next: I believed.

I remember thinking how handsome Jesus was in those watercolor pictures and how I had never seen a man with long hair before. I wondered if my daddy, the Army major, would approve. My favorite picture was the familiar one with the children climbing all over Jesus' lap. As I recall, it was the only one I ever saw that captured Him smiling. I determined quickly that big people bored and upset Him and little people made Him quite happy.

As I recount this simple, unexciting testimony to you, a lump wells in my throat and tears burn in my eyes. Jesus is the most wonderful, most graceful, most exciting, most redemptive thing that has ever happened to me. He is my life. I cannot express on paper my love for Him. It is a love that has grown in incongruous bits and pieces, baby steps, leaps, bounds, tumbles, and falls, . . . decade after decade.

A romance with Christ differs so dramatically from a romance between mortals. I do not wish any other woman to love my husband, Keith, the way I do. How different my romance with Christ! I want all of you to love Him . . . at least as much as I do. I'm jealous for us to want Him more than we want blessing, health, or even breath. I want to know Him so well that my undivided heart can explain, "Because Your love is better than life, my lips will glorify You" (Ps. 63.3). Better than life! God invites mortal creatures — you and me — into a love relationship with the Son of glory. That, my friend, is the meaning of life. Let's partake. Fully. Completely.

We will never spend our time more valuably than in the pursuit of knowing Jesus Christ. My deepest prayer is that this offering would take you another step closer in the noblest pursuit of life. I have very little doubt that I will leave more lacking in this particular book than any God has entrusted to me simply because there is no end to what could be said. And, indeed, must be said. If not by mortal creatures, then by those invisible to our eyes, encircling the throne and in a loud voice, singing, "Worthy is the Lamb!"

He is Jesus.
The One and Only.
Transcendent over all else.
To know Him is to love Him.
To love Him is to long for Him.
To long for Him is to finally reach
soul hands into the One true thing
we need never get enough of.
Jesus.
Take all you want.
Take all you need.
Till soul is fed.
And spirit freed.
Till dust is dust.
And Face you see.
Jesus Christ.
He's all you need.

Part 1

The Word Made Flesh

I am so glad to have you along on this ride, dear one! I would willingly take this particular journey all by myself, but you make it far more wonderful. We have several hundred miles ahead of us, so grab your Bible, a jug full of Living Water, and a durable pair of sandals. Our journey will take us all over Galilee, Jerusalem, Judea, and even across the lake to the "other side." Our goal is simply to walk with Jesus wherever He goes through the pages of Scripture. You and I will drop in on His journey just a few months before His earthly arrival. Interestingly, His trek toward earth began much sooner — "In the beginning," in fact. God's perfect plan of redemption through the "Word made flesh" was already in motion before He breathed the first soul into man. May God astound you with a fresh glimpse of the greatest story ever told.

Commit, dear student of God's Word! Let's see this journey to the very last page! Let's welcome God to completely transform our image of His Son. Let's fall in love with Jesus all over again. Author's Note: Throughout this book many Hebrew and Greek words are defined to clarify the meaning of certain Scripture references. Unless otherwise noted, these definitions are taken from *The Complete Word Study Dictionary of the Old Testament,* Spiros Zodhiates, et al., eds., (Chattanooga, Tenn.: AMG Publishers, 1994) and *The Complete Word Study Dictionary of the New Testament,* Spiros Zodhiates, et al., eds., (Chattanooga, Tenn.: AMG Publishers, 1992).

Chapter 1

Unexpected Company

Luke 1:1–25

"Do not be afraid, Zechariah; your prayer has been heard." (Luke 1:13)

Our study will focus on the Gospel of Luke. In his first verses the "beloved physician" wrote that while many others had also written about Christ, Luke "carefully investigated everything from the beginning." His resulting "orderly account" began in the time of Herod, king of Judea. A priest named Zechariah and his wife Elizabeth were godly people, but they had no children. Elizabeth was barren; and they were both well along in years (Luke 1:6–7). Zechariah's time came to serve as priest, and while he was serving in the temple: "an angel of the Lord appeared to him" (Luke 1:11).

Picture that morning with me. Zechariah

rose from his bed in a small room outside the temple, amazed at the once-in-a-lifetime priestly privilege he feared would never come; after all, he was no spring chicken.

Zechariah's mind surely detoured to his wife of many years. Unlike most of the other priests, he had no children. When his temple service took him from home, Elizabeth was all alone. She handled her empty home with grace, but he knew her childlessness still stung terribly. Jewish homes were meant for children.

Zechariah took extra care to smooth out the white linen fabric and carefully tie the sash of his priestly garments. Not all the priests took their responsibilities so soberly, but Zechariah was a righteous man. He walked through the temple gate with all senses magnified and beheld a sight to take your breath away — the cream-and-gold temple bathing in the morning sun. A few early risers probably already gathered for worship in the courtyard. Little did Zechariah know that the gentle breeze was blowing in far more than just another morning.

First Chronicles 24 provides the detailed background for the story of the priesthood. Aaron had many descendants. Each of the twenty-four divisions of priests served in the temple for one week twice a year and at major festivals. An individual priest could offer the incense at the daily sacrifice only once in his lifetime. Zechariah's only turn had come. Surely he was overwhelmed.

Luke 1:10 tells us that worshipers assembled outside the temple at the time for the burning of the incense. Their custom was to pray individually and simultaneously in the courtyard as the priest was praying for them corporately inside. After he finished his duties, he would come out to them and give them a blessing.

As Zechariah was praying, the angel Gabriel appeared to him saying: "Do not be afraid, Zechariah; your prayer has been heard. Your wife Elizabeth will bear you a son, and you are to give him the name John" (Luke 1:13).

Obviously, the fragrance of the incense wasn't the only thing that ascended to the throne of God that day. Don't miss the significance of the statement "*your* prayer has been heard." The responsibility of the priest on duty was to offer the incense and to pray for the nation of Israel. His purpose was to offer a corporate prayer. Furthermore, the priest's intercession for the nation undoubtedly included a petition for the Messiah, Israel's promised Deliverer and King.

Zechariah would have petitioned the throne of grace on behalf of the nation of Israel and for God to send its long-awaited Messiah.

The old priest could not have known that God had purposely manipulated his appointment that day for a revolutionary reason. Later we will see that many of those who served in the priesthood were not like Zechariah. Many priests could have offered the incense that day with little respect and voiced a repetitious prayer void of anxious expectation. Luke 1:6 tells us that Zechariah and Elizabeth were "upright in the sight of God." The Creator and Sustainer of the universe was ready to answer a prayer that had been prayed for hundreds of years, but He purposely chose a man who could pray an old prayer with a fresh heart.

I don't believe Zechariah's prayers that day were limited to corporate petitions. Whether or not he planned to make a personal request, I believe he did. I think he poured the perfectly mixed ingredients on the fire, inhaled the aroma of incense rising toward heaven, asked God's blessing over the nation of Israel, passionately pleaded for the coming of the Messiah, then, before he turned and walked away, voiced an age-old request from the hearth of his own home.

I will never forget the first time I had an

opportunity to go into the "old city" in Jerusalem. As much as I had enjoyed the trip, it would have been terribly incomplete without going to the Wailing Wall. I knew from my studies that the Wailing Wall is considered to be virtually the most sacred place on earth to an orthodox Jew. As a portion of the sacred temple structure, it signifies the place of most intimate physical closeness to God. Droves of people pray at the Wailing Wall. Many write their requests on small pieces of paper and literally wedge the notes in the wall's crevices. I rose early that morning and had a lengthy time of preparation in prayer. I knew I would have only a few minutes at the wall, and I gave serious thought to the petitions I would make there.

After deep consideration, I recorded the most important requests I could possibly make on a small sheet of paper. Later I stood at that wall as overcome in prayer as I have ever been. After I voiced my petitions through sobs, I wedged my requests in a crack in the wall and left them there. Why did I take it so seriously when I can boldly approach the throne of grace twenty-four hours a day? Because in a common, godless world, I was standing at an uncommon, sacred place. A place where more collective petitions have been poured out to the one true God than any other in the world . . . and I had one chance.

I believe that's why Zechariah may have grasped the most sacred moment of his life to let his personal prayer ascend like incense to the throne of grace. The prayer at that exact moment may not have been for a son. At their ages, perhaps Zechariah and Elizabeth had given up. Or perhaps he remembered Abraham and Sarah, and he knew God could do the impossible. Either way, I believe Zechariah voiced something about the void in their lives and the hurt or disappointment of their own hearts. What the old priest could not possibly have known was how intimately connected would be his corporate prayer for the Messiah and his personal prayer for a son.

Have you almost given up on God answering an earnest, long-term prayer of your heart? Not becoming hopeless over a repetitious request can be terribly challenging. God never missed a single petition from the children of Israel to send their Messiah; nor did He miss a solitary plea from the aching hearts of a childless couple. God does not have some limited supply of power, requiring that we carefully select a few choice things to pray about. God's power is infinite.

God's grace and mercy are drawn deeply from the bottomless well of His heart.

When Zechariah stood at the altar of incense that day and lifted the needs of the nation to the throne, an ample supply of supernatural power and tenderhearted compassion remained in the heart of God to provide not just his needs, but the desire of his heart. God was simply waiting for the perfect time.

Do you have a long-standing prayer concern? If you have received a definitive no from God, pray to accept it and trust that He knows what He's doing. If you haven't, don't grow weary or mechanical. Like Zechariah and Elizabeth, continue to walk faithfully with God even though you are disappointed. Walking with God in the day-in/day-out course of life swells your assurance that God is faithful and enjoyable even when a request goes unmet. Recognizing all the other works God is doing in your life will prevent discouragement as you await your answer. Zechariah waited a long time for God's answer, but when it came, it exceeded everything the priest could have thought or asked.

God gave Zechariah some assurances about this promised son. He said, "He will be a joy and delight to you, and many will rejoice because of his birth, for he will be great in the sight of the Lord. . . . And he will go on before the Lord, in the spirit and power of Elijah, to turn the hearts of the fathers to their children and the disobedient to the wisdom of the righteous — to make ready a people prepared for the Lord" (Luke 1:14–15, 17).

How would you have responded to the words of the angelic messenger? I somehow think I might have been just like Zechariah. The message was just too much for the old priest. He asked for a sign.

Apparently Gabriel was in no mood for Zechariah's doubt. Those were the last words out of the priest's mouth for a while. Zechariah's transgression wasn't terminal. The promise was still intact, and the old man would still be a father. He just wouldn't have much to say until his faith became sight.

Luke's account of Zechariah's news concludes with his return home and the record of Elizabeth's pregnancy. The woman in me fusses over the lack of details. How did Zechariah tell her the news? What did she say? Did she laugh? Did she squeal? Did she cry? If age had already closed her womb, what was her first sign of pregnancy? Why did she remain in seclusion for five months?

Lastly, I wonder if Zechariah somehow shared with Elizabeth every last detail of the prophecy concerning their son. Can you even imagine being told in advance of your child's conception that he or she would bring joy and delight to you and be great in the sight of the Lord? We breathe a huge sigh of relief over a sonogram showing all the right appendages. What we'd give for a few guarantees about their character!

Without a doubt, Zechariah and Elizabeth would think this answer was worth waiting for. God is so faithful. One reason He may have given them such assurances about their son's future greatness is because they would probably not live to see all the prophecy come to fruition. Like few of the rest of us, this set of parents would not die hoping. They would die knowing.

Chapter 2

Give Him the
Name Jesus

Luke 1:26–38

"You will be with child and give birth to a son, and you are to give him the name Jesus." (Luke 1:31)

Picture the omniscient eyes of the unfathomable *El Roi* — the God who sees — spanning the universe in panoramic view, every galaxy in His gaze. Imagine now the gradual tightening of His lens as if a movie camera were attached to the point of a rocket bound for planet Earth. Not a man-made rocket, but a celestial rocket — of the living kind.

Gabriel has been summoned once again to the throne of God. At least six months have passed since God last sent him to Jerusalem. Gabriel's previous assignment took him to Herod's temple, one of the wonders of the civilized world. This time heaven's lens focuses northward. Imagine Gabriel plunging earthward through the floor of the third heaven, breaking the barrier from the supernatural to the natural world. Feature him swooping down through the second heaven past the stars God calls by name. As our vision "descends," the earth grows larger. God's kingdom gaze burns through the blue skies of planet Earth and plummets like a flaming stake in the ground to a backward town called Nazareth.

Luke 1:26 tells us that in the sixth month of Elizabeth's pregnancy Gabriel made his appearance to Mary. Miles and decades separated an expectant senior adult from her kid-cousin up north. Jewish families were close-knit, but these women, presumably related by marriage, inhabited very different cultures. A few constants would have permeated their family lives, however. The practices of the ancient Jewish betrothal were consistent.

Luke 1:27 tells us that Mary was a virgin "pledged to be married to a man named Joseph." Betrothal compares more to our idea of marriage than engagement. The difference was the matter of physical intimacy, but the relationship was legally binding. Betrothal began with a contract drawn up by the parents or by a friend of the groom. Then at a meeting between the two families, in the presence of witnesses, the groom would present the bride with jewelry. The groom would announce his intentions to firmly observe the contract. Then he would sip from a cup of wine and offer the cup to the bride. If she sipped from the same cup, she was in effect entering covenant with him.

The next step was the payment of the *mohar,* or dowry, by the groom. This occurred at a ceremony, ordinarily involving a priest. Other traditions were also practiced, but these were the most basic and consistent. By the time a couple reached this step, their betrothal was binding, though a marriage ceremony and physical intimacy had not yet taken place. An actual divorce would be necessary to break the covenant. Furthermore, if the prospective groom died, the bride-to-be was considered a widow.

Betrothal traditionally occurred soon after the onset of adolescence, so it is probably accurate to imagine Mary around age thirteen at the time of the announcement. Remember, in that culture a thirteen- or fourteen-year-old was commonly preparing for marriage.

Don't miss the one fact we're told about Joseph in Luke's introductory account — he was a descendant of David. How awesome of God to purpose that Christ's royal lineage would come through His adoptive father. We shouldn't be surprised at the profound significance with which God views adoption.

Ephesians 1:4–6 tells us something profound about God's view of adoption. It identifies us as the adopted children of God. In a peculiar kind of way, God the Father allowed His Son to be "adopted" into a family on earth so that we could be adopted into His family in heaven.

Luke's Gospel doesn't tell us much about Joseph, but we have plenty of information to stir our imaginations about his bride-to-be. I love to imagine where Mary was when Gabriel appeared to her. I wonder if she was in her bedroom or walking a dusty path fetching water for her mother. One thing for sure: she was alone.

No matter where the angelic ambassador appeared to Mary, he must have stunned her with his choice of salutations: "Greetings, you who are highly favored! The Lord is with you." Prior to Zechariah's encounter, four centuries had passed since God had graced the earth with a heavenly visitation. I doubt the thought occurred to anyone that he would transmit the most glorious news yet heard to a simple Galilean girl.

How I love the way God works! Just when we decide He's too complicated to comprehend, He draws stick pictures.

I'm sure Mary wasn't looking for an angelic encounter that day, but if a town could have eyes to see, Nazareth should have been looking. Nazareth means "watchtower."[1] A watchtower was a compartment built at a strategic place on the city wall for the designated watchman. He was one of the most important civil servants in any city. From the watchtower, the watchman stayed on red alert for friend or foe. Two thousand years ago, Nazareth received an unfamiliar friend.

Matthew 2:23 records a prophecy handed down orally through the generations: "So was fulfilled what was said through the prophets: 'He will be called a Nazarene.' "

Indeed, if towns could see, Nazareth would have been looking. But the recipient of the news was totally unsuspecting. Humble. Meek. Completely caught off guard. Luke 1:29 tells us "Mary was greatly troubled at his words." The phrase actually means "to stir up throughout." You know the feeling: when butterflies don't just flutter in your stomach but land like a bucket at your feet, splashing fear and adrenaline through every appendage.

Mary felt the fear through and through, wondering what kind of greeting this might be. How could this young girl comprehend that she was "highly favored" (Luke 1:28) by the Lord God Himself?

The angel's next statement was equally stunning: "The Lord is with you." Although similar words had been spoken over men such as Moses, Joshua, and Gideon, I'm not sure they had ever been spoken over a woman. I'm not suggesting the Lord is not as present in the lives of women as He is men, but this phrase suggested a unique presence and power for the purpose of fulfilling a divine kingdom plan. The sight of the young girl gripped by fear provoked Gabriel to continue with the words, "Do not be afraid, Mary, you have found favor with God" (v. 30). Not until his next words did she have any clue why he had come or for what she had been chosen.

"You will be with child and give birth to a son" (v. 31). Not just any son — "the Son of the Most High" (v. 32). Probably only Mary's youth and inability to absorb the information kept her from fainting in a heap!

Then came my favorite line of all: "you

are to give him the name Jesus" (v. 31). Do you realize this was the first proclamation of our Savior's personal name since the beginning of time? *Jesus.* The very name at which every knee will one day bow. The very name that every tongue will one day confess. A name that has no parallel in my vocabulary or yours. A name I whispered into the ears of my infant daughters as I rocked them and sang lullabies of His love. A name by which I've made every single prayerful petition of my life. A name that has meant my absolute salvation, not only from eternal destruction, but from myself. A name with power like no other name. *Jesus.*

What a beautiful name. I love to watch how it falls off the lips of those who love Him. I shudder as it falls off the lips of those who don't. *Jesus.* It has been the most important and most consistent word in my life. Dearer today than yesterday. Inexpressibly precious to me personally, so I am at a loss to comprehend what the name means universally.

Jesus. The Greek spelling is *Iesous,* transliterated from the Hebrew *Yeshu'a* (Joshua). Keep in mind that Christ's earthly family spoke a Semitic language closely related to Hebrew (called Aramaic), so He would have been called Yeshu'a. One of the things I like best is that it was a common name. After all, Jesus came to seek and to save common people like me. Most pointedly, the name Jesus means "Savior." Others may have shared the name, but no one else would ever share the role. We have much to learn about Jesus, the Savior. I can hardly wait!

Like Zechariah, Mary also had a question, but the angel responded differently to her inquiry. She asked, "How will this be, . . . since I am a virgin?"

Gabriel met Mary's question with a beautifully expressive response. "The Holy Spirit will come upon you, and the power of the Most High will overshadow you." The Greek word for "come upon" is *eperchomai,* meaning "to . . . arrive, invade, . . . resting upon and operating in a person." Only one woman in all of humanity would be chosen to bear the Son of God, yet each one of us who are believers have been invaded by Jesus Christ through His Holy Spirit (see Rom. 8:9). He has been invading the closets, the attic, and the basement of my life ever since I accepted Him. How I praise God for the most glorious invasion of privacy that ever graced a human life!

I wonder if Mary knew when He arrived in her life . . . in her womb. Brothers in the faith might be appalled that I would ask such a question, but female minds were created to think intimate, personal thoughts like these! I have at least a hundred questions to ask Mary in heaven.

No doubt Mary would have some interesting stories to tell. Part of the fun of heaven will be hearing spiritual giants tell the details of the old, old stories. Mary certainly wouldn't have thought of herself as a spiritual giant, would she? I would love to know the exact moment this young adolescent absorbed the news that she would carry and deliver God's Son.

Gabriel ultimately wrapped up the story of the divine conception with one profound statement: "So the holy one to be born will be called the Son of God" (v. 35). The term *holy one* has never been more perfectly and profoundly applied than in Gabriel's statement concerning the Son of God.

Could a teenager have fathomed that she was to give birth to the Son who was the radiance of God's glory and the exact representation of His being? (Heb. 1:3). Perhaps Mary's age was on her side. When my two daughters were teenagers, and when they would tell me something, I always had more questions than they had answers. I'd say, "Did you ask this question?" to which they'd invariably say, "No, ma'am. Never even occurred to me." I want to know every detail. They were too young to realize any were missing!

Mary only asked the one question. When all was said and done, her solitary reply was: "I am the Lord's servant. . . . May it be to me as you have said" (v. 38). The Greek word for servant is *doule,* which is the feminine equivalent to *doulos,* a male bond-servant. In essence, Mary was saying, "Lord, I am Your handmaid. Whatever You want, I want." Total submission. No other questions.

We might be tempted to think: *Easy for her to say! Her news was good! Who wouldn't want to be in her shoes? Submitting isn't hard when the news is good!* Oh, yes, the news was good. The best. But the news was also hard. When the winds of heaven converge with the winds of earth, lightning is bound to strike. Seems to me that Gabriel left just in time for Mary to tell her mother. I have a feeling Nazareth was about to hear and experience a little thunder.

Chapter 3

Kindred Hearts

Luke 1:39–56

"Blessed is she who has believed that what the Lord has said to her will be accomplished!" (Luke 1:45)

Imagine that you are Mary, thirteen or fourteen years old, but in a very different culture. You awakened to the sun playing a silent reveille over the Galilean countryside. Among your first thoughts was a Hebrew benediction of thanksgiving for God's covenant reflected in another day. You are oblivious to the selection of this day on God's calendar.

You dress in typical fashion, a simple tunic draped with a cloak. A sash wrapped around the waist allows you to walk without tripping over the long fabric. You are the virgin daughter of a Jewish father, so you have draped your veil over your head and crossed it over your shoulders for the duration of the day. You have never known another kind of dress, so you are completely accustomed to the weight and the constant adjusting of a six-foot-long, four-foot-wide veil. Beneath the veil, thick, dark hair frames a deep complexion and near-ebony eyes.

Without warning, a messenger from God appears and announces that you have been chosen among women to bear the Son of God. You can hardly believe, yet you dare not doubt. As suddenly as the angel appeared, he vanishes. You are flooded with emotions.

What do you imagine you would be thinking and feeling right now? What in the world does a young woman do after receiving such life-altering news? Often God allows the space between the lines of His Word to capture our imaginations and prompt us to wonder. Not this time. He told us exactly what Mary did next.

Remember Gabriel's declaration. The most revolutionary news since Eden's fall: "the Savior is on His way." Announcing the soon-coming Messiah, he offered the stunned adolescent an almost out-of-place slice of information. By the way, "Elizabeth your relative is going to have a child in her old age, and she . . . is in her sixth month" (v. 36).

How like God! In the middle of news with universal consequences, He recognized the personal consequences to one girl. For years the scene of Mary running to Elizabeth has tendered my heart. I'd like to share my thoughts on this moment from my first book, *Things Pondered: From the Heart of a Lesser Woman.* These words were never meant to provide doctrinal exegesis, but to invite us to the momentary wonder of being a woman.

How tender the God who shared with her through an angel that someone nearby could relate. The two women had one important predicament in common — questionable pregnancies, sure to stir up some talk. Elizabeth hadn't been out of the house in months. It makes you wonder why. As happy as she was, it must have been strange not to blame her sagging figure and bumpy thighs on the baby. And to think she was forced to borrow maternity clothes from her friends' granddaughters. But maybe Elizabeth and Mary were too busy talking between themselves to pay much attention. Can you imagine their conversation over tea? One too old, the other too young. One married to an old priest, the other promised to a young carpenter. One heavy with child, the other with no physical evidence to fuel her faith. But God had graciously given them one another with a bond to braid their lives forever.

Women are like that, aren't they? We long to find someone who has been where we've been, who shares our fragile places, who sees our sunsets with the same shades of blue.[1]

Though wonderful, Mary's news was traumatic. How kind of God to provide someone to share her joy, her peculiarity, her belief in the impossible! I don't think Mary let the dust settle before she headed to Elizabeth's.

Luke 1:39 says, "At that time Mary got ready and hurried . . ." The words *got ready* offer us a delightful possibility. The Greek word for this phrase is *anistemi,* meaning "to stand again; to cause to rise up." Certainly the word could mean that Mary simply rose up and departed. The wording could also imply that she got up off her face where she had fallen after the angel departed. The rest of the definition adds "particularly spoken of those who are sitting or lying down; rising up from prayer." If she didn't fall on her face, she was the exception to the rule in such visitations. Both Ezekiel and John the revelator had to be placed back on their feet! Mary may not have taken the news standing up either.

Elizabeth lived fifty to seventy miles from Nazareth. Mary had no small trip ahead of her and no small amount of time to replay the recent events. She probably joined others making the trip, but we have no reason to assume anyone traveled with her. Can you imagine how different she was already beginning to feel? How did it feel to finally enter the village Zechariah and Elizabeth called home? What do you imagine was going through Mary's mind as she passed village merchants and mothers with children?

Finally, Mary entered Zechariah's home and greeted Elizabeth. Mary's words of salutation may have been common, but Elizabeth's reaction was far from common. The infant John jumped within his mother's womb, and Elizabeth was suddenly "filled with the Holy Spirit" (v. 41). Elizabeth proclaimed Mary and her child "blessed" and asked a glorious question: "Why am I so favored, that the mother of my Lord should come to me?" (v. 43).

Mary and Elizabeth shared not only tender similarities but also vital differences. Elizabeth pointed out the most profound difference: she was expecting her son; Mary was expecting her Lord. The concepts seem almost unfathomable even with the complete revelation of the Word. Don't miss the riches that follow Elizabeth's inspiring question. She went on to announce: "As soon as the sound of your greeting reached my ears, the baby in my womb leaped for joy. Blessed is she who has believed that what the Lord has said to her will be accomplished!" (Luke 1:44–45).

Verses 46 through 55 are often called "Mary's Song." Many scholars also refer to this section as the Magnificat, derived from her words, "My soul glorifies the Lord" (v. 46). "Glorifies" is translated from the Greek *megaluno,* which means "magnify." Mary's unparalleled experience caused her eyes to see evidences of God as if through a magnifying glass. Her wonderful words offer us an opportunity to catch a glimpse of several facts about Mary.

Mary's excitement. God used Elizabeth to confirm what Mary had experienced. Mary had probably been too scared to celebrate, but Elizabeth's confirmation set her free! How do I know? Behold verse 47: "My spirit rejoices in God my Savior." The original word for "rejoices" is *agalliao,* meaning "to exult, leap for joy, to show one's joy by leaping and skipping denoting excessive or ecstatic joy and delight. Often spoken of rejoicing with song and dance." Whether or not young Mary began physically jumping up and down with joy and excitement, her insides certainly did! I am totally blessed by the thought. Nothing is more appropriate than getting excited when God does something in our lives. I think He loves it!

Mary's love of Scripture. Mary's song reflects twelve different Old Testament passages. She didn't just hear the Word; she held it to her heart and pondered it. Scripture draws a picture of a reflective young woman with an unusual heart for God. A young Hebrew girl believed nothing to be as important as motherhood. I believe she must have recalled a favorite Old Testament story when she received the news. Mary sang praises to God just as Hannah had done over the birth of Samuel.

I see Mary's humility in the account. Her statement "all generations will call me blessed" (v. 48) was not voiced in pride but from shock. Mary reminds me of David, who said: "Who am I, O Sovereign Lord, and what is my family, that you have brought me this far? . . . Is this your usual way of dealing with man, O Sovereign Lord?" (2 Sam. 7:18–19). In a way, the answer to his question is yes. God seems to love little more than stunning the humble with His awesome intervention.

Mary's experience. Please don't lose the wonder of it. Marvel with me at the fact that she was plain, simple, and extraordinarily ordinary. I always felt the same way growing up. Still do deep down inside. That's part of the beauty of God choosing someone like you and me to know Him and serve Him. May we never get over it.

Mary was obviously aware of the covenant being fulfilled before her eyes. I'm not sure we can comprehend the mind-set of the ancient Hebrews. Their belief system was not just a religion to them — it was life. God was as much a part of their politics as their religious practices. We can't separate Mary from her culture. To get to know her is to gain insight into the home in which our Savior was reared.

Once again, Luke concluded the segment with the pen of a man rather than a woman. Verse 56 reads, "Mary stayed with Elizabeth for about three months and then returned home."

Wait a pair of minutes! Did Mary stay

until John was born or not? Did Mary get to enjoy with her cousin the precious time of the birth? Did she see the baby? If not, why did she leave just before he was born? I feel like stomping my foot and demanding an answer. Wouldn't do me any good. The answer is not there. Add that to the list of things we want to ask in heaven. One thing is for sure: During that three months Elizabeth and Mary had all the quality time in the world to share their hearts and chat about the babies. After all, Zechariah couldn't interrupt.

Chapter 4

His Name Is John

Luke 1:57–80

"And you, my child, will be called a prophet of the Most High; for you will go on before the Lord to prepare the way for him." (Luke 1:76)

Time has a way of passing quickly . . . unless you're with child. Pregnancy seems to expand everything — the calendar, the waistline, the hormonal anxiety — turning nine months into a lifetime. Finally the little one arrives and usually the only remaining trace of the longest tenure of a woman's life is stretch marks. Elizabeth's pregnancy flew by in our first chapters of study, but for her, no doubt time dragged its swollen feet.

Nothing brings out family dynamics like a wedding, birth, or funeral. Perhaps God has given me a peculiar sense of humor, but

Elizabeth and Zechariah's run-in with the relatives makes me laugh out loud. On the eighth day following the birth, the neighbors and relatives gathered for the circumcision and naming of the baby. The relatives took it upon themselves to name the new baby after his still-silent father. Elizabeth spoke up: "No! He is to be called John" (v. 60). In Hebrew the name was Johanan, meaning "the Lord is gracious."[1]

How did the relatives respond to Elizabeth's unyielding response? "There is no one among your relatives who has that name" (v. 61). Listen closely to the narrative and you can almost hear those beloved busybodies whispering ear-to-ear, "John? Who's John?"

Names were not a big deal in my family, so I didn't feel much pressure over naming our babies, but my husband's family had treasured certain names for generations. To make matters a little more emotional, Keith's dear grandfather was ill at the time of our first expectancy, prompting Keith to announce to me, "If the baby is a boy, I think we should name him after my grandfather."

I'm as sentimental as anyone, but Keith's grandfather's name was Leon. I have no idea what prompted me to think so quickly, but I responded: "Honey, that sounds wonderful, but I think it's only fair that if the baby is a girl, we name her after my grandmother." Being the just man he is, Keith said: "OK, that sounds fair. What was her name?" Minnie Ola. The thought of naming our firstborn child Minnie Moore proved too much for Keith. The subject never came up again.

Elizabeth's relatives were not as easily dissuaded. They weren't taking John for an answer. I love verse 62: "They made signs to his father, to find out what he would like to name the child." Right here I believe we have the first recorded game of charades. They made signs to Zechariah because he made signs to them. The difference was, they weren't mute and he wasn't deaf! Makes me howl every time. Finally, "to everyone's astonishment he wrote, 'His name is John' " (v. 63). Subject closed.

Immediately Zechariah's mouth opened, his tongue was loosed, and he began to speak, praising God. The Judean hill country hadn't had this much excitement in years. Everyone got an earful of good news . . . and had a mouthful to say about it.

Theologians call the words that fell from Zechariah's loosed tongue "the Benedictus." You will find the old priest's words in Luke

1:67–80. A benediction was a prayer that God might bestow certain blessings on a person or a people. Interestingly, a benediction was customarily spoken over the people by the priest performing the temple service. Don't miss the significance!

Zechariah fell silent before he could complete his final temple duty. The priest would customarily return to the courtyard after completing his tasks and bless the people. On Zechariah's big day, the people waited outside for a blessing they didn't get. He had accomplished everything else, but he never got to speak that benediction. For nine months a benediction had been mounting in the old priest with every fresh evidence of God's faithfulness. When God finally loosed that tongue, it was like a calf loosed from a stall.

Sometimes we praise because we choose to; other times we praise because we want to. Occasionally we praise because we have to — because, if we don't, the rocks will cry out! That's compulsory praise!

Among the many things Zechariah declared was his explanation in verse 78. He stated clearly why God enacted this intricate, redemptive plan: "because of the tender mercy of our God."

The Greek word for "tender" is

splagchnon, meaning, figuratively, "the inward parts indicating the breast or heart as the seat of emotions and passions." The original word for "mercy" is *eleos,* meaning "mercy, compassion, active pity . . . special and immediate regard to the misery which is the consequence of sin."

God is many things: a ruling God, a righteous God, a judging God, a holy God. He is also a feeling God. Please meditate on the depth of feeling portrayed through the words *tender mercy.* He feels for us not only when we are the innocent victims of a depraved world. He also feels for us when we are drowning in misery as a consequence of our own sin. He who knows no sin feels for us who do.

God possesses active pity — He not only feels for us, but He also does something about it. God throws out the lifeline to every soul drowning in the consequences of sin. "Amazing grace, how sweet the sound that saved a wretch like me."

Listen closely as we conclude our chapter. You are God's passion. God's tender mercy is as fresh today as it was in the home of an elderly set of new parents. Our Scripture concludes with a profound synopsis of John's life: "And the child grew and became strong in spirit; and he lived in the desert until he appeared publicly to Israel" (v. 80). Please note: John was set apart from birth, yet God used time to mature him into a servant who knew how to wield the power of the Spirit he'd been given. Can you see any parallels to the fact that you have likewise been set apart from the time of your "second" birth?

Beloved, God is into growth. We are set apart from our supernatural births, but God uses time to teach us what to do with all we've been given. We learn through many processes how to apply the Spirit's strength to and through our own lives. John will prove to be a man worthy of our meditation. We have much to learn from him . . . for the Lord's hand was with him.

Chapter 5

A Savior Is Born

Luke 2:1–20

"Today in the town of David a Savior has been born to you; he is Christ the Lord." (Luke 2:11)

As long as I live I will treasure the Christmas of 1981. Amanda was two years old and totally enraptured by the lights, ornaments, wrapping paper, and bows celebrating the season. Strangely, she was also swept up in the wonder of the story. She could have understood only the tiniest fragment, but true to her nature, she received what she knew with tender contemplation.

Melissa was tucked secretly inside me. The timing of the pregnancy announcement was just right to give Keith a Christmas surprise. For my grand finale a pair of booties lay strategically under the tree. My parents' small home bulged with excitement. Most of my family members share my personality. We are not small on enthusiasm . . . or volume. The swirling scents of baking turkey and sweet potatoes bathed in cinnamon, butter, and brown sugar filled the air. Someone announced, "It's time!" and all of us made our gleeful way to the living room and gathered around the tree to hear the old, old story.

I've heard the questions thousands of times: Why do we celebrate this time of year? How do we know when the birth of Christ took place? Why celebrate Christmas at a time originally set for ancient pagan celebrations?

The scrooges are right; we don't know when Christ was born. But I happen to think His is a birth worthy of celebrating at some time of year. God did not just tolerate celebrations and festivals commemorating His faithfulness — He commanded them. His idea! Some were solemn; others were for the pure purpose of rejoicing before the Lord.

On one such occasion Nehemiah said, "Go and enjoy choice food and sweet drinks, and send some to those who have nothing prepared. This day is sacred to our Lord. Do not grieve, for the joy of the Lord is your strength" (Neh. 8:10). The Book of Esther also speaks of an annual day set aside for "joy and feasting, a day for giving presents to each other" (Esther 9:19). The most concentrated list of Old Testament feasts appears in Leviticus 23. The chapter describes seven different feasts. In verse 5 we read, "The LORD's Passover begins at twilight on the fourteenth day of the first month."

The first month falls, according to the new moon, over the last half of March and the first half of April. The timing has significance to all of us who have carried children in our wombs. In the Jewish calendar, the fourteenth day of the first month is called the day of conception. If our God of perfect planning and gloriously significant order happened to overshadow Mary on the fourteenth day of the first month of His calendar, our Savior would have been born toward the end of our December. We have absolutely no way of knowing whether or not He did, but I would not be the least bit surprised for God to have sparked His Son's human life on one Passover and ended it on another.

No, I don't believe in Easter bunnies, and I don't have much of an opinion on Santa Clauses, but I'm a hopeless romantic when it comes to celebrating Christmas, the birth of my Savior. Until a further "Hear ye! Hear ye!" from heaven, December 25 works mighty fine for me.

Back to 1981. It was my brother's turn to read the Christmas story. He was a college boy with a deep, passionate voice. Scarcely before he could say, "And it came to pass in those days," Amanda rustled to her knees, shut her eyes, and cupped her plump little toddler hands together as if praying a bedside prayer. She remained frozen in that position throughout the entire Christmas story, her eyes never opening, but her face changing expressions with every event. The tears streamed down our cheeks as we listened to the story as if for the very first time through her ears. Oh, yes, it's a wonderful story! You can find the words in Luke 2:1–20.

Factual to its finest detail, Luke's narrative places the dot on the time line. Caesar Augustus was the ruler of the Roman Empire. From Matthew we learned that Herod the Great was king of Palestine. Herod's reign ended in 4 B.C., so Jesus had to have been born prior to that time.

God purposed that His Son would come out of Nazareth but be born in Bethlehem. So He caused a census to require everyone in the Roman world to return to the place of his or her family's origin. Probably the timing was too close to the birth of the child for Joseph to leave Mary behind. One commentary tenderly suggested that Joseph may not have wanted Mary left behind and subjected to gossip.

Joseph had to leave Galilee to be registered at his ancestral home of Bethlehem, because he was a descendant of David. How much did the young couple understand the full implications of Mary's pregnancy? Did they ponder over Micah 5:2, with its clear statement that out of Bethlehem would come "one who will be ruler over Israel, / whose origins are from of old, / from ancient times"? Or did they reflect on the words of Jeremiah that promised " 'The days are coming,' declares the LORD, 'when I will fulfill the gracious promise I made to the house of Israel . . . will make a righteous Branch sprout from David's line; he will do what is just and right in the land' "(Jer. 33:14–15).

Fulfilled prophecy demonstrates the incredible veracity of the Word of God. In the specific promises fulfilled by Jesus' birth, we have enough fact to build our faith from now till Christ returns. Bethlehem is about five miles south of Jerusalem, quite a distance from Nazareth, with chains of hills and mountains in between. Theirs was no easy trip.

Women could be tempted to picket the New International Version for leaving out one little detail that had a profound influence on Mary's trip: "Mary . . . being great with child" (v. 5 KJV). We have to appreciate the fact that the verb tense indicates a continuous action. We might say she was getting greater by the minute.

I certainly remember feeling that way. I'll never forget catching a glimpse of myself, great with child, in the distorted reflection of the stainless-steel faucet on the tub. My stomach looked huge, and my head and arms appeared like nubs. From then on I took showers. Taking "great with child" on the road is no easy task.

Whether or not Mary and Joseph planned Christ's birth this way, God certainly did. One of my favorite phrases in the birth narrative is humbly tucked in verse 6: "The time came for the baby to be born." The time. The time toward which all "time" had been ticking since the kingdom clock struck one.

The words in Luke 2:6 refer to the most important segment of time since the first tick of the clock. The second hand circled tens of thousands of times for thousands of years, then finally, miraculously, majestically — the time came. God's voice broke through the barrier of the natural realm through the cries of an infant, startled by life on the outside. The Son of God had come to earth, wrapped in a tiny cloak of human flesh. "She wrapped him in cloths and placed him in a manger, because there was no room for them in the inn" (v. 7).

The story just gets better. Luke 2:8–19 identifies the first persons to receive the glorious birth announcement. Why do you think God first proclaimed the good news to a motley crew of sheepherders? He seems to enjoy revealing Himself to common people rather than to those who feel most worthy. He often uses the foolish things of this world to confound the wise (see 1 Cor. 1:28). Maybe God had a soft place in His heart for the shepherds watching over their flocks.

Don't miss the fact that the announcement came to the shepherds while they were watching over their flocks at night. Sometimes in the contrast of the night, we can best see the glory of God. Verse 9 tells us that "the glory of the Lord shone around them." Notice the Scripture does not say that the glory of the Lord shone around the angel but around the shepherds. As you picture the scene, keep in mind that only one angel, an angel of the Lord, appeared to them first. The other heavenly hosts did not join the scene until after the birth announcement. Most definitely, the glory shone around the shepherds.

Try to imagine for a moment what happened. How do you think the glory of the Lord looked around the shepherds? We don't know for sure; I'm just asking you to picture it in your mind right now.

I am convinced that God wants us to get involved in our Scripture reading. Using our imaginations and picturing the events as eye-witnesses can make black ink on a white page spring into living color. No matter how the glory of God appeared, it scared the shepherds half to death. The words of the angel are so reminiscent of my Savior. Often He told those nearly slain by His glory not to be afraid.

Oh, how I love Him. The untouchable Hand of God reaching down to touch the fallen hand of man. "I bring you good news of great joy that will be for all the people" (v. 10). I am convinced our witness would be far more effective if we brought our good news with great joy. Notice the shepherds wasted no time before embracing the news.

The angel then proclaimed the special delivery: "Today in the town of David a Savior has been born to you; he is Christ the Lord" (v. 11). In other words, He is the *Christos,* the Anointed One, the Messiah! "This will be a sign to you: You will find a baby wrapped in cloths and lying in a manger" (v. 12).

I think you will cherish the meaning of the word *sign.* The Greek word *semeion* means the "finger-marks of God, valuable not so much for what they are as for what they indicate of the grace and power of the Doer." You see, a sign is a fingerprint of God, given not so that we will be consumed by the sign itself but by the invisible hand that left the visible print. The angel sent the shepherds to embrace the baby, not the sign.

The Scriptures tell us that suddenly a great company of heavenly host appeared with the angel, praising God and saying, "Glory to God in the highest, / and on earth peace to men on whom his favor rests" (v. 14). Behold the awesome proclamation: through this Child, the God of the highest heaven has graced the earth.

The shepherds hurried and found Mary, Joseph, and the baby. After they had seen Him, they spread the word about the angelic message, and all who heard it were amazed.

At first glance, God seems to give more attention to the shepherds' responses to the birth of Christ than to Mary herself. On a more probing look, however, we discover that while the shepherds went away praising God, "Mary treasured up all these things and pondered them in her heart" (v. 19).

Chapter 6

In the Stable
with Mary

Luke 2:19

In the beginning was the Word, and the Word was with God, and the Word was God. . . . The Word became flesh and made his dwelling among us. We have seen his glory, the glory of the One and Only. (John 1:1, 14)

I so much desire for you to experience the life of our Christ on this journey. I want you to feel the lap of the waves on the sea of Galilee. To hear the cries of the needy crowds that came to Him. To see the expressions on the faces in the stories of Luke's Gospel.

For now, I want to invite you into the stable for a personal look. We know Mary treasured the things she saw and heard.

How do you suppose she felt on the night of nights after Jesus had been born, when the astounded shepherds had gone to spread their tale and Joseph's care for her gave way to sleep?

I have a pretty active imagination, and I have tried to wonder what that night was like. Men may not be constantly wanting to know more details, but women do. One of the things we want to know is what happened during that night after Jesus was born. What was it like? What conversations took place? What did Joseph say? What did Mary say? Was it a long labor? Was it a short labor? I want to know those things. And don't think one of these days I'm not going to ask!

I remember so well what my first moments were like with my oldest daughter, my firstborn. I'd seen her, of course, in the delivery room. I kept expecting for them to come put some kind of gold medal on me, or one of those wreaths of roses that they put around a horse's neck, at the end of all of that labor. But no! They were all taken with the baby instead.

Back in those days they still kept the baby in the nursery and sent Mom on to her room after she had held her baby for a little while. Finally they brought her to me at 4:30 in the morning. She was wrapped so tight that it took me fifteen minutes to unwind her! But I did exactly what you do if you're a parent. I looked at every single finger and toe, studied that precious little body, and introduced myself formally to my firstborn. Can we imagine that Mary did anything much different than that? I don't know about you, but I couldn't sleep a wink. I was so exhausted. I bet you that Mary didn't get a wink of sleep either.

Now the following are just some thoughts that God gave me as I tried to imagine what it would have been like over those next couple of hours. But I want to be very clear here: this is strictly fiction. I just invite you to imagine with me what Mary's first moments might have been like as a mother. Here are my thoughts:

Her body lay sapped of strength, her eyes were heavily closed, but her mind refused to give way to rest. She ached for her mother. She wondered if she yet believed her. She heard the labored breathing of the man sleeping a few feet from her. Only months before he was little more than a stranger to her. She knew only what she had been told and what she could read in occasional shy glances. She had been told he was a good man. Over the last few days, she found out he was far more than a good man. No man, no matter how kind, could have done what he had done. She wondered how long it had been since he'd really rested.

A calf, only a few days old, awakened hungry and could not find its mother. The stir awakened the baby who also squirmed to find His mother. Scarcely before she could move her tender frame toward the manger, He began to wail! She scooped Him in her arms, her long hair draping His face, and she quietly slipped out of the gate. She gingerly sat down and leaned against the outside of the stable, propped the baby on her small lap, and taking a strip of linen and tying back her hair, she began to stare into His tiny face. She had not yet seen Him in the light. She had never seen the moon so bright. The night was nearly as light as the day. Only hours old, His chin quivered, not from the cold, but from the sudden exposure of birth. His eyes were shaped like almonds and were as black as the deepest well. She held Him tightly and quietly hummed a song she'd learned as a child. She had been so frightened of this moment, so sure she would not know what to do. She had never held an infant so small, and He was God, wrapped in soft, infant flesh, with bones so fragile she felt like He could break. She had pictured this moment so many times. What would the Son of the Spirit look like? She never expected Him to look so normal, so common. Must have been the part He inherited from His mother. She was so sure she'd feel terribly awkward. So afraid she'd drop Him, the Messiah, and God would be awfully sorry He had given Him to her! Instead, every fear, every doubt, every inadequacy was momentarily caught up in the indescribable rapture of a mother's affection.

She remembered asking Elizabeth things she dared not ask her father and mother. Once when they were walking together at the end of the day, the wind blew her cousin's robes against her, and like a curious teenager, Mary tried her hardest to catch a good glimpse of Elizabeth's rounded middle. At the time she herself had no physical evidence that God's promise was true. But she had enough faith to ask endless questions. *What am I to do when He comes?* Her cousin's reply would remain etched upon Mary's heart long after He had saved the world. *He will tell you what He needs from you. Beyond what He needs, all He wants is for you to embrace Him and talk to Him.*

She looked back into His delicate face and watched Him closely as He seemed to stare deeply into the moonlit sky. And she began to talk. "Sweet baby boy. Do You know who Your Daddy is? Do You know Your name? Do You know why You're here? What do You see when You look out there? Can You see the stars? Do You remember their names? Do You think I'll do OK? Will You love me too?" A tear dropped from her chin to His. He yawned and made such a funny expression she grinned, wiping her face on the yellowed rags she'd draped around Him. The fussing calf had obviously found its mother. Not a sound was coming from inside the stable. The earth stilled. The infant slept. She held the babe next to her face, and for just a moment, all the world was silent to the breath of God.

She closed her eyes and listened, stealing time like a hidden metronome, as high and as wide as she dared to think, but she still could not begin to comprehend. She, a common child of the most humble means who had never read the Scriptures for herself, was embracing the incarnate Word. The fullness of the Godhead rested in her inexperienced arms, sleeping to the rhythm of her heart. This time she hummed a song she did not know, a song being sung by the choir of angels hovering over her head but hidden from her carnal senses. The deafening hallelujahs of the heavenly hosts were silent to mortal ears except through the sounds of a young woman's voice who had unknowingly given human notes to a holy score. The glory of God filled the earth. Heaven hammered a bridge, but one young woman sat completely unaware of all that swelled the atmosphere around her. The tiny baby boy had robbed her heart. "So, this is how it feels to be a mother," she mused.

She crept back into the stable, wrapped Him in swaddling clothes and laid Him in the manger. Just down the path, the sun peeked gently over the roof of an inn full of barren souls who had made Him no room.

Emmanuel, the "with" of God, in the most intimate moments. Sometimes perhaps He is most obvious in aloneness and in darkness. He is with us to embrace, to hold so close we can hear His heart beat.

Part 2

The Son of God

I hope the fresh reminder of the birth of Emmanuel was as precious to you as it was to me. God is with us! May we never take the news lightly! The next portion of our study unfolds while the Son of God is still wrapped in a tiny blanket of warm, wriggling flesh. Picture a newborn with me. Beautiful dark eyes and skin, squirming in a young mother's inexperienced arms. Hear the sounds He makes. Gurgles. Coos. Hungry cries. The Savior of the world has come. That's where we begin, but our study will accelerate quickly. Because God chose to share only tidbits of information about the young life of Christ, this section will conclude with Christ's induction into ministry at around thirty years of age. As you can see, we have lots of ground to cover; and at times we'll have to use our imaginations, under the sound guidance of Scripture, to picture what Jesus was like. He was no doubt the apple of His Father's eye. May He become ours too.

Babies have a way of grabbing your attention, don't they? I sense One in particular vying for ours this moment. Let's get started and give it to Him.

Chapter 7

The Lord's Christ

Luke 2:21–38

"For my eyes have seen your salvation, which you have prepared in the sight of all people, a light for revelation to the Gentiles and for glory to your people Israel." (Luke 2:30–32)

We concluded part 1 with Mary gathering memorable moments and holding them to her heart. Now the incarnate Christ is only a few days old. Picture Him with me. The infant Christ. Tiny. Deep olive skin. Ebony eyes. Soft, fuzzy hair, probably black as pitch. Fitting in one of Mary's small, young arms. No doubt she rubbed His soft, little head with her cheek, just as every mother nestles an infant.

Few things are sweeter than a new mom and her baby. Just a few days ago, I leaned over to peek at a total stranger's newborn in a stroller, and I looked back up at the mother and said, "Oh, how precious she is!" Tears welled in her eyes, and she couldn't even respond. I embraced this darling mom and said, "I so remember how easily the tears come after the birth of a child." I think we are safe to picture Mary the same way. Not only had she experienced the miracle of childbirth with all the physiological changes that make a new mother so emotional, but she also was a virgin giving birth to the Messiah. Can you imagine being Mary — assigned to care for the Son of God? Every new mom battles fear and insecurity. Multiply those emotions tenfold. After all, this days-old infant was God's only Son. Don't you imagine she felt pressure to get it right? An imperfect mom with a perfect child.

Pictures of Covenant and Redemption

Jesus' parents had Him circumcised on the eighth day of His young life. Then they presented Him at the temple and offered the sacrifices required of new parents. Each of the steps Mary and Joseph took after Christ's birth was typical of devout Jewish parents. What made these events atypical is that their infant would ultimately fulfill the prophetic representation of each of these rituals. Let's take a brief look at all three rites: circumcision, redemption, and purification.

The Rite of Circumcision

We read about circumcision in Genesis 17:1–14. It was so important that verse 11 says, "it will be the sign of the covenant between me and you." Verse 14 says an uncircumcised male "will be cut off from his people; he has broken my covenant." The rite of circumcision was God's way of requiring the Jewish people to become physically different because of their relationship to Him.

A careful reading of Colossians 2:9–15 sheds light on how the infant Jesus would later be used to fulfill a different kind of circumcision in believers. Verse 11 says: "In him you were also circumcised, in the putting off of the sinful nature." If you have walked with Jesus for any time, you can point to ways in which our spiritual circumcision results in proof that we are different than the persons we originally were.

Colossians 2:15 goes on to proclaim that

this Christ "disarmed the powers and authorities, he made a public spectacle of them, triumphing over them by the cross." When the infant Jesus was circumcised at eight days of age, I'm not sure His parents could fathom that He was the physical manifestation of the covenant God had made thousands of years earlier.

Second Corinthians 1:20 says, "No matter how many promises God has made, they are 'Yes' in Christ." The infant Joseph held during that circumcision was the very Yes of God to the promise of the covenant being symbolized. But this infant was more. He was also the fulfillment of the rite of redemption.

The Rite of Redemption

In Luke 2:22–24 two distinct rites were observed by Mary and Joseph. Before we research them, please note that a segment of time has passed between the circumcision and the presentation. According to Leviticus 12:1–8 a woman was to wait thirty-three days after the circumcision before presenting a son at the temple. Exodus 13 tells us the reason why every firstborn male was to be redeemed. The redemption was a reminder "that the LORD brought us out of Egypt with his mighty hand" (Exod. 13:16).

Mary and Joseph went to Jerusalem in obedience to this command. Like all devout Jewish parents, they presented their infant to the Lord to depict sacrifice and redemption. When Jewish parents presented their firstborn son to the Lord, they were symbolizing the act of giving him up by saying, "He is Yours and we give him back to You." Then they would immediately redeem him or, in effect, buy him back.

Few teachings are more important and consistent in God's Word than the doctrine of redemption. The Hebrew word is *padhah,* meaning "to redeem by paying a price." The New Testament tells us Christ came to fulfill for us the very rite Mary and Joseph observed as they presented the Christ child to the Lord.

Ephesians 1:7 says, "in him we have redemption through his blood, the forgiveness of sins, in accordance with the riches of God's grace." Consider the verse from the apostle Paul's Jewish perspective. He drew a parallel to our entrance into the family of God. Since most of us are Gentiles, we are considered the "adopted ones" in God's family. What was true in a tangible sense after the birth of a Jewish son is true of us in a spiritual sense after our rebirth as "sons" of God. We all must be redeemed. The wonderful picture for us, however, is that we are not bought from God by our natural parents. Rather, Christ buys us from our natural parentage, which is sinful flesh, to give us to His Father. If the concept is too confusing, just celebrate that Christ has redeemed you!

Before we turn our attention to the third rite Mary and Joseph observed, look back at the last phrase of Luke 2:22: "Joseph and Mary took him to Jerusalem to present him to the Lord." Centuries of parents had presented baby boys to the Father. He loved them all, but that day in Jerusalem two new parents presented God with His One and Only Son. I'm about to cry just thinking about it. Do you think God smiled? Or do you think He cried? Don't you think He thought Jesus was the most beautiful baby He had ever seen?

An unimpressive-looking couple walked into a temple built for the very presence of God — and God had never been more present. No cloudy pillar. No consuming fire. The Word made flesh first entered the temple wrapped in a baby blanket. His earthly parents lifted Him to His Father and, in essence, purchased Him from heaven — for a while — for a lost world. One day that baby would buy them from earth for the glory of heaven. Wow. Now we see a third aspect of their observance that day.

The Rite of Purification

The rite of redemption was distinct from the rite of purification. This purification is described in Leviticus 12:1–8. The prescribed sacrifice included a lamb, but the law made provision for impoverished parents. Verse 8 says, "If she cannot afford a lamb, she is to bring two doves or two young pigeons." Luke told us that Jesus' parents offered the poverty version of the sacrifice.

Have you ever considered what Christ's earthly poverty has to do with us? Second Corinthians 8:9 proclaims that though Christ "was rich, yet for your sakes he became poor, so that you through his poverty might become rich."

Mary and Joseph offered the least sacrifice permitted by Jewish law for the rite of purification. How fitting that they held in their arms the greatest sacrifice a holy God could ever make for their eternal purification. Titus 2:14 tells us that Jesus Christ "gave himself for us to redeem us from all wickedness and to purify for himself a people that are his very own."

Revelation of Messiah

Next we see two touching scenes in Luke 2:25–38. Two deeply discerning people — Simeon and Anna — were at the temple the day Jesus was presented. Both were watching and waiting for the Messiah.

God had revealed to Simeon that he would not die until he had seen the Lord's Christ. The Scripture does not say how God made this revelation, but I suspect that He did it the way He usually does — through His Word. The prophecy of Daniel points to the period of time when the Messiah would come. I think God may have used Daniel 9 to communicate to Simeon.

Simeon honored the promise he had received by living a devout life and waiting for the promised day. God probably won't reveal to us the time of Christ's return (Matt. 24:36), but the same principle is true for us: God constantly reveals His glory to us. The more we prepare ourselves through devotion, prayer, worship, watching, and expectantly waiting, the more likely we will be to see the glory of God (see John 14:21).

I revel in Simeon's response and prophecy when he beheld and held the baby Jesus. "Simeon took him in his arms and praised God, saying:

'Sovereign Lord, as you have promised,
  you now dismiss your servant in peace.
For my eyes have seen your salvation,
  which you have prepared in the sight
  of all people,
a light for revelation to the Gentiles
  and for glory to your people Israel' "
    (Luke 2:29–32).

One of my favorite titles for my Savior came from this devout man; He called Jesus "the Lord's Christ" (Luke 2:26).

Simeon didn't proclaim only the joy of Jesus as the Lord's Christ. He also spoke painful prophecy. He blessed them and said to Mary, "This child is destined to cause the falling and rising of many in Israel, and to be a sign that will be spoken against, so that the thoughts of many hearts will be revealed. And a sword will pierce your own soul too" (vv. 34–35). Imagine all that Mary had experienced during the past year. How could she have understood that the infant Son of God would one day cause the piercing of her own soul? Surely the greatest callings of God are the gravest as well.

Are you wondering why we are researching seemingly irrelevant Jewish customs? Luke stated our purpose: "according to the Law of Moses" (Luke 2:22); "as it is written in the Law of the Lord" (v. 23); "in keeping with what is said in the Law of the Lord" (v. 24); and "what the custom of the Law required" (v. 27).

Luke was the only Gentile inspired by God to write a Gospel, and he reminded his readers of something we must never forget: our incarnate Christ was Jewish. We cannot begin to picture Jesus' earthly walk without becoming a student of His world. This will be one of our chief goals as we walk through the life of Jesus the Messiah.

Untold treasures await us. Some jewels will sparkle visibly like diamonds on red velvet; others will become obvious only by digging in the dark mines. But when our journey is complete, we will have arms filled with treasures to hold in our hearts forever. Come ye who are poor and needy. Unfathomable wealth is hidden in Him.

Chapter 8

The Child Jesus

Luke 2:39–50

"Didn't you know I had to be in my Father's house?" (Luke 2:49)

Have you ever wondered what Christ was like as a child? Now that both my children are young adults, I treasure the moments when I catch glimpses of their childhood in something they do or say. Every now and then an expression crosses Amanda's face that looks exactly like when she was a toddler. Sometimes when I sit beside Melissa, stroking her long hair as she sleeps, I see her as a four-year-old all over again.

Let's wonder together what Christ was like as a child. Did His adulthood reflect His childhood? We will attempt to draw a portrait of the child Jesus from Scripture, Jewish tradition, and supposition. We'll consider a few things that may have been typical in Christ's boyhood; then we'll consider a few that were obviously atypical.

Matthew 13:54–58 tells of Jesus' rejection by the people of His hometown. They considered Him too ordinary to be worthy of their attention. These verses remind us that Christ grasped average humanity by experiencing it. He grew up in a small town with parents who possessed little wealth but came to be rich in offspring. We know that Christ had at least four younger brothers and more than one sister. I'm no math whiz, but seven children would have filled Joseph's modest household to the brim.

The events of Luke 2:39–52 give us our only glimpse of Jesus' childhood. His family traveled to Jerusalem for the Passover. On the trip home they did not realize that the twelve-year-old Jesus was not along. Frantically returning, they found Him in the temple conversing with the elders.

These events demonstrate that Jesus was an exceptional child, but amazement over His miracles as an adult demonstrates that God shielded Jesus' young life from the complications of divine acts. Jesus probably did not walk until He was ten or twelve months old, and He certainly didn't walk on His bathwater. He probably gleefully splashed water all over His mother just like our children splashed theirs.

As the oldest child, Jesus probably begged to hold a baby brother or sister just like other preschoolers. I don't think Mary left Him to baby-sit from the time He was two or three just because He was the Son of God. I'm certain she watched Him cautiously as He played and explored the outdoors just as we watch our children. When He fell, He bruised. When He burst His lip, He bled. When He needed a nap, He cried.

Interestingly, other elements of Christ's childhood would be normal in a Jewish home but very atypical to Gentiles. Certainly Jesus was reared according to Jewish law and tradition. Joseph took a primary role in His religious upbringing. Jesus read Scripture by the time He was five. At six He probably attended the school of the local rabbi. While still quite young, Christ began memorizing lengthy Scripture passages. At age ten He would have begun training in the oral law. Long before Christ turned twelve, He would have been reciting certain prayers as He arose in the morning, other prayers when He ate and dressed, and still others when He crawled into bed in the evening.

I'm not sure we who are Gentiles can begin to comprehend the religious life of the

Jews. Judaism was not a label used to identify where they attended church. Being Jewish was a completely unique way of life that permeated every move they made. Also, by the time we again catch up with Christ at twelve years old, He would already have begun learning His father's trade. From Matthew 13:55 we know that Joseph was a carpenter, and from Mark 6:3 that Jesus followed His earthly dad. Jesus was probably little more than a toddler when He began to hang around His father's workshop and to hammer a nail into anything standing still. Some of the first blood ever drawn from Emmanuel's veins may well have been when a hammer and a nail struck the tender flesh of a tiny apprentice.

Jesus was a little boy, a human little boy, with a little boy's childhood. But consider what made His childhood unique — the "otherness" of Christ. One of Mary and Joseph's children was God incarnate. The rest were not. Can you imagine calling the Son of God for supper? Or telling Him to wash His hands? If you knew one of your children was the divinely born Son of God, would you want to be certain He ate His vegetables? How in the world would earthly parents rear the perfect Son of God in an imperfect household?

Luke 2:41 suggests another way Christ's boyhood was very atypical compared to our modern existence. Luke tells us His family observed certain annual practices common to Jewish culture.

Strict Jews observed three annual pilgrimages to Jerusalem: Passover, Pentecost, and the Feast of Tabernacles. Virtually every Jewish family in a community made the trip. The trip was long, and parents allowed children to run between families and relatives, amusing themselves along the way. They didn't have televisions built into their SUVs in those days. Jesus was twelve years old — only a year from being considered a young man. Mary and Joseph simply assumed He was somewhere in the caravan.

I had the joy of raising my children alongside my best friend of twenty-plus years. Numerous times we thought one of our children was with the other only to find the child in the dog bowl or splashing in the toilet. We feel fortunate we didn't leave any of ours while on a vacation somewhere.

Jesus' parents found Him on the third day. He was sitting in the temple, conversing with the teachers. I'm not sure anything prompts emotions like finding a lost child. Fear surges through your heart during the search. Relief floods over you when you find the child safe. Then if the child discounts parental concern, emotions surge to vengeance!

Luke 2:48 tells us His parents were astonished. I think you'll appreciate what the word *astonishment* means. *Ekpletto:* "to strike out, force out by a blow, but found only in the sense of knocking one out of his senses or self-possession, to strike with astonishment, terror, admiration."

When one of our children does something we perceive as wrong, Keith or I will say, "What do you plan to do about your daughter?" Notice Mary and Joseph were both astonished, but Joseph may have given Mary that "go ahead and deal with Him" look.

Mary was understandably hurt and asked, "Why have you treated us like this?" (v. 48). Yep, this was their first brush with preadolescence. Mary was feeling a tiny prick of that sword Simeon prophesied. She had no idea how much deeper it would one day plunge.

Christ's response suggests that He was as mystified that they'd expect to find Him anywhere else as they were mystified to find Him there: "Didn't you know I had to be in my Father's house?" (v. 49). The words "had to" come from the Greek word *dei,* meaning "is inevitable in the nature of things." Likely this word has never been used more literally. After all, the Father and the Son had the same nature. Christ was drawn to God, not as a devout believer, but as an overpowering magnet — as two pieces of the same whole.

Even though I feel compassion concerning Mary's and Joseph's fear, I love what they found their son doing! "After three days they found him in the temple courts, sitting among the teachers, listening to them and asking them questions" (v. 46).

"Listening." I'm so thankful Christ not only speaks, but He also listens. We don't know if God allowed twelve-year-old Christ to exercise His full omniscience or to unleash just enough wisdom to astound His listeners. I love the fact that Christ still listens — but not to learn, since He knows all things. Rather, He allows us to pour out our hearts.

"Asking them questions." Christ not only listened, but also He asked questions. Contrary to popular belief, faith is not the avoidance of questions. Our faith grows when we seek answers, and we find many between Genesis 1:1 and Revelation 22:21. We may hear a gentle, "Because I said so," to those God chooses not to answer, but I don't be-

lieve our heavenly Father is offended by questions. Part of Christlikeness is learning to listen and ask appropriate questions, even of those you respect in the faith.

"His answers." My favorite part! Not only did Christ listen and ask questions, but Luke 2:47 tells us He answered them! As we study, we may see several examples of Him posing a question that only He could answer. Christ certainly uses that teaching method with me. Sometimes He'll cause me to dig through Scripture for a question He seemed to initiate. Other times the question may come as a personalized whisper in my heart: "Beth, why are you acting that way?" Often my honest answer is: "I don't know, Lord! Can You tell me why?" If I really search His heart, sooner or later He'll give me insight into my reactions. As He reveals my insecurities and fleshly defense mechanisms, understanding makes me more cooperative with the subsequent changes. Can you relate?

If the boy Christ could answer difficult questions, surely we can trust the immortal One seated at the right Hand of God to make intercession for us (see Heb. 7:25). Whether or not you receive a speedy answer, I believe you are always free to ask questions.

Before we move on, please understand one more thing about questions and answers. In verse 48, Mary asked Christ a question. In verse 49, Christ gave her an answer. Verse 50 tells us, however, that she didn't understand the answer He supplied. There you have it. Another very real possibility: we might ask Christ a question and receive an answer, though we still may not understand the answer — until later. Maybe much later.

In my opinion, Christ's response was quite interesting. I've searched every Greek translation I can find, and none of my resources have an original word that directly translates to *house* (NIV) or *business* (KJV) in verse 49. From what I can gather, a more precise translation of Christ's response might be: "Didn't you know that I had to be about my Father?"

That question implies the desire of my heart more than any other I can imagine. I just want to be about God. Not about ministry. Not about my own agenda. Not about writing Bible studies. Not about me at all. When all is said and done, I would give my life for people to be able to say, "She was just about God." That would be the ultimate legacy. "Not that I have already obtained all this, . . . but I press on" (Phil. 3:12).

Dear student, may we live lives that would cause others to be surprised to find us any other place than to "be found in him" (Phil. 3:9).

Chapter 9

Picturing Jesus

Luke 2:51–52

And Jesus grew in wisdom and stature, and in favor with God and men. (Luke 2:52)

We have come to an important point in our study because we begin to form mental images of what Jesus was like physically and personally. My hope is that the pictures we create will remain with us throughout the study.

We will tread carefully because we want to capture as accurate a visual as we can even though we will be using our imaginations. I don't want the Jesus we study to remain faceless and devoid of personality. I am asking the Holy Spirit to help each of us form some kind of image of Jesus that we can picture throughout our study. I am praying that you will picture a face and imagine its changing expression with each encounter in Scripture. I believe we have God's full approval to use our imaginations and picture His Son as real and vivid flesh and blood. After all, that's what He sent Christ here to be.

When we first began planning this study, my editor asked, "Beth, have you given some thought to what your primary goal will be as you write about the life of Christ?" This is my response: I want you, the reader, to feel like an eyewitness to the life of Christ. I want you to feel the arid, Middle-Eastern breezes as Jesus teaches and ministers and to imagine the expressions on His face.

With all my heart I believe God approves of this type of approach because it reflects the very mind-set He seemed to birth in His own people. Ray Vander Laan described a major difference between Western and Eastern thought. He said: "A Westerner like me learns in the Greek way, in the Greek tradition. Truth is presented in words and in careful definitions and explanations. We love bullets . . . lists and points. An East-erner, however, is much more likely to describe truth in pictures and in metaphors, in the meaning of places and structures. For example, a Westerner might describe God as powerful or loving or all-knowing. An Easterner would be much more likely to say God is my Shepherd or a Rock or Living Water."[1]

I hope, like proper Westerners, we learn through our bullet points and word definitions, but let's also seek to learn through pictures and metaphors. Right now let's try to see Christ as an Easterner might. Our purpose in using our imaginations is to picture Christ and His encounters as real and vivid, not to worship an inaccurate image. We cannot begin to picture Christ as He is this moment, seated at the right Hand of God. We have absolutely no reference point to imagine His holiness. His earthly stature, however, is different. We do have a few reference points to help us create His human visage. Our goal is to lightly sketch a possible picture, not to draw one with permanent ink.

Luke 2:42 tells us Jesus was twelve at the recorded visit to the temple. Luke 3:23 says He was thirty at the beginning of His ministry. The Gospel writer supplies only two verses spanning the eighteen years in between. During these years, Christ Jesus went from boy to mature man. Luke 2:52 appears brief and to the point but actually broadens dramatically our concept of

Christ. It tells us our Lord "grew in wisdom and stature, and in favor with God and men."

Jesus Grew in Wisdom

The Greek word for "wisdom" is *sophia.* Consider two segments of the definition. Each applies to Christ in Luke 2:52: (1) *Sophia* is skill in the affairs of life, practical wisdom, wise management as shown in forming the best plans and selecting the best means, including the idea of sound judgment and good sense. (2) *Sophia* is, in respect to divine things, wisdom, knowledge, insight, deep understanding. As you seek to formulate an impression of what Christ was like in His earthly form, please view Him as completely practical and deeply spiritual. In fact, Christ came to show us that the deeply spiritual is very practical.

I am affectionately teased at times by those who love me for not necessarily being the poster child for common sense. I can spend hours researching ancient language translations, then get lost on my way home from work. In fact, the verse they sometimes laughingly apply to me around my office is Luke 1:20: "Behold, thou shalt be dumb"

(KJV). I, on the other hand, simply say I am blonder than I pay to be.

When it comes to the Word, however, I have learned both the hard way and the delightfully pleasant way that the spiritual is deeply practical. I encourage you to avoid imagining Christ as so deep you'd have to dig to find Him or so spiritual His head is in the clouds. He came bringing heaven to earth. In today's terms, He was a man who could preach an anointed sermon, then change a flat tire on the way home from church.

No wonder Christ became such a rare teacher! Believing people are starving for a wisdom that is both deeply spiritual and vastly practical. Christ embodied every dimension of wisdom in His earthly life, even before He officially began His public ministry.

Jesus Grew in Stature

This phrase tells us the obvious: Christ grew physically (and mentally) in the vigor and stature of a man. What is, of course, less obvious is what He grew to look like. God's Word lets us use our permanent markers only once as we try to imagine Christ's appearance. Our solitary source happens to be one of my least favorite verses. God knows my heart and why I feel this way.

Isaiah 53:2 predicts about the coming Messiah: "He had no beauty or majesty to attract us to him, / nothing in his appearance that we should desire him." I simply cannot imagine Christ not being beautiful, but I also believe beauty is in the eye of the beholder. All of us can think of people who are beautiful to us but whose faces might never be chosen for a magazine cover. Don't read more into Isaiah 53:2 than is there, however. The intent of the original terms is that He didn't have a magnificent, godlike physical appearance that attracted people to Him. The descriptions don't necessarily imply that Christ was unattractive but that His looks were most likely ordinary.

Now let's put down the permanent marker for a moment and pick up our light lead pencils. We can sketch a few more details on our mental canvas through supposition. His people and part of the world offer a few clues about His physical appearance. His skin was most likely very brown, as were His hair and eyes. The men of His culture and era usually wore their hair almost touching the shoulders. They wore it longer if they had taken a vow of consecration (see

Num. 6). The texture of their hair was probably as varied as the Caucasian hair of the Western world. Christ's hair could have been wavy or straight, thick or thin. The most common appearance was probably dark, thick, and wavy hair to the shoulders. Jesus almost certainly wore a beard. His facial features were probably strong, bony, and masculine. The biggest error many painters have probably made in their interpretations of Jesus is portraying a small, almost scrawny stature. He was a carpenter, used to manual labor.

Jesus' daily dress was much like you probably imagine. He would have worn the traditional tunic, girded with a belt, and at times a large cloak called a mantle, which served somewhat as an overcoat. The climate and terrain meant His feet and sandals were more often dusty than muddy. In public Jesus probably wore a turban made of linen. The colors men most often wore on an ordinary day were tan, beige, brown, and amber tones. Right about now, our men readers are wondering who cares, while our women readers are wondering what He wore to church! So I'll stop while everyone is dissatisfied.

Jesus Grew in Favor with God

Oh, how I love picturing the relationship Christ shared with His heavenly Father. I will limit my comments for now because I don't want to steal the joy of discovery as we search out dimensions of their relationship in the chapters to come. For now, note what the word *favor* means. The Greek word is *charis,* which is often translated "grace" in the New Testament. *Charis* means "grace, particularly that which causes joy, pleasure, gratification, favor, acceptance." Jesus' growing in favor with God basically implies that their relationship became an increasing delight to both of them. Without a doubt, the relationship between God the Father and God the Son is totally unique. Indeed Jesus is the One and Only — the only begotten of the Father. And the relationship the two of them shared while Christ was earthbound is unparalleled.

Jesus Grew in Favor with Men

As we attempt to formulate a picture of Christ's stature and personality, this description is extremely important. Isaiah 53:3 tells us that He was despised and rejected by men. Understand that He was not despised and rejected until He became a complete threat to the establishment. Actually, His popularity was the driving force behind Jesus' opponents' lust for His blood.

In Luke 2:52, God states Christ's favor with men, but throughout the Gospels He demonstrates it. Fishermen don't leave their nets to follow someone void of personality. People didn't just respect Him — they liked Him. The word *favor* is undeniably related to the word *favorite.* I don't believe we are stretching the text in the least to say that Christ was a favorite of many who knew Him.

Think for a few moments of the different characteristics of people who tend to capture your favor. Unless those characteristics are inconsistent with godliness, in all likelihood Christ possessed them. I can readily share a few of my favorite characteristics in people: godly, warm and personable, at least somewhat demonstrative, knowledgeable in a specific area so I can learn from them, trustworthy, and funny!

Let's explore some of our favorites for a moment, assuming we probably share a few of the same ideas. I have the utmost respect for anyone who characterizes godliness, but if they don't also possess some semblance of warmth, my feelings toward them may not progress much further than respect. I know lots of people who are funny, but if their humor is unkind or inappropriate, I am very resistant to choose their company.

Although God's Word tells us that we are not to show favoritism, all of us have favorite characteristics we enjoy in people. I think you can safely assume that Christ possessed many of the dimensions you would favor most. Work with me here while I make one more suggestion that you may or may not choose to sketch on your pencil portrait.

I believe Christ had a warm smile and a great sense of humor. If you can't imagine a godly person as funny, I know some folks you need to meet. The older I've become, the more I've asked God to purge my personality of anything that is inconsistent with godliness. I stopped giving place to inappropriate humor a long time ago, yet dozens of times a week I laugh so hard I can't sit up. Not only are my husband and children hilarious, but also my coworkers and I laugh hysterically over things that are neither off-color nor unkind. I am convinced laughter is as much a gift of expression as tears.

Proverbs 17:22 says "a cheerful heart is good medicine." Can you imagine that

Christ, the Great Physician, would not have used such an effective medicine? Good humor and laughter are far too wonderful not to come straight from the heart of God. One of the surest characteristics of a healthy little one is cackling laughter and smiles. Christ dearly loves for us to come to Him as little children.

I pray that this chapter will help you pencil a picture of Christ on the canvas of your mind. He was real. His sandals flapped when He walked down the road. His hair was misshapen when He awakened. He had to brush the bread crumbs off His beard after He ate. The muscles in His arms flexed when He lifted His little brothers and sisters. He had hair on His arms and warmth in His palms. He was the Son of God and the Son of man. Fathom the unfathomable.

Chapter 10

Waist Deep in Jordan

Luke 3:1–23

John answered them all, "I baptize you with water. But one more powerful than I will come, the thongs of whose sandals I am not worthy to untie. He will baptize you with the Holy Spirit and with fire." (Luke 3:16)

Our gloriously deliberate God orchestrated the lives of two extraordinary men, born six months apart, to converge waist-deep in the waters of the Jordan River. For John the Baptizer, it was the beginning of the end. He had prepared God's way, and now God was preparing his. For Jesus, it marked the end of the beginning. His life would descend on Galilee, Judea, and Jerusalem like a desert storm. That day, in the river of promise, John baptized Jesus with water, and Jesus baptized the Jordan with glory.

Preparation

John proclaimed, "Prepare the way for the Lord, / make straight paths for him" (Luke 3:4). The original Greek word for "paths" is the word *tribos,* which means "a beaten pathway." In a personal way God wants us to prepare a path. Have we made a path for Him to come and do a major and powerful work in our lives?

I have personal experience with a beaten pathway. I lived up on a hill in Arkadelphia, Arkansas, and one of my very best buddies by the name of Stacie Morris lived way down at the bottom of the hill. We had all sorts of pine trees on the way, and I had beaten a path down to her house because I had been there so many times.

I believe God's word to us is, *Make a beaten pathway. Come to Me. Make it your practice to approach Me over and over again, so that when I am ready to pour out a fresh work, the way will be made clear.* Do you have debris standing in the way of God doing a powerful work in your life? In exactly the situation you're in, in exactly the state of health you may be in, whatever your circumstances may be, God wants to work powerfully. In John 5:17, Jesus tells us that His father is always at work, and He too is working with Him. I want you to see this in conjunction with the next point because they go together.

Visitation

After a task of preparation, notice with me an unexpected visitation. Matthew tells us Jesus came to the Jordan to be baptized by John. "But John tried to deter him, saying, 'I need to be baptized by you, and do you come to me?' Jesus replied, 'Let it be so now; it is proper for us to do this to fulfill all righteousness.' Then John consented. And as soon as Jesus was baptized, he went up out of the water. At that moment heaven was opened, and he saw the Spirit of God descending like a dove and lighting on him" (Matt. 3:14–16).

Just imagine what was going on in the mind of Christ as He was walking to the river Jordan. I wonder if He stopped to watch the scene for awhile, with the people confessing their sins. Did He watch this mighty servant of God preaching the Word with boldness? I'm just picturing somehow that horizon and His figure overlooking the scene. Then He walks up to the shore, and John sees Him.

I've written something that is strictly fiction. I was just reflecting on what might have been going through John's mind as Jesus approached him. These thoughts came to me. Perhaps they will help us to see these as very real people encountering the Son of God.

My tongue had been like a flame that day. The Word of God came to me in the desert like fire from heaven. If I hadn't preached it, it would have consumed me. I had no fear. No intimidation. God sent me to those Jordan waters, and I knew they'd come. No prearranged meeting. Just the wind of the Spirit wooing, drawing, then blowing away the debris of sin, preparing the way for the Deliverer. No matter who came to the shore to hear or to jeer. The message was immutable, "Repent! For the kingdom of heaven is near!"

The fruit of repentance pierced the wind with cries of confession and waves of grief. I hardly stepped out of those waters that day. My voice grew raspy and hoarse but never quiet. Boldness was the marrow in my bones. Funny how stunned we are when the future we prophesy suddenly becomes present. I had told them I was unworthy to loose His sandals and that I would only baptize with water for repentance. He would baptize with the Holy Spirit and with fire. I spoke like an authority. Like an associate of the closest kind. Like someone who knew it all. I didn't.

I was just raising a repentant man from the waters when I saw someone out of the corner of my eye walk to the water's edge. As I think back, how those waters kept from parting that day, I'll never know. Numbers were gathered on the shore. Others were waist-deep in the water. Suddenly I became oblivious to all but the overpowering presence of the One. There He stood, looking straight at me, through me. Oh, it was Him all right! I had been preparing for Him all my life, and yet I was not ready. All I could do was look at Him and shake my head, "No. Please, no! Not me. I have need to be baptized by You!"

Suddenly I was overcome by my own compulsion to flood the shore with waves of repentance, and He answered, "Let it be for now. It is proper for us to do this to fulfill all righteousness." So I consented, shaking all over. I placed my left hand on His back and my right hand on His chest. I felt the heartbeat of the Son of God. As if in slow motion, I leaned Him back into those waters, His weight submitting to my hands.

All of a sudden the Jordan chilled me to the bone. I raised Him from the waters, and He stood before me drenched in the river of promise. The water dripping from His beard seemed to drop like diamonds, proclaiming His endless perfections. He alone had no confessions to make that day. Only one was made over Him, the confession of His holiness enthroned in heaven. "This is my Son whom I love and with Him I am well pleased." The blessing of the Father fell like a dove from heaven. He walked out of those waters and into our lives, interrupting a fallen world with grace and truth. My name is John. I am the son of a simple man and woman. I baptized the Messiah that day.

Can you imagine? He had prepared all his life. When we set apart our lives unto Him, He will do wonders with us the likes of which we cannot imagine.

Representation

Next look with me at a third element of the event, a glorious representation. People from the entire region came to John confessing their sins, and he baptized them in the Jordan. We can almost picture him waist-deep in water with people streaming out to be baptized. First they were confessing their sins because they weren't being baptized unto salvation. John was baptizing them unto repentance, preparing them to encounter the Savior, the only One who could bring them salvation.

I believe they were quite specific confessing their sins. In all likelihood they were crying out these confessions, maybe even wailing them. They may have been weeping over their sins. Then came Christ. We know He was not coming to be baptized unto repentance. He was the spotless Lamb of God. Complete perfection. The only One who had no confessing to do that day in those waters. He came for John to baptize Him.

I just want you to get the picture here. I'm not trying to make a doctrinal statement or an interpretation of Scripture. I'm just asking you to see a picture. We know that God was baptizing His Son into ministry.

The representation of the death, the burial, and the resurrection. I also see something so precious in the fact that they had confessed their sins standing in those waters and then were baptized. Christ comes after they've made this confession. He is baptized — drenched in the same waters where they had confessed their sins. I'm just talking symbolism here, but do you almost see Him wearing the sins they had confessed in those waters?

I love the practice of daily coming to the line with Christ and naming my sins. I don't practice a "Lord forgive me for all of my sins." I don't see true biblical repentance in that. Repentance assumes we are naming the sin to acknowledge it. Then I like to discuss with God why it doesn't agree with His Word. Why the sin isn't what He wants for me. That kind of repentance begins to get those precepts down into my soul. I love Acts 3:19: "Repent, then, and turn to God, so that your sins may be wiped out, that times of refreshing may come from the Lord." Those of us who have already received Christ have been baptized into Him. Now daily confession is like refreshment to our souls. We come away from repentance cleansed. Ready to be filled. Ready to walk in the Spirit.

Divine Demonstration

In Matthew 3:16 we're told, "At that moment heaven was opened, and he saw the Spirit of God descending like a dove and lighting on him." Try to picture that with me. What in the world does heaven look like open? I mean somebody just explain that to me. Back in Genesis 1 God created the heavens and the earth, and He separated the expanse from the waters, and He called that expanse the sky. I can't help but think, *He called it into being. He put it in its place. He can open it if He wants to!* He opened up the sky like a window, and showed Christ the vision through it.

This event also makes me think of Stephen, the very first martyr, because heaven was opened to him and he saw Jesus Christ standing at the right hand of God on his behalf. What I want you to understand is that heaven is right there. We look up at that sky and the expanse of the stars. He is literally just an open window from us, sitting on His throne, and His presence is in us and on us. God upon His throne is near. We just cannot see it.

On this special occasion God did something unusual. He opened up that window, and Christ looked straight into heaven. It had been a long time since He had seen that vision. I believe part of God's purpose for sending Jesus here is to experience life as we do. That means I don't believe He had X-ray vision every single second into the throne room of God. I believe that many times He prayed, meditated, and had relationship in the very same ways we do today. So what a time that must have been to capture that moment when He could see heaven open and the Holy Spirit descend.

Paternal Proclamation

His Father proclaimed a blessing as He said, "This is my Son, whom I love; with him I am well pleased" (Matt. 3:17). I want to suggest to you again that I don't think God spoke audibly to His Son every day He was on earth. I think maybe Jesus was called here to sympathize with us and to take part in the kind of relationship we do. A whole lot of His prayer was Him talking to God, knowing in His own Spirit and through God's Word what the Father was answering Him. The audible voice of His Father must have just fallen on Jesus with the dearest of familiarity. That was the love of His life. I want to think that through the night, He replayed that voice and blessing in His own mind a thousand times. "He loves me. Life is hard here, but He's proud of me. I have the blessing. I have the blessing."

I want to share with you the most unforgettable baptism I have ever seen. I will share a number of times in this study about my experiences in India, because God has seared my heart with that country. Part of my soul is right there in that place.

A few years ago we were in northern India at a small church. Because that part of India is Muslim and Hindu territory, it is illegal to testify of Christ in any way. I mean they are serious about it. Very soon after we left, that entire area was closed down to people like us. While we were there, I got an opportunity to speak to that precious church. At the end of the service, the minister of that church came back to the pulpit and said, "Now would our candidates for baptism please come forward."

With great sobriety, several people walked to the front and stood before the congregation. I remember so distinctly one man and one woman. The woman was in full Indian dress, just as you'd imagine that she was, with a veil over her head. The pastor presented them before the body.

They had been through all sorts of classes

so they could understand. Because this would be making a public profession of their faith, it could easily mean exclusion from their family, all sorts of persecution, maybe imprisonment, and possibly death. It is a serious thing to profess Jesus Christ in Northern India.

You could hear a pin drop in that room. The pastor told their names and shared a little bit about them. Then they were led, in their clothing, up to the baptismal waters. First the pastor baptized the woman.

I already had begun to cry because they are such a humble people. She was baptized in her veil. In her culture she would not have dreamed of taking off that veil. Yet as soon as she came up, she was pulling the veil back over her head.

The man came next. He looked to be in his late twenties. A tall, lanky man with very dark hair, very dark skin, and a little bit of a beard. Much taller than the pastor. It was a very, very sober moment. He was a Hindu. Try to appreciate how many millions of gods the Hindus must please. They live in complete fear. To them everything is a god.

But there he was, professing Jesus Christ as his Savior, the One and Only. Completely sober. The pastor baptized him back into those waters and brought him up.

The pastor's facial expression did not change one iota. But the man looked at the congregation, threw his arms up in the air, and began to jump up and down in that water. Water was splashing everywhere, even over the Plexiglas. The pastor was standing back. The man was just jumping up and down.

I couldn't even begin to understand what he was saying, but for that moment, I believed that I had the spiritual gift of interpretation. Something told me that he was saying, "Free! I am free!" It wouldn't have mattered if they came and took him. He had been in bondage to pleasing all of those gods. How could they hurt him? How would they judge him? Now finally, finally he had one true God! Through His Son, Jesus Christ.

I will never forget that moment because it reminded me that I, too, have been in terrible bondage. I knew what that man was saying to us: "Nothing they could do to me now compares with where I have been. Let me die free. But I am free." How we take for granted that we have identified with Jesus in the death of our bondage and the resurrection of freedom in Christ.

Jesus and John. Cousins. Waist deep in the Jordan. A beginning for one. An ending for another. Death awaiting both . . . and freedom for you and me. Oh can't you see beauty in that glorious encounter?

Chapter 11

Wilderness Welcome to Ministry

Luke 3:24–38

Jesus, full of the Holy Spirit, returned from the Jordan and was led by the Spirit in the desert, where for forty days he was tempted by the devil. (Luke 4:1)

We now reach a pivotal point in the life of Christ: His thirtieth year on planet Earth. As if Christ's ministry had been contained in an alabaster box, God broke the seal and began to pour Him forth like fragrant oil. But I don't believe Christ was sitting by idly until God took the box off the shelf. Perhaps it is more accurate to picture Christ being suddenly thrust from private to public ministry.

After Jesus' baptism, the Spirit led Him

into the desert to be tempted by the devil. Why did God lead Christ into the desert immediately following His baptism? Likely God's purpose was multifaceted, but I want to offer one possibility: before Christ went public, He had to determine what type of Messiah He was going to be. Christ's baptism represented His initiation into public ministry. God was about to present Jesus as His Son and Israel's Messiah.

Satan is very shrewd. He probably won't tempt you to turn stones into bread, assume authority over the kingdoms of the world, or throw yourself off the highest point of the temple. He tailors the temptations to each person's challenges. Hebrews tells us that Christ was tempted just as we are. I believe that long before He was thirty years old, Christ had numerous other temptations exactly like those we face in our day-to-day struggles. God's Word says He was tempted in all ways like us, yet was without sin. What thirty-year-old hasn't been tempted? Let's resist seeing this encounter as Christ's only grapple with temptation.

Christ's experience in the desert represented an intense season of temptation that was tailored by the enemy for the challenges of messiahship that lay ahead. I believe some issues were meant to be settled from the very beginning of Christ's ministry. God placed Jesus with His adversary in a lab of sorts to establish the ground rules. With this idea in mind, let's briefly consider each temptation in Luke 4:1–13.

"Tell this stone to become bread" (v. 3)

Could Christ turn a stone into bread? Undoubtedly! So why shouldn't He? After all, He was famished. Matthew 4:2 tells us Jesus was hungry because He had been fasting for forty days. Nothing is wrong with eating when a person is hungry, unless a greater issue is involved. Luke 2:37 beautifully describes the most probable purpose for the kind of fasting Jesus practiced in the desert. It describes Anna, the prophetess, who "served God with fastings and prayers night and day" (KJV). No doubt Christ's fast was for similar purposes. Most likely His intent was to seek God and refrain from all distractions. Since we know He was filled with the Spirit and led by the Spirit, we can assume the Spirit prompted the fast; therefore, the fast wasn't over until God said so.

What did this temptation have to do with Christ's imminent ministry? Robert Stein says the issue was whether or not Christ would use His power for His own ends. "Would He live by the same requirements of faith and dependence on God as everyone else in the kingdom?"[1] Satan's strategy wasn't all that different from what he used tempting Eve in the garden (see Gen. 3:1). In both cases, Satan wanted to sow doubt . . . but certainly not because he had any. He knew what God had said to Adam and Eve, and he definitely knew Christ was the Son of God. Why in the world would Satan have tried sowing doubt in Christ?

At this point in Christ's wilderness temptation I can really relate. Think of the questions we would have if we encountered an intense battle right after we entered a place or time of ministry:

- Did I misunderstand God?
- If He really loves me, why would He appoint me to such a struggle?
- How could this happen right after my finest moment with God?

We see a second similarity in that the temptation involved food. Christ was hungry. Eve was hungry for something different. Our appetites are ferocious. They are fodder for much temptation.

I find Paul's description of the enemies of the cross of Christ very interesting in Philippians 3:19. He not only said their minds are on earthly things, but he also said "their god is their stomach." Although you and I are not enemies of the cross, we certainly know the temptation of making our stomachs gods. Christ didn't fall to the temptation. He responded with two critical phrases.

Christ's first phrase of response was universal because Scripture applies to every temptation we can ever face. He said, "It is written" (Luke 4:4). In those words He clarified the matter of authority. Jesus subjugated Satan's words to God's Word.

The second phrase of Jesus' response was issue specific. "Man does not live by bread alone." Christ applied the specific word from Scripture to meet His need. So Satan moved on to the next temptation.

"If you worship me, it will all be yours" (v. 7)

We cannot imagine Christ ever being the least bit tempted to worship Satan, but can we not imagine that He might have been tempted to rip Satan's authority out of his hands?

Christ didn't challenge Satan's ability to make such an offer. We can assume Satan had the authority as the prince of this world.

It's true the authority God has allowed Satan is limited and temporary, but it is nonetheless very real.

Can you imagine how Christ must feel as He watches the state of the world under the influence of the evil prince's authority? Oppression, violence, and deception characterize the world God loves. Surely Christ is counting the days until He grabs the deed restriction to the world and reigns in righteousness.

Satan was hoping Christ would be so anxious to secure the world that He'd worship him. Needless to say, Satan was wrong. Christ will most assuredly reign over this world, but not until all things have happened according to God's kingdom calendar.

Once again Christ called on Scripture, this time with the specific application: "Worship the Lord your God and serve him only" (v. 8). Christ adamantly resisted worshiping Satan as a way to gain the world. So Satan moved to his third temptation.

"Throw yourself down from here" (v. 9)

"Jesus answered and said to him, 'It is said, "You shall not put the Lord your God to the test"'" (v. 12 NASB). Based on Christ's response to this temptation, we know that at least one of Satan's intentions was to tempt Christ to put God to the test. One way of putting God to the test might be disguising a dare by calling it faith. Challenging God is not only void of faith; it is also foolish. A self-prompted refusal to seek medical attention for serious illness followed by a public proclamation of God's obligation to heal you could be putting God to the test. Racing a car and saying God is responsible for keeping you from injury or believing rules of accountability don't apply to you could also be forms of testing God.

Satan may have had a second intention in this particular temptation. The placement of the temptation at the temple suggests that the enemy may have been hoping a dramatic scene would cause the Jews to hail Jesus as their king before He faced the cross. If Christ had foregone the cross, He would have been no less God, but we would be lost.

In conclusion, I believe our hypothesis was correct. These were no ordinary temptations. They appear to be direct assaults on the messiahship of Christ. We can, however, draw a few closing applications.

• Seasons of intense temptation are not

indications of God's displeasure.
- Satan is tenacious. Don't expect him to give up after one or two tries.
- Scripture is the most powerful tool in our fight against temptation. Don't fight back with your words, fight back with God's!

Chapter 12

The Preacher

Luke 4:14–21

"The Spirit of the Lord is on me, because he has anointed me to preach good news to the poor." (Luke 4:18)

I was a mess before the Savior set me free. That's why my dearest life passages are the ones found in Isaiah 61:1–2 and quoted again in the Gospel of Luke. Jesus went to His home synagogue in Nazareth and declared both the fact and the nature of His call and ministry — to preach good news to the poor . . . to proclaim freedom for the prisoners . . . sight for the blind . . . to release the oppressed . . . to proclaim the year of the Lord's favor (Luke 4:18–19).

Do you know this Jesus? Once you do, you can't get over Him. God allowed me to write an entire study based on these verses; yet even now as I read them, I cannot help but cry. I owe Jesus everything. Every breath. Every word out of my mouth. Not because I can repay Him, but because I love Him so. Even as a believer, I continued to live in defeat. Abundant life was not mine until I let the Healer set me free, not just from hell but from myself.

OK, I'll get a grip and we'll see what fresh word God will bring us. First consider verse 14: "Jesus returned to Galilee in the power of the Spirit." Don't miss the significance! Jesus went into His wilderness temptation full of the Holy Spirit. He returned from the wilderness in the power of the Spirit. After all He had suffered? We picture ourselves emerging from intense seasons of temptation or trial "by the skin of our teeth." Wounded. Half dead. Limping forever.

Jesus, on the other hand, came from the battle with an anointing of power. He taught in various synagogues, and word of Him spread through the whole countryside. Christ then set His sights on Nazareth — His hometown. I wonder what He was thinking as He rounded those familiar hills and gazed upon the village, no longer as a fellow citizen but as a saving servant.

No doubt Jesus received warm embraces, even kisses on His cheeks, as He walked the village streets. Merchants probably called His name and welcomed Him back, not because He was the Son of God but because He was a native son. We can safely assume Christ ducked His head through His family's own front door and probably slept there until He went on the road with His disciples.

By this time most of His siblings probably were grown with families of their own. His brothers' homes were most likely "add-ons" to their father's. Jesus' family members probably had feelings toward Him ranging from curiosity and confusion to animosity and jealousy. A single Jewish man making the road His home was highly irregular. They probably loved Him, but they most assuredly didn't understand Him.

Jesus returned to Nazareth with power He had never manifested there. Still, He didn't throw the defining explosive until the next Sabbath. Although Jesus regularly went to the synagogue, on that day a fresh breeze blew in. He stood up to read.

Old Testament Scripture was meticulously copied by hand onto parchment. The parchment was then rolled into scrolls and placed in cabinets or what is called a Torah ark. They removed one scroll of Scripture at a time. Luke's description accurately reflects the custom of the designated reader. Jesus stood up to read. He was then handed the scroll that, not coincidentally, was Isaiah, the book containing more prophecy about Christ than any other.

Picture the scene. The synagogue was the center of Jewish community life, so it was undoubtedly buzzing with activity. The structure was rectangular, and its typically ornate triple doors usually faced Jerusalem. As Christ walked through the doors, He passed three or four pillars and several stone benches on the edges of the room. Most of those attending sat cross-legged in the floor. Undoubtedly, many of them knew Him personally. Customarily, the designated reader was handed the scroll chosen for the day and, after reading the passages at a lectern, he handed the scroll back to the attendant, sat down in front, and offered instructional commentary. Imagine the authority and power that must have accompanied Christ's voice that day.

With every eye glued to Him, Jesus began with a stunning eight-word synopsis: "Today this scripture is fulfilled in your hearing" (v. 21). The Greek word for "fulfilled" is *pleroo,* meaning "particularly, to fill a vessel or hollow place." To demonstrate His play on words, read aloud Luke

4:18–19 and insert the name *Jesus* every time you see the word *me*. Could anyone else in all of history fill this position? No matter how many priests, prophets, and kings had served the nation of Israel, this calling was Christ's alone. Until then, the long-awaited position remained unfilled. How aptly this applies to us as well. We remain hollow until the only One suited for fulfillment is allowed to take His proper place. Luke 4:18–19 constitutes the job description God assigned to His chosen One.

If you compare Luke 4:18–19 with the original job description of the Messiah in Isaiah 61:1–2, you will notice a few differences. One very clear difference between the two texts is that Jesus abruptly stopped reading without saying "and the day of vengeance of our God" (Isa. 61:2). He had a very good reason. He read only what God was immediately fulfilling through Him. When Christ returns, He will come for His own, but He will also come with a vengeance. In His first advent, however, God purposely sent Christ with a different agenda. Let's briefly discuss each part of that description:

1. "The Spirit of the Lord is on me, because he has anointed me to preach good news to the poor" (Luke 4:18). Christ didn't mean the financially destitute. The Greek word for "poor" is *ptochos,* indicating "utter helplessness, complete destitution, afflicted, distressed." I think God is far too faithful to let anyone make it through life without confronting seasons of utter helplessness. Look at the remainder of the definition: "subsisting on the alms of others."

God created us to need something or someone else. Sooner or later, any healthy individual discovers that autonomy doesn't cut it. Once we confront our need for someone or something beyond ourselves, we will subsist on the alms of others if we don't discover Christ. Like beggars we go from person to person with our empty cup, crying, "Can't you add anything to my life?" They might throw in a coin or two. In fact, a few may be weekly . . . and probably weary . . . tithers. But when we shake the cup, the tinny echo reminds us how empty we remain. Until we allow Jesus to fill our cups daily, we simply subsist. The good news Christ may want to preach to you today is that you don't have to subsist. You were meant to thrive. Sooner or later, God will make sure we confront the poverty of living on the alms of others so that we may learn to feast on Him.

2. *"To heal the brokenhearted" (Luke*

4:18 KJV). Unless you're using a King James Version, this phrase probably came from the Isaiah reference. Some New Testament translations include it, while others don't. Either way, the phrase was in the original job description and is worthy of our consideration. The original word for "brokenhearted" is *suntribo,* meaning "to break, strike against something . . . to break the strength or power of someone." The Greek word for "heal" is *iaomai,* meaning "to heal, cure, restore." I love the Hebrew word translated "heal" in Exodus 15:26 when God introduced Himself by a new title: "I am the Lord, who heals you." The word *raphah* means "to mend (by stitching), repair thoroughly, make whole." I picture God focusing steadily on the object of repair. One stitch follows another. It takes time. I picture painful penetrations of the healing needle. I don't know about you, but I'm quite sure if my healing processes had been painless, I would have relapsed.

3. "To proclaim freedom for the prisoners" (v. 18). In many ways long after my salvation I was like the prisoners in Psalm 107:10–16, 20, "suffering in iron chains, / for they had rebelled against the words of God" (vv. 10–11).

Many people sincerely love God, but I

136

don't think anyone stands to appreciate the unfailing love of God like the believer finally set free from failure. This captive can undoubtedly testify: He sent forth His Word and healed me. Stitch by stitch. Please notice that Christ proclaimed freedom. He didn't impose it. It remains an offer.

4. *"Recovery of sight for the blind" (v. 18).* Although Christ would heal many from physical blindness, I believe His intent here was a far more serious kind of blindness. Second Corinthians 4:4 says, "The god of this age has blinded the minds of unbelievers, so that they cannot see the light of the gospel of the glory of Christ, who is the image of God."

I found the original word for "blind" in both Luke and 2 Corinthians to be so interesting. *Tuphlos* means "to envelop with smoke, be unable to see clearly." Perhaps none of the enemy's attempts to cloud our vision compare to our fiery trials. His job is to keep us blinded to the One who walks with us through the fire. Oh, believer, God is there whether or not our spiritual eyes discern Him.

5. *"To release the oppressed" (v. 18).* I looked up every definition for *oppressed* in the Greek and Hebrew dictionaries. A half dozen original words are translated in the

137

Bible with our single word *oppressed,* and all but one have the word *break* in the definition. I'm becoming more and more convinced that heavy-duty oppression is Satan's counterfeit for biblical brokenness.

At times I've fought back the tears as I've heard testimonies of people who had been utterly unable to function, describing themselves as broken by God. I don't think God's brand of brokenness is total emotional wreckage. God's intent in breaking us is to bend our stiff knees so that we will submit to His authority and take on His yoke. His aim is our abundant and effective life. Being totally unable to function because the mind and emotions are in shambles is Satan's counterfeit. Praise God, Christ can certainly use Satan's counterfeit brokenness to bring us to a place of accepting His own, but I think we credit some things to Christ that He doesn't do.

6. *"To proclaim the year of the Lord's favor" (v. 19).* That year those gathered in the Nazarene synagogue were staring in the face of the Lord's favor — His blessed gift of grace, Jesus Christ. The word *year* can be translated as "any definite time." God places before each of us a definitive period of time to accept the Lord's favor. He wills for none to perish but for all to come to re-

pentance (see 2 Pet. 3:9). The world has until His return. The individual has a definitive period of time known by God alone. I am not past begging people not to wait too long for salvation, because eternal life in heaven is at stake, or for freedom, because abundant life on earth is at stake. He longs to be your champion now.

Part 3

The Way and Life

Ministry is never easy. It's also rarely uncomplicated. You and I are called to ministry whether or not it is a full-time vocation. Keep in mind a point so obvious it's almost obscure: Christ was the first person God ever assigned to "Christian" ministry. He set the precedent. We can learn much from watching how He handled fickle crowds and difficult circumstances. That's what our third section of study is all about. Mark 10:45 tells us Christ didn't come to be served but to serve. However, not everyone Christ met wanted what He had to serve. We can certainly expect the same response at times. But we'll never see a situation cause Christ to flinch from what His Father called Him to do. He had a "made-up mind." His example will challenge us as we take deep stock of His goals and His methods. May "His way" become ours.

I love this point in a Scripture journey. The foundation has been poured, and fresh habits are forming. Let's not miss a single truth as we continue on. Let your mind and heart be completely immersed by the Spirit of God through His Word.

Chapter 13

"What Is This Teaching?"

Luke 4:22–37

All the people were amazed and said to each other, "What is this teaching? With authority and power he gives orders to evil spirits and they come out!" (Luke 4:36)

Our previous chapter centered on the glorious job description of the anointed One. After Jesus declared the prophecy fulfilled in their presence, the people spoke highly of Him. Jesus' next words seem surprising. He seemed to invite rejection in declaring that a prophet is rejected in His hometown. If I hadn't studied Scripture for a number of years and learned to recognize behavior that was characteristic of Christ, I might have thought He was picking a fight with the people. I tend to cheer for the underdog, and strictly from appearances, I might have been tempted to think Jesus didn't give them a chance.

Since we know Christ's heart was perfect and patient, something more was going on in that encounter than meets the eye. Murky waters like these force us to dive in and see what's stirring on the bottom. Two considerations may help us to understand Christ's prophetic confrontation.

First, consider the original wording. Verse 22 tells us that "all spoke well of him." The translation "spoke well of" comes from the Greek word *martureo,* meaning "to be a witness, bear witness . . . to be able or ready to testify." "Amazed" is the Greek word *thaumazo,* meaning "struck with admiration." Either of these words could be used by spectators after attending any rock concert and being impressed by a talent. The wording suggests that they were impressed by Christ's delivery — not so much what He said, but how He said it.

Let me draw on my experience and offer a possible explanation. After delivering a message, nothing hits me like cold water more than someone saying, "You are a great speaker." First of all, I know better than that. I have a thick accent and use tons of country colloquialisms. Far more important, though, if someone makes a statement like that, I know either I failed miserably or the person didn't get it. In the case of Jesus' teaching, we know He can't fail, so obviously, they didn't get it. In Jesus' seemingly harsh words, He may have been responding to their grading His speech rather than receiving His message.

Notice a second consideration: the velocity of the crowd's change of mood. The crowd's mood went from admiration to a murderous rage in the moments of Christ's confrontation. Luke describes them as furious. The word in the text for "furious" comes from the word *thuo,* meaning "to move impetuously, particularly as the air or wind, a violent motion or passion of the mind." The north wind of their admiration suddenly reversed into a south wind of tornadic proportions. When a mood can change in a matter of moments from admiration to murderous fury, something is amiss.

I have learned some very hard lessons in ministry. One is that some people in the religious world make idols or stars out of Christian speakers or singers. A fan can turn to foe with mind-boggling velocity. You don't have to be in a ministry that places you in front of people to know what I'm talking about.

Have you seen a dramatic and sudden mood swing in an individual or group? If so, you know what I mean. Unsettling, isn't it? Don't forget that the people Christ addressed in Luke 4 were very religious. Unchecked anger can easily lead to uncontrolled behavior regardless of how much we attend church. The synagogue members tried to kill Jesus. They grabbed Him and took Him to the brow of the hill to hurl Him to His death. "But he walked right through the crowd and went on his way" (v. 30).

Allow these words to represent far more than a simple getaway. Based on what follows in the chapter, I believe Christ's experience in Nazareth was a pivotal moment in His life. He had to choose to perform ministry either their way or His way.

The types of crowds Christ encountered two thousand years ago still fill many churches today. Many congregations want to hear impressive A+ messages, but the messenger better keep his confrontational thoughts to himself. The same committee that throws out the red carpet to a new preacher may eventually roll him out the door in it! Meanness at church sometimes exceeds anything that occurs in secular sur-

146

roundings. As James 3:10 says, "My brethren, these things ought not so to be" (KJV).

For the next several chapters we're going to watch Jesus do things His way. You can be sure His way won't likely be conventional.

After departing His hometown, Christ went to the village of Capernaum. Luke 4:31–37 contains the first account of Christ's miraculous works recorded in the Book of Luke.

Christ's earthly ministry was hardly launched before the demonic world confronted Him — in a synagogue, no less. Thank goodness, Christ isn't spooked by the demonic world. No matter what authority Satan and his subjects have been temporarily allowed in this world system, Christ can pull rank any time He wants. On that day in Capernaum, He wasted no time. A demon-possessed man shouted loudly and declared Jesus to be the Holy One of God.

The demon appeared to desire attention. We can assume the demon was loud because Christ adamantly told him to "Be quiet!" I'm certainly not suggesting that all demonic activity is loud. I am asking you to consider that when allowed to penetrate a place meant for practices of devotion to

God, one of the chief tactics of demons is to divert attention.

I've seen this tactic. At a recent conference a woman began to shriek right after someone prayed and before I was to speak. The wise and godly woman leading the conference immediately went to the microphone and dealt graciously but firmly with the outburst. Although I've not often observed that type of behavior, the few times I've experienced it, I discerned a tactic of the demonic world to divert attention. I'm not talking about precious children rattling papers or innocent babies crying. I'm talking about intrusive disruptions that leave little doubt of origin.

Note that the demon seemed to be telling some semblance of the truth, but we see a distortion or misuse of the truth in the demonic testimony. He was acting as a counterfeit preacher of sorts. He could not stop the truth so he hoped to disqualify the message by the instability or insanity of the apparent messenger.

Some years ago, a strange thing happened at our church. Each Sunday, for six or seven weeks, a man who appeared to be mentally ill would stand outside the main doors and "preach" to us using a megaphone as we left the building after worship. Some of the statements he made were technically scriptural, but his appearance and his approach demonstrated such instability that he did more to distract people from the truth than attract. The typical listener's tendency would be to disbelieve anything he said simply because he was the one saying it.

A new dimension of spiritual warfare was erupting as Christ began His earthly ministry. Let's have a quick history lesson so we can recognize the new dimension. Thousands of years ago, war was declared in the heavenlies when Satan was booted out of heaven.

The Bible is not about Satan, but several passages hint at his origin. Many Bible scholars believe the following passages apply to Satan. Ezekiel 28:11–17 describes him as the anointed guardian cherub on God's holy mount. He was a creature of great beauty and power until he became proud and corrupted. Then he was driven from heaven. In Isaiah 14:12–15 he is called Lucifer. Before he fell from heaven Lucifer wanted to make himself like the Most High.

Revelation 12:3–4 also speaks of Satan's banishment from heaven. Obviously the dragon in Revelation represents the devil (see Rev. 12:9). Many commentators also believe that the "third of the stars" in verse 4 represents a third of the angels in heaven. These fallen angels are now called demons. Remember, unlike God, Satan cannot be in all places at once; therefore, many demons do his worldwide bidding.

We saw earlier that Satan is presently the "prince of this world." Christ had not come in human form to challenge the devil on his own turf until now. We don't even have to wonder how unwelcome Christ's presence was to the demonic world. Christ's power is obvious in Luke 4:35. The moment He commanded the demon to "come out," the demon received a compulsory expulsion.

Luke supplies us one specific bit of information not contained in Mark's account of this exorcism. Luke couldn't help telling us that the man wasn't injured. Matthew, a former tax collector, had much to say about stewardship. In the same way, Dr. Luke, more than any other Gospel writer, pointed out more about the physical condition of the people Christ encountered.

Christ's encounter with the demon-possessed man concludes with the introduction of a vital word. The crowds remarked that Jesus' teaching possessed a totally distinctive element: He taught with authority.

No greater concept exists where you and I are concerned than the authority of Jesus

Christ. Even more than the atonement. For if He has no authority, His act of atonement would have been sacrificial but powerless. The life of Christ unfolding in our study to come will say volumes about authority. From this point forward, be on the lookout because what we do with Christ's authority determines what He does with us. He's not just good. He's God.

Chapter 14

A House Call

Luke 4:38–44

He bent over her and rebuked the fever, and it left her. She got up at once and began to wait on them. (Luke 4:39)

This study is the first God has given me that focuses entirely on the life of Christ, and that's a problem because I want to begin every entry with, "Oh, how I love Him." No new words. Nothing creative, nor even particularly profound. Just true. I keep telling myself, "You can't start every single chapter with the same words!" Fine, then. But that's what I'm thinking.

Now we're going to look at Jesus as He leaves the synagogue, heals people with all kinds of diseases beginning with Peter's mother-in-law, and silences the demons who sought to comment on His actions.

These passages lend themselves to at least five insights into the life of Christ.

Jesus Made House Calls

We see the platform for Christ's ministry broaden from the synagogue to include the home. What a relief to know that God doesn't just go to church, He goes to our homes! When I was a little girl, I was fairly certain God lived in our church baptistry. My vivid imagination turned dressing-room doors into secret passages into the mysterious dwelling of the divine boogie man. I am happy to report that God doesn't live in the baptistry. He lives in the hearts of those who trust Him and in the homes of those who provide Him room. Sometimes we don't bother to summon Jesus Christ into our homes until we are overwhelmed by threatening circumstances.

One person suffering in a home is enough to affect all who live within. Simon's mother-in-law was suffering from a high fever and "they asked Jesus to help her" (v. 38). Understandably, she would not have been in a position to seek help for herself.

Aren't you thankful we can summon Christ's intervention on another person's behalf? Aren't you also thankful that others have summoned Him on yours? Our homes today are threatened by fevers of all sorts — far beyond the physiological: unresolved conflict, unforgiveness, unfaithfulness, compromising media communications, pornography, and more. We need Jesus in our homes.

Do you have a sense of Christ's activity in your home? I've a good reason for asking you this question. Almost every spiritual marker of Christ's heightened activity in my home came as a direct result of some threatening situation. Right now both my daughters are walking with God, but I assure you this did not simply happen in the natural evolution of their lives. I've watched their relationships grow through situations in which some threat convinced them to cleave closer to Christ.

God is so faithful. He can use the worst of circumstances to introduce us to the best of relationships. I am intrigued by the fact that Simon's mother-in-law immediately began serving Christ and the others. Few people are more compelled to serve than those who have experienced the healing power of Christ.

Jesus Engaged Himself in People's Lives

When Jesus went to help Simon's mother-in-law, Luke 4:39 tells us He "bent over her." I don't think I'm reading too much into the picture to imagine a close encounter suggesting deep concern. I react in a similar way any time one of my children is sick. I don't remain upright and stoic, checking off a list of symptoms. I bend over them and draw close. I learned from my mother how to better gauge a temperature with my cheek on their foreheads than with a thermometer. I cannot keep my distance from a sick child even if her malady is contagious. Christ could have healed Simon's mother-in-law from the front porch. He didn't. He came to her and drew down close. Also, don't miss the strong implication that Christ involved Himself one-on-one with those He helped.

Once again we have a detail from Luke the physician. Mark also tells of Jesus healing many on this occasion, but only Luke adds the phrase "laying his hands on each one" (v. 40). We will study several encounters in which Christ healed people. Be forewarned against drawing a particular formula for healing based on any one incident. For now, the point is that Christ Jesus had a hands-on approach to ministry — just like He does today. His hands may currently be invisible, but His prints appear in countless restored lives.

Jesus Rebuked the Fever, Not the Patient

Not all illnesses are the patient's fault. I oppose teaching that suggests the opposite. Sometimes we do things or fail to do things that cause poor health. At those times, we probably could use a good rebuke. Often, however, the cause and effect is something only God understands. Thank goodness, the only One who knows absolutely is the One who reigns absolutely.

Jesus Encountered Much Desperation

This passage gives us two snapshots of desperation that no doubt pierced the heart of Christ. First, the people came only after the sun had set. To those of us who are Gentiles, the reason is not so obvious. Verse 38 tells us Christ had previously left the synagogue when He went to the home of Simon. Verse 31 tells us it was the Sabbath day.

Remember, at this point Christ primarily has been ministering in various synagogues to Jews. It was unlawful for them to carry the sick on the Sabbath. The Jewish "day" ends at sundown; therefore, God-fearing people counted the moments until the sun would set over the Sea of Galilee. As the darkness of a new day fell, they bundled their sick and brought them to the Light. The thought almost makes me cry. It was as if they watched the clock of the law tick until it finally struck grace . . . and they raced to Him with their need. How blessed we are to live in the liberty of a completed Calvary! The pharmacy dispensing God's grace is open 24/7.

A second snapshot of desperation appears in our passage. The next morning Jesus rose early and went out to pray (Mark 1:35), but the needy people searched Him out. I wish I had words to express the feelings such scriptural moments stir in me. The thought of Christ ducking out the door while it was still dark to find a place to be by Himself with God floods my soul with emotion. I love every glimpse of the unique relationship Father and Son shared while Christ was on earth and His Father was in heaven. Never before had such a bridge connected the celestial and the terrestrial. I always wonder what Christ said to His Father in those intimate moments and what He saw. Did God the Father speak audibly to Him? Or did He speak in His heart like He does to you and me through His Word? I can't wait to find out someday in glory.

We have no idea how many moments Jesus got to steal with His Father, but Scripture seems to imply He was soon interrupted: "When they came to where he was, they tried to keep him from leaving them" (v. 42). I'm convinced we don't give enough thought to how challenging a prison of flesh must have been to Christ. Prior to His advent, He was completely unencumbered by the natural laws governing the human body. Suddenly He experienced for Himself the pull to be in many places at once and the challenge to prioritize not just the good but the goal. He stated the goal as nothing less than to "preach the good news of the kingdom of God to the other towns also, because that is why I was sent" (v. 43). Healing the sick seems like an awfully important ministry to me, but the Savior plainly said that it was not the priority work He came to accomplish.

Jesus Was Determined

Luke 4 concludes with a definitive statement in verse 44: "He kept on preaching in the synagogues of Judea." He kept on — no matter how many directions He felt pulled. No matter how many needs remained in each town. No matter what others prioritized for Him — He kept on. Why? Because every other need humanity possessed was secondary to the need to hear and receive the gospel. Not unimportant, mind you. Just secondary. Physical healing affects this life alone. The kingdom is forever. Then why did Christ spend time and energy performing miracles of healing on such temporal bodies? Probably for three primary reasons:

- Because He could. He can do whatever
- He wants. Before that fact makes you nervous, remember: what He wants is always consistent with who He is. Among many other wonderful things, He is the healer. In one way or another He heals every single person who comes to Him by faith.
- *Because He is compassionate* — beyond anything we can imagine.
- *Because the miracles helped authenticate the messenger.*

Preaching the good news of the kingdom of God was Christ's absolute priority. One of the biggest temptations even mature believers face is being sidetracked by the urgent. Many situations need our attention. They tempt us to let them steal our focus. Christ may have faced the same temptation when the people came to Him and tried to keep Him from leaving.

The word for "keep" is *katecho,* meaning "to hold fast, retain, or hold down, quash, suppress." The people's attempts to hold onto Christ may not have been limited to the vocal and emotional. They may have hung onto Him physically too. How His heart must have broken for them. I believe He may have been torn emotionally, but He was not dissuaded. The best thing He could do for them was to stay true to the goal.

Can you imagine how Jesus longed for the time when His work would be accomplished and He could dwell within the hearts of all who would receive Him, never to leave them? Until then, He had a job to do. Christ ignored neither the urgent need nor the ultimate goal — but He never allowed the former to hinder the latter. Oh, how I love Him.

Chapter 15

A Catch in Deep Waters

Luke 5:1–11, 27–32; 6:12–16

Then Jesus said to Simon, "Don't be afraid; from now on you will catch men." (Luke 5:10)

Next we get to celebrate a fact that continually staggers my imagination: Christ calls mere mortals to join Him in His work. He doesn't need our help. Christ could save the world through dreams and visions, but He doesn't. He delights in asking us to join Him. I am convinced that every believer is summoned by Christ to work with Him here on earth. His is the only work we do that is for keeps.

I love my family, but sometimes after I have worked maniacally on the house and twenty-four hours later it is a wreck, I want to bawl! Other times at the office I'll finally get through a stack of paperwork and clean off my desk just in time for another stack to appear in its place. You can no doubt relate. My tasks at home and at work are important, but when I pour my life into God-things, such as boasting in the Lord with my children or teaching a Bible class on Sundays, those activities are for keeps.

Before we study our passages in Luke, note the words of John 5:17: "Jesus said to them, 'My Father is always at his work to this very day, and I, too, am working.' " I believe Christ calls disciples not so much to work for Him as with Him. What a difference I have found exists between those two concepts. Throughout this section of our study we are emphasizing how Christ did things His way, especially with those whom He called to join Him.

Peter had been out fishing all night and had caught nothing. In the morning, as they were washing their nets, Jesus told Peter to return to the lake and prepare for a great catch. We know this was probably not Christ's first encounter with Simon (Peter) because Jesus had healed Simon's mother-in-law. Simon obeyed Christ's instructions, with two dramatic results. First, they caught so many fish that the boat began to sink under the load. Second, Simon recognized he was in the presence of holiness. "When Simon Peter saw this, he fell at Jesus' knees and said, 'Go away from me, Lord; I am a sinful man!' " (Luke 5:8).

We don't know the previous vocations of each of Christ's twelve apostles, but we know for certain two vocations were among them. Peter, James, and John were fishermen; Matthew (Levi) was a tax collector.

Jesus moved with absolute purpose in His ministry. Already He had attracted many disciples who considered themselves His followers, but Christ was about to do something more. We have no idea how many disciples Christ had at this point, but He had enough to draw out the twelve from among them after an intense night of prayer. The twelve did not cease being disciples, but they had an additional function as apostles. The Greek word for "apostles" means "one sent, apostle, ambassador . . . it designates the office as instituted by Christ to witness of Him before the world (John 17:18). It also designates the authority that those called to this office possess." We will most often see them referenced as the twelve disciples, but keep in mind that their distinction was an apostolic ambassadorship and authority assigned them by Christ.

More than any other one-on-one relationship in his Gospel, Luke developed the relationship between Christ and Peter. Let's focus now on their first encounters. Earlier we noted that Luke 5 most likely does not represent their initial meeting. Actually, even Luke 4:38 does not represent their first encounter. John chapter one tells about the events that surrounded their very first meeting.

Jesus first met Andrew with some other disciples of John the Baptist. Andrew took Jesus to see Simon. When He first saw the man who would one day lead the disciples, Christ declared: " 'You are Simon son of John. You will be called Cephas' (which, when translated, is Peter)" (John 1:42). By the time Jesus taught on the shore in Luke 5:1, Christ and Peter had already shared at least two encounters. This one, however, was more than an encounter. It was a call. Picture Christ on the shore of the Sea of Galilee, pressed from all sides by people listening to the Word of God.

Can you see Him? In an attempt to capture His meekness, artists often portray Jesus as a skinny, mealy-mouthed weakling, but biblical meekness never equals weakness. Meekness is submission to the Father's will. Few things require more strength than submission. The incarnate Jesus, preparing to teach the crowds, was a powerful and authoritative speaker.

Luke 5:2 tells us Jesus saw two boats at the water's edge, one of which belonged to Simon Peter, who was rinsing his nets. Jesus got into the boat and asked Peter "to put out a little from shore. Then he sat down and taught the people from the boat" (v. 3). Christ taught from the boat probably for two reasons: (1) the boat provided a platform that made Him more visible, and (2) the breeze coming off the lake provided acoustics that made Him more audible. The spiritual does not always operate apart from the logical.

When Jesus had finished teaching, He told Peter to put the boat out into deep water for a catch. Peter replied that he had fished all night and had caught nothing, but he obeyed Jesus' words. How shocked he must have been when the nets filled with more fish than he could handle. Then shock gave way to insight as Peter fell at Jesus' feet and declared, "Go away from me, Lord; I am a sinful man!" (v. 8). Let's draw a series of applications from the events on the lake that day:

1. Christ knows more about our jobs than we do. In our previous chapter we learned that Christ makes house calls. Now we see

Him expand His ministry into the workplace. He told Peter how to fish. Had Peter not already known Christ, he might have thought: *Me fisherman, You carpenter. I won't tell You how to build, and You don't tell me how to fish.* Instead, he submitted with only one brief disclaimer: we've done this all night and caught nothing.

One of the most critical reasons believers experience defeat is because we categorize only a few areas of our lives as Christ's arena. Many Christians think Christ's jurisdiction doesn't extend into certain areas. As if to save Him the extra trouble of dealing with things that don't concern Him, they leave Christ at church to deal with areas related to His expertise.

Satan is greatly defeated when we start living the truth that every area is Christ's specialty. Whether you're a homemaker, steelworker, or CEO, Christ knows every detail associated with your job. Jesus knows accounting, movie-theater managing, banking, drafting, engineering, nursing, real-estate brokering, and anything else we could do. For crying out loud, the One who knows the numbers of hairs on your head could also style them if He wanted. Not one of us does anything for a living that He can't do better.

2. Christ honors our submission even when our only motivation is obedience. If there was one phrase I wasn't going to say as a parent, it was "because I said so." I heard those words from my army-captain dad more times than I could count. I wasn't about to repeat them. After all, I had studied child development. I vowed to explain things to my children as if they were little adults. I almost got away with it too. Then I had Melissa — the proverbial "but, why?" child. One day she pushed me too far. Something in me snapped. I suddenly exploded, "Because I said so!" Not just once. I screamed it over and over like a mad bull on a rampage. I even screamed it at the dog. Four-year-old Melissa shrugged her shoulder, said "OK!" and skipped off happily.

I called my dad and thanked him. Sometimes God allows us to explore the "whys" of His instructions. Other times He wants us to obey "because He said so." Has God asked you to obey in a specific matter that still awaits your obedient response? (Always remember that He never leads us to do anything inconsistent with His character as expressed through His Word.) Would you consider the following statement? "Master, I've had a lot of excuses for doing this my way, but because You say so, I will . . ." You finish the sentence. Follow through, then wait on the Lord to bless your act of obedience, no matter how long it takes. He is faithful.

3. The same job subjected to Christ's authority can yield entirely different results. Peter had no doubt fished in every level of water in the lake. The key to his enormous catch was not the deep water. It was the authority of Christ. Beloved, if your job has grown stale, you may not need a new occupation. You may need a new partner. Make Colossians 3:23–24 your motto, and you'll have a different attitude: "Whatever you do, work at it with all your heart, as working for the Lord, not for men, since you know that you will receive an inheritance from the Lord as a reward. It is the Lord Christ you are serving."

Every hour you do your job as working for the Lord gets punched on a time clock in heaven. You get paid by God Himself for the hours you work as unto the Lord. I'm not being cheesy. Our future inheritance is real, and it far exceeds minimum wage. As you partner with Christ at your job, you will be more efficient. No matter whether your new efficiency increases your earthly dividends, it most definitely will increase your eternal dividends, where moth and rust cannot destroy or thieves break in and steal (see Matt. 6:19).

4. Christ's willingness to empower us can overwhelm us. Simon Peter already knew Jesus possessed extraordinary power, but he felt the real impact of Christ's power when that authority worked through his own hands. Suddenly the fisherman fell at Jesus' knees and said, "Go away from me, Lord; I am a sinful man!" (Luke 5:8).

What blessed condescension that the God of glory would use us! What humility the realization should bring! Isaiah cried, "Woe to me! . . . I am ruined" (Isa. 6:5). Peter cried, "Go away from me, Lord; I am a sinful man!" (Luke 5:8). Both men were overwhelmed, not just by what they had done. They were overwhelmed by what they were: sinful men. Do not miss the fact that neither was prepared to receive their call until they confronted their sin.

I've certainly never experienced an encounter like Isaiah's or Peter's, but I have assuredly faced moments of such stark realization of my own sin that I felt unbearable pain. Interestingly, those moments did not come during times of rebellion, but rather, they came during close encounters with God when I drew close enough to get an eyeful of myself.

I will never forget the realizations that brought me to surrender to the crucified life. Suddenly I realized that even if I could cease all sinful behavior, I would continue to battle sin throughout my life because I don't just commit sin. Apart from God, I am sinful. My problem is not just what I do; it's who I am without His nature.

Those realizations were both harrowing and liberating. The surrender resulting from the realization of my own innate unholiness did more to activate the holiness of God in me than anything I've ever experienced. How like God! Even our painful realizations of sinfulness are to mortify us to new life.

In conclusion, if you've had an encounter with Jesus that shed a harrowing and liberating light on you, praise Him for it. If you have not had that encounter, here's a tip: Don't seek an experience. Seek Jesus. Get apart to Him. He has a promise for all who seek Him: "If from there you seek the Lord your God, you will find him if you look for him with all your heart and with all your soul" (Deut. 4:29). (See also Matt. 7:7–11)

Chapter 16

If You Are Willing

Luke 5:12–26

" 'That you may know that the Son of Man has authority on earth to forgive sins.' " (Luke 5:24)

As much as I wish we could, we won't be able to delve into every segment of Luke. Instead, I am praying for God to draw out specifically the precepts that are critical to accomplishing His goals for us. If I pass over a Scripture passage you were hoping we'd dissect, slice into it yourself and ask God to tutor you. He wants to talk just to you!

Our next Scripture involves two miracles of healing. Either could teach volumes, but the second introduces concepts so critical that we dare not miss them. The first miracle in Luke 5:12–16 involves a leper who approached Jesus. The leper's approach reveals insight into God and His complex ways. First, the leper humbly approached Christ in absolute belief: "Lord, if you are willing, you can make me clean" (v. 12). He had no doubt Christ could heal him. He just didn't know if He would — which brings us to our second consideration.

The leper also realized another issue: Would this healing be God's will? . . . In essence, the leper said: "Lord, I have no doubt You possess the power to heal me. If You, in Your wisdom and plan, see purpose in it, then please do it." I believe with all my heart that eternal purposeis the central issue involved in whether or not God heals a believing(see Matt. 9:28) and requesting (see James 4:2) Christian's physical illness. Although I don't pretend to understand how or why, some illnesses may serve more eternal purpose than healing, while other healings serve more purpose than illness.

I cannot imagine what purpose some illnesses and premature deaths serve, but, after years of loving and seeking my God, I trust who He is even when I have no idea what He's doing. Above all things, I believe God always has purpose in every decision He makes.

How much like the leper are you? Are you convinced that Christ can do absolutely anything, and are you also seeking His purposes in everything? If so, don't lose courage. As long as this remains the desire of your heart, come to Christ as the leper did — humbly making your request while seeking His purposes for your life.

Next consider with me the account in Luke 5:17–26. Verse 17 almost casually includes an odd phrase. Jesus was teaching, surrounded by the Pharisees and teachers of the law. Then Luke added: "And the power of the Lord was present for him to heal the sick." What? Did Christ sometimes lack the power to heal? Meanwhile, some men came carrying a paralyzed man on a mat. When they could not get in the house because of the crowd, they climbed on the roof, tore open a hole, and lowered their friend. Luke 5:20 says of the paralytic and his friends, "Jesus saw their faith." Two concepts surface in this account. Consider each one with me:

The Power of the Lord

Reconsider my question: Did Christ sometimes lack the power to heal? I hope this causes you to really think. A good student is not afraid to explore challenging passages. This statement causes us to wonder if times existed when Christ did not have the power to heal the sick. Dissecting the original language provides a key to understanding this statement. The word for "power" in this statement is *dunamis,* meaning "power, especially achieving power." Another Greek word often translated "power," "strength," or "might" in Scripture is *ischus.* This word will help us understand what *dunamis* is and is not. *Ischus* expresses the fact that God possesses divine power. *Dunamis* expresses God's earthward application of His divine power. *Dunamis* is divine *ischus* applied to achieve certain earthly results.

I hope you catch that Christ was ready and willing to apply His *ischus* to specifically achieve (*dunamis*) healing that day. Christ healed many times, but the implication is that healing was part of a far more specific agenda in certain instances. We can break it down this way: Christ is always able. He is often willing. Sometimes He is more than willing — He is utterly resolved.

Our fresh insight makes the scene even more provocative. Do you remember the identified audience? The King James Version offers an interesting twist that changes the climate of the room. "There were Pharisees and doctors of the law sitting by . . . *and the power of the Lord was present to heal them*" (v. 17, emphasis mine). The power of the Lord was present to heal the Pharisees and teachers and anyone else who would fall under the power of His Word in that place! Christ hadn't just come to heal those who were physically sick. He came to heal those who were sick with sin! We can be sure because of the nature of the conflict that ensued. Are you with me? Then let's continue with the next concept.

The Authority of the Lord

Do you love picturing the paralytic being lowered through the roof into the crowded home-classroom? When was the last time you were trying to concentrate on a sermon when something terribly distracting occurred? Imagine the Pharisees trying to look scholarly while the roof is falling on their heads. How long do you think they waited before looking up? Doesn't the thought make you grin?

Then imagine the paralytic descending into the distinguished crowd like a puppet on a string. You can be fairly certain that the

175

smell of a man unable to bathe himself was unwelcome. In their culture, the chronically ill or debilitated also tended to be the chronically outcast and poor. What a contrast of characters! Before the Pharisees' proper eyes, the paralytic was dropped smack in front of Jesus.

Jesus gave us another troublesome passage in verse 20: "When Jesus saw their faith, he said, 'Friend, your sins are forgiven.' " Does Christ's statement mean that all sickness results directly from the individual's sin? Fortunately John's Gospel gives us a case study to shed light on the question. The apostolic band encountered a man born blind. They wanted to know who had sinned. Jesus replied, "Neither this man nor his parents sinned, . . . but this happened so that the work of God might be displayed in his life" (John 9:3).

The only absolute connection between sin and physical infirmities is that we live in a fallen world. Our assumption from Scripture is that problems such as disease and poverty resulted from the fall into sin. Beyond that we can make no other assumptions.

Sometimes Christ emphasized forgiveness of sin when He healed, but other times He didn't. Perhaps our safest supposition is that sometimes sin was an issue and other times it was not.

Whether or not sin has ever made you physically ill, couldn't we each say that we've been somehow paralyzed by it at one time or another? One situation involving sin in my past literally paralyzed me with fear. I found healing and began to walk as a healthy believer again when I finally "heard" Christ say, "Friend, your sins are forgiven." Christ's forgiveness caused me finally to be healed from the crippling fear that resulted from sin.

For the remainder of our chapter, we'll concentrate on verse 24. Jesus said to the paralyzed man, "I tell you, get up, take your mat and go home." What we're about to discuss was pivotal to me after an unexpected and harrowing detour into sin years ago. I would still be paralyzed except for the truth God presented to me out of this exact Scripture.

Jesus came as the Son of man to rescue us from the plight of man. We have a sin problem. We are powerless to help ourselves. Given the right set of circumstances and the wrong state of mind, each of us is capable of just about anything. Even if we could get our external lives under perfect and legalistic control, we'd probably rot on the inside with the heinous sin of pride. Let's face it, we're all hopeless — except that Jesus came as the Son of man.

"The Son of Man has authority on earth to forgive sins" (Luke 5:24). I can remember being so devastated over a sin I had allowed to ensnare me that I repeatedly begged God to forgive me. I was repentant the very first time I begged. I confessed my sin with great sorrow and turned radically from it. Still I continued to plead for forgiveness.

One day in my Bible reading, God revealed these Scriptures to me. He spoke to my heart and said: "Beth, My child, you have an authority problem. You think you can do your part, which is repent. You just don't think I can do My part, which is forgive."

I was stunned. I began to realize that my sin of unbelief was as serious as my prior sin of rebellion. I wept and repented for my failure to credit Him with the authority He possessed to forgive my sins. It was eye-opening!

In *I Should Forgive, But . . .*, Dr. Chuck Lynch says when we keep confessing the same sin "each subsequent time that sin is confessed, rather than the confession bringing relief, it only reinforces the false belief

178

that it has not been forgiven. Double, or re-confession, only deepens the false belief that we have not been forgiven."[1] I know he's right because my constant re-confessions did not bring me relief. They only made me more miserable and self-loathing! Relief came when I decided to take God at His Word!

If you have truly repented — which means you have experienced godly sorrow and a subsequent detour from the sin — bathe yourself in the river of God's forgiveness. The Son of man has authority to forgive sins right here on earth. You don't have to wait until heaven. You can experience the freedom of complete forgiveness right here. Right now. Fall under Christ's authority and accept His grace.

Chapter 17

The Lord of the Sabbath

Luke 6:1–11

Then Jesus said to them, "The Son of Man is Lord of the Sabbath." (Luke 6:5)

In Luke 5:17–18 the Pharisees and doctors of the law were "sitting by" (KJV). Matthew Henry wrote, "How many are there in the midst of our assemblies, where the gospel is preached, that do not sit under the Word, but sit by! It is to them as a tale that is told them, not as a message that is sent them; they are willing that we should preach before them, not that we should preach to them."[1]

Can you recall a time you attended a Bible study or church service that profoundly affected a few of the people you were with, while others were completely unmoved? Like the Pharisees and teachers of the law, sometimes the unaffected can be the most "religious" people in the room. Could the difference be sitting by rather than sitting under God's Word?

One of my favorite congregations to visit is an African-American church in New Orleans. I've fellowshiped with these wonderful people after a number of services, and not one of those times has a solitary person been critical or even untouched by the message. It's not the preacher because I've never heard the same person preach there twice. What, then, is the difference? The listeners involve themselves in the message. They are not spectators. They take responsibility for the effectiveness of the message by actively engaging themselves in it.

I've been in many other settings where members basically gave the preacher an anointing rating over lunch. This discovery startled and affected me. I began praying that God would motivate me to actively engage myself in every message I hear or read. Since that time I've not heard or read a single ineffective message. Our next text shares two more prime examples of attitudes of people who sit by rather than sit under the power of God's activity.

Luke 6:1–11 describes two scenes involving the issue of working on the Sabbath. The first involved the disciples' eating grains of wheat. Try to fathom the pettiness of the complaint that the disciples were threshing wheat because they were rubbing it in their hands. They preferred that the disciples ache with hunger rather than break the Sabbath law.

Jesus watched as the Pharisees sunk their proud feet into the quicksand of legalism and stood their sinking ground. What a ridiculous scene they created. They presumed to tell the lawgiver Himself how to obey the law.

Those who caught Christ's disciples threshing grain in their own palms weren't the first to be presumptuous. Through the centuries religious leaders had taxed God's laws with so many of their own that God's original purposes were often obscured. By the time Christ came to earth to accomplish His work, the Pharisees and teachers of the law had turned the Sabbath into the hardest day of the week.

Like yours, my job can be exhausting. Those who think ministry is easy would be wise to keep that opinion to themselves lest they be hit by a Catholic candlestick, a Lutheran communion plate, or a Baptist hymnal. Exhaustion is an interdenominational, equal-opportunity vocational hazard. The travel this ministry necessitates is one of the biggest contributors to exhaustion. Strange hotel rooms are not conducive to sleep, especially when you're accustomed, like I am, to sleeping with a fan on.

Just as I was preparing this study, my staff gave me a delightful gift they knew I could use to make a hotel room "sound" more like home. It is a compact noisemaker. You can choose from several "tranquil" sounds such as rain or gentle wind. We nearly died laughing when we discovered that one of the tranquil sounds was a vacuum cleaner! What a perfect example of a way to make your rest remind you of work!

Remember, God established the concept of regular work/rest cycles during Creation. The need for authentic rest and the demonstration of trust in God is for all people, not just the ancient Jews. For the remainder of our chapter, let's draw our attention to the second Sabbath controversy in the text.

On another Sabbath, Jesus encountered a man with a withered right hand. Think of all the jobs that would have been difficult, if not impossible, for this man. A shepherd had to be adept at using a rod and a staff. A farmer needed both hands to plow. A carpenter had to hold a hammer in one hand

and a nail in the other. A merchant would have had a difficult time securing and displaying goods with only one hand. Even a tax collector needed his right hand! In a discourse on rest versus work, I don't think it's a coincidence that the man involved had lived a humiliating life of unwelcome rest from effective labor. Christ granted him a rest from his incapacity and futility. The One who created the Sabbath used it to bring restoration to a man weary of uselessness.

Meanwhile the Pharisees and teachers of the law were watching Jesus, just looking for some basis to condemn Him (v. 7). Their primary reason for attending that day was to see if Jesus would heal.

I love the fact that they were convinced Christ would heal, even on the Sabbath, if He encountered a need. What a healer He is! No amount of laws could keep Him from being Himself! The Pharisees and teachers of the law caught Christ in the act of being God. Hallelujah!

The most merciful people are those who have been sitting under the faucet of God's mercy instead of sitting by with a critical eye. Please note this sad fact, which was emphasized by the events following the Pharisees' and teachers' speculations: those who look for reasons to accuse will undoubtedly find some. They quickly found basis to accuse Jesus.

In my own life and ministry, I've accepted that, sooner or later, anyone looking hard enough to condemn will be accommodated. I really do believe that more people in the body of Christ are generally accepting than accusing, but one mean-spirited person is practically enough to ruin anyone's day. Francis Frangipane wrote something so powerful on the subject, I immediately committed it to memory. He said of the Lord:

To inoculate me from the praise of man,
He baptized me in the criticism of man,
until I died to control of man.[2]

Beloved, one thing I know for sure on this subject: nothing will squelch our efforts to seek the approval of others like not receiving it! Furthermore, those who approve one day can be the same ones who accuse the next day. I encourage you to break free from the traps set by approval and accusation. We are called to live our lives above reproach but expect it anyway. Christ was blameless yet was blamed continually. I think you can trust me on this one: blameless people are rarely those who cast blame.

When the man with the shriveled hand stood before Him on the Sabbath, Jesus knew the Pharisees and teachers of the law were looking to accuse Him. Remember, He could read their minds. (Incidentally, aren't you glad we can't?) Christ did not allow Himself to be controlled by potential accusations nor even by the law that He, Himself, instituted. He was indeed the Lord of the Sabbath.

Anyone who tried to put Christ on the hot seat usually ended up getting burned. (Thankfully, not necessarily in the eternal sense.) His public question to His accusers made them look terribly foolish: "I ask you, which is lawful on the Sabbath: to do good or to do evil, to save life or to destroy it?" (v. 9). Picture the scene described in verse 10: "He looked around at them all." Eye to eye. Just waiting for someone to give Him an answer. They were struck dumb. Or maybe dumber. Then He said to the man, "Stretch out your hand" (v. 10). And he did. Right there in front of all those perfect and pious-looking people, the man — who all his life had probably hidden his handicap under the sleeve of his garment — stretched forth his humiliating infirmity — and was healed.

"Now, Lord, . . . stretch out your hand to

heal and perform miraculous signs and wonders through the name of your holy servant Jesus" (Acts 4:29–30).

Part 4

The Esteem of Man

I'm already finding myself completely immersed in our story line. Are you? I hope so. Let's be willing to go even further, asking God to involve us emotionally, mentally, and spiritually in every single Scripture and to help us picture each scene with the spiritual sight of an eyewitness. We have an extremely interesting study ahead. I love watching Christ operate in relationships. He did not come to redeem the earth. Sand and water were not His priority. He came to redeem people. Study Him carefully in the coming chapters. Watch the kinds of things that impressed Him. Let's allow Him to move us, to change us. As remarkable as this may seem, you and I can have lives that "impress" Christ. Let's learn how.

Let's dive in even deeper with Jesus. If

I don't go as deep as you desire, take off with Jesus on your own! Allow my commentary to be a catalyst for your own encounters with Christ. Ask Him questions and search for the answers. Hold nothing back from Him. Treasures await you, my friend.

Chapter 18

Amazing Faith

Luke 7:1–10

"I tell you, I have not found such great faith even in Israel." (Luke 7:9)

One of my most heartfelt personal petitions to God is for Him to develop in me His taste. I want to grow to love what He loves, hate what He hates, and marvel at the things He finds marvelous. I'm a long way from His gloriously discriminating palate, but this lesson gives a refreshing bite of heaven's taste. In this and the coming chapters, we're going to learn what impresses Christ. As we grow in grace, may we each develop His taste and marvel over the things He considers marvelous.

We find a story in Luke 7:1–10 about a Roman centurion who had been especially kind to the Jewish community. He had built the local synagogue. The Jews, who normally hated their Roman captors, loved this man. The centurion had a servant who was very ill, so he sent Jewish elders to Jesus asking for the servant's healing.

As Jesus drew near to the centurion's house, however, "the centurion sent friends to say to him: 'Lord, don't trouble yourself, for I do not deserve to have you come under my roof. That is why I did not even consider myself worthy to come to you. But say the word, and my servant will be healed. For I myself am a man under authority, with soldiers under me. I tell this one, "Go," and he goes; and that one, "Come," and he comes. I say to my servant, "Do this," and he does it' " (Luke 7:6–8).

Luke tells us that when Jesus heard this He was amazed and said, "I tell you, I have not found such great faith even in Israel" (v. 9). Of course when the friends returned to the centurion, they found the servant well.

Awesome story. Christ almost seems delightfully shocked in this encounter — almost caught off guard by such faith. I'm so glad God purposed for Christ to know all things, yet know the thrill of sudden amazement. It's one of life's sheerest joys. Don't you agree?

The original word for "amazed" in verse 9

is *thaumazo,* meaning "to wonder, marvel, be struck with admiration or astonishment." Perhaps you've bought into the "wretched worm that I am" mentality enough to be uncomfortable thinking about Christ being impressed by anything wretched man can do. Since we're attempting to develop God's taste, perhaps we could all use a little adjustment in our perception of the divine.

A word God used in Isaiah 66:2 blows my mind. The verse says, "This is the one I esteem: / he who is humble and contrite in spirit, / and trembles at my word." The word *esteem* means to "regard with pleasure, . . . have respect." God is clearly saying that He respects certain people.

Do you see the like-mindedness of Christ and His Father? Our difficulty imagining that God could have respect for a mortal is because we confuse attitudes of respect with feelings of inferiority. We tend to view respect as a feeling we have for those we perceive as superior to us, and on our best day, we are so inferior to Christ that, if not for the Lord's great love (see Lam. 3:22), we would be consumed by holy fire.

If we're to have a balanced perception, we must keep in mind that God created us. We are His "workmanship" (Eph. 2:10). He loves us. At times, He actually delights in us.

God could have created us void of weakness and with a complete inability to sin. He didn't. He purposely created us with free will and affections so that we could choose Him and love Him in the midst of many options and much opposition.

God didn't create robots. He created humans. When God sees humans cooperate with His good work and fulfill what they were created to be, He sees something very good. Perfect? No. Respectable? Yes. When the Father sees a human who is prone to selfishness, pride, and arrogance humble himself or herself and tremble at God's Word, He esteems that person. Hallelujah! Oh, how I want to be someone God could respect!

Christ's encounters on earth show our mortal minds the stuff of heaven by transplanting them onto the soil of earth. In essence, Luke 7:1–10 is an earthbound interpretation of Isaiah 66:2. Let's spend the remainder of our chapter considering two amazing things about a man whose faith amazed the Son of God.

The centurion valued his servant highly. Please don't miss this! The person who was dying was not a family member or a good friend. He was a slave. Slaves were certainly not hard to come by under the Roman rule of that day. The typical mentality in that culture was the immediate replacement of an infirm slave. The attitude of the centurion, however, was that his servant was virtually indispensable to him. In fact, "valued highly" is translated from the Greek word *entimos,* meaning "honored . . . dear, precious, costly." Look at another place in Scripture where *entimos* is used but rendered with a different English word: "As you come to him, the living Stone — rejected by men but chosen by God and precious to him" (1 Pet. 2:4).

Years ago a friend discerned that I was beginning to be overwhelmed by the sudden demands of a writing ministry. She said something that made both of us laugh: "I can't write the Bible studies for you, but I could answer some of your mail. All I'd have to do is say *precious* a lot." Ever since I've been aware of how much I say and write the word *precious!* But you see, it's a very biblical word. First Peter 2:4 tells us that Christ is precious to God. Keeping this fact in mind, read John 15:9. "As the Father has loved me, so have I loved you." Can you see that you are also precious?

The centurion revealed a dimension of godly character in the high regard he felt for his servant. Christ, however, doesn't just display godly character. He *is* godly character. Be blessed by knowing that Christ Jesus values His servants highly. We are precious to Him. Even in our frailties. Even though we can't reach perfection in this lifetime.

Luke 7:8 defines a highly valued servant as one who does the master's will: "I say to my servant, 'Do this,' and he does it." The centurion's slave was so important because he revealed his complete devotion through obedience. Likewise, Jesus Christ is building a spiritual household out of devoted servants willing to offer spiritual sacrifices. These living stones are as precious to Jesus as He, the Chief Cornerstone, is to His Father.

The centurion was a man of good works. The centurion was a Gentile, yet the Jewish elders pleaded with Jesus on his behalf. They said he deserved to have his servant healed. Thank goodness, our works do not measure how much we "deserve" the activity of Christ in our lives. His grace is entirely unmerited favor. No, works don't reveal worthiness, but they can reveal something else. Our fruits reveal our character.

The centurion's works reveal a good character. He built the synagogue. He had many friends. Impressively to me, he loved his servant, but he didn't believe his own press. No matter how others viewed him, the centurion knew himself. Apparently the more he thought about what he sent the elders to request, the more overwhelmed he became. He sent his friends with the message: "I do not even deserve to have You come under my roof." Christ was not far from the house when the centurion sent this message. I can't help drawing this parallel: the closer Christ's presence comes to us, the more humble a discerning person becomes.

Please notice that even though the centurion was greatly humbled, he still presented his request! Again, let's keep a balanced perspective! The "wretched worm that I am" mentality might say, "I can't even ask such a thing" and end up having not because he asked not (see James 4:2). Those who are truly humble and discerning know that we can approach Christ with our petitions, not because we deserve to approach but because He has graciously made Himself approachable!

The most impressive statement the centurion made was, "Say the word, and my servant will be healed" (Luke 7:7). The centurion's understanding of authority may be unparalleled in the Gospels. He seemed to be saying, "If I am who I am and people under my authority do as I say, You, being who You are, need simply say the word and the act is accomplished." I seriously doubt the centurion knew Jesus' full identity, but he understood that Jesus possessed an authority that was ignited into action by His word.

Child of God, Christ's word is action. What He commands He also accomplishes. What impresses Christ, however, is when we believe it. In one way, we face a situation similar to the centurion. We are challenged to believe what Jesus Christ can do without seeing Him with our own eyes. The centurion never laid eyes on Christ, but he witnessed His incomparable power when his dear servant sat up in the bed, fully recovered. I have a feeling it may have taken the centurion a little longer to get up. I can almost picture the blood returning to the servant's deathly pale cheeks while it drained from the centurion's!

Somehow, even if we've asked and believed, God also allows us the wondrous delight of total amazement when He works. We simply weren't meant to recover from certain things. A miracle of God is one of them.

Chapter 19

Compassion without Restraint

Luke 7:11–17

When the Lord saw her, his heart went out to her and he said, "Don't cry." (Luke 7:13)

Luke 7:11 tells us that after Christ healed the centurion's servant, He and His disciples went to the town of Nain. Forgive me if this seems unimportant, but I can't help noting their physical condition. Nain was twenty-five miles southwest of Capernaum. No short walk.

Not only did Christ and His disciples walk a great distance to get to Nain, but the large crowd went along. Picture the scene with me. Two crowds met that day in Nain. Christ, His disciples, and a large crowd approached the town gate just as a funeral procession was leaving the city.

Western funeral customs leave us little to compare to those of the ancient East. For us, even in the most tragic situations, cries of any volume are rare, and when they occur, their sounds are almost more than a Western soul can bear. Contrast that to the scene Christ met. In the ancient East, the depth of concern for the dead and the grieving could be measured by the volume of the wails and the physical demonstrations of grief.

I can't think of a situation they would have considered more tragic in those days than a widow losing her only son. Her double portion of grief would have been compounded by an utterly hopeless future. The sound of the processional would have been as unsettling as the sight.

Christ may have been more unsettled by the sight and the sound than anyone present. This kind of funeral processional was the people's custom, but I'm not sure Christ has ever grown accustomed to death, no matter how many millions of times He's seen it. It's too contrary to His nature.

In 1 Corinthians 15:26 Paul wrote that "the last enemy to be destroyed is death." Although Satan is certainly Christ's animate foe, I believe Scripture suggests that His ultimate archenemy is death. He hates it. He longs for the time when death will be swallowed up in victory and we will sing, "Where, O death, is your sting?" (1 Cor. 15:55).

With Christ's transcendent hatred of death, He had an entirely different angle on the sight in Nain. Jesus viewed death from a heavenly perspective: earthly life is but a breath. Eternity holds riches for the trusting. Christ knew that death, for the faithful, is the door for a greater reality of life. I have a feeling, however, that occupying a cloak of human flesh and staring grief straight in the face from street level was momentarily staggering for Christ. I believe Scripture suggests such a thing. "When the Lord saw her, his heart went out to her and he said, 'Don't cry' " (Luke 7:13).

How hard must it have been for Christ to possess all authority but stick to a kingdom plan requiring its timely exercise? He could sneeze on Satan and blow him to oblivion, but that's not the plan. Satan's prompt demise would spare us trouble, but it would also spare us growth resulting in many rewards. Until the right time for Satan's disposal, Christ restrains Himself. Other areas of restraint must have also been challenging for Jesus as He walked on this pavement. Imagine the thoughts a funeral procession must have provoked in the mind of the author of life.

I think the very lordship of Christ overwhelmed Him at that moment in Nain. No one else in the crowd could do anything about the widow's plight. They possessed no power. Christ was the only one present who had lordship over the living and the dead. His heart went out to her. He felt deeply. He spoke only two words to her: "Don't cry." We've all said those two words to someone who was brokenhearted, but I believe Christ probably meant something a little different.

I don't know about you, but most of the time when I've said, "Don't cry," my heart was saying, "Please stop crying. I can't bear to see you in so much pain!" Usually the words come from one who can't stand to see the hurt because she is powerless to help. Christ, on the other hand, is never helpless. When He said, "Don't cry," He meant, "Not only do I hurt for you, but also I'm going to do something about the cause of the hurt."

Verse 14 records Jesus' initial action: "He went up and touched the coffin." Picture the structure more like a stretcher than our Western concept of a coffin. The body was placed on a board and shrouded with burial linens. Now imagine Christ walking up and touching this burial slate.

The first thing we read after Christ touched the bier is that "those carrying it stood still" (v. 14). They probably stood there bug-eyed. You see, for anyone unnecessary to the interment process to risk touching the dead body was a serious no-no. Jesus was ritually defiling Himself. What they couldn't have realized is that the Son of God could not be defiled no matter what He touched. One day soon He would literally take on the sins of the entire world while still remaining the perfect Lamb without spot or blemish.

We've already seen that Christ did not need to touch to heal. He did not even need to be present. He seemed to touch because it came natural to Him. I'm anxious to share with you what *touched* means in today's context. The word is *haptomai,* from the word *hapto,* meaning "to connect, bind." *Haptomai* means "to apply oneself to, to touch." The word "refers to such handling of an object as to exert a modifying influence upon it." Christ Jesus literally connected Himself to the situation. We apply all sorts of medication for hurts. Christ took one look at this woman's grief and applied Himself.

I hope you'll be blessed by the Greek antonym or opposite term for "touched," *egkrateuomai.* You will find the English translation of this word at the very end of the list of the fruit of the Spirit in Galatians 5:22–23. The word is "self-control."

In today's text, imagine Christ acting out of exactly the opposite of self-control. Stick with me here until you grasp the meaning. When Christ saw the woman in such agony and faced with such hopelessness, I'm suggesting He literally cast off self-restraint and reacted! The difference between Jesus and us is that He doesn't sin even when He casts off self-control! Christ does not depart from the Spirit whether He responds or reacts.

Herein lies the most profound difference between the miracle in Nain and the previous miracle in Capernaum. In the second case, the only prerequisite was her pain. Unlike the centurion, she made no request. She exhibited no faith. In fact, we have no idea if the grieving mom even realized Christ existed. She was probably too enveloped in her own agony to notice. He awaited no conditions nor apparently had any intention of using the moment for instructional purposes.

Jesus ran into a woman in hopeless despair and just reacted with what came most naturally to Him — healing mercy. Oh, how I praise Him! I believe we possibly have a small glimpse into what Christ would do in every one of our despairing situations if a greater plan was not at stake. I believe what comes most naturally to Christ every time He encounters need is to instantly fix it. Is it possible He exercises great restraint to work any other way in the face of devastation? I think so.

A plan of profound importance exists that sometimes overrides the miracle we desperately desire. I am comforted to know that instantaneous healing and resurrection power come even more naturally to our Christ than waiting and working through long but necessary processes. The biggest reason why I can trust in the sovereignty of God is because I am so utterly convinced of the sweetness of God.

How about you? Are you convinced God is sovereign? Are you convinced God is kind, even sweet? I believe we will see both these dimensions appearing side by side many times throughout our study.

After touching the coffin and stunning the unsuspecting carriers, Christ said emphatically, "Young man, I say to you, get up!" (v. 14). What I'd give to view this moment on videotape! Picture the expressions on the pallbearers' faces. This stranger had not only come close to touching the dead body, but also He began talking to it. They didn't have long to make a mental diagnosis before movement erupted on the tabletop. Imagine what they were doing down below as the weight shifted and the dead body sat up. Now take the scene one step further — imagine their faces when the dead man spoke. The second wonder is that they didn't drop him like a hot potato.

Who had ever heard of such a thing? Actually, they had, which adds another interesting twist to this story. Just on the other side of the hill from Nain was a town called Shunem. Several centuries earlier Elisha had restored life to a dead boy (see 2 Kings 4:8–37).

Surely the villagers must have noted at least one very important difference between the miracles — the amount of effort involved. Elisha got on the bed and lay on the boy until the boy's body grew warm. Then Elisha turned away and walked back and forth in the room and then got on the bed and stretched out upon him again. Jesus, on the other hand simply spoke: "Young man, I say to you, get up!" No contest. A wide gulf of difference lay between Elisha the prophet and Jesus Christ, the omnipotent Son of

God. With the same expediency of "there was light" in Genesis 1:3, there was life in Luke 7:15. Nothing gradual. No gradual warmth as blood began pumping through thousands of capillaries. No pacing, waiting, or wondering. No garbled nonsense from a patient slowly regaining consciousness. Jesus said, "Get up!" and the dead man did. Instantaneously.

As the curtain draws on the scene, two crowds became one and all were filled with awe, praising God. Their words? "A great prophet has appeared among us," they said. "God has come to help his people." Far more than a great prophet had appeared among them that day. God had come in human flesh to help His people.

If you have received Christ as Savior, in many ways this is your story, too — only yours is even better.

Chapter 20

A Bout with Doubt

Luke 7:18–28

"I tell you, among those born of women there is no one greater than John; yet the one who is least in the kingdom of God is greater than he." (Luke 7:28)

People who seem to live out the faith almost flawlessly inspire me; but I am also moved to meditation by those who grapple and wrestle with it. I find that rather than give me "permission" to doubt, their stories usually give me permission to move through my doubt to a place of spacious faith. May God use this chapter toward such an end.

Luke tells us that John the Baptizer sent messengers to Jesus asking if He was the Messiah. Jesus told them to return to John and tell him just what they had seen: "The blind receive sight, the lame walk, those who have leprosy are cured, the deaf hear, the dead are raised, and the good news is preached to the poor" (Luke 7:22).

Matthew gives us one additional piece of information about the situation. John sent his disciples all right . . . from his prison cell (Matt. 11:2). Mark 6:17–18 tells us that John was there because he confronted King Herod about his adultery. Do you suppose John's location may have influenced the question he sent his disciples to ask Jesus?

My heart is awash with compassion for a man who sat in prison two thousand years ago. Four walls closing in surely must limit your vision. The facts to support Christ's messiahship were all there, and I'm pretty certain John knew it. Furthermore, the baptizer knew Jesus was the Messiah the moment he saw Him at the Jordan River.

I don't believe John's sudden bout with doubt had anything to do with public merit. It was a private matter. John had heard the wonders Christ had done for others. I think maybe his faith was shaken because he could have used a wonder for himself, and he didn't appear to be getting it. John knew with his head that Jesus was the Messiah. Sitting in that prison cell, I think he was having a little trouble knowing it with his heart.

I don't think we have trouble relating here. Have you known Christ long enough to witness His marvelous works? Have you heard testimonies of His intervening power? Even after such evidence, has your faith ever been greatly shaken because of something He didn't do for you personally? Like John, have you ever found yourself waiting and waiting on Christ to come through on a certain matter while hearing all sorts of wondrous works He was doing elsewhere?

It hurts, doesn't it? We can be believers in Jesus for years, literally seeking Him, finding Him, and serving Him — then suddenly have a staggering bout with doubt. Overwhelmed with guilt and fear, we'll think, *How in the world could I be doubting after all this time?* It's a horrible feeling! I'd like to suggest, however, that these kinds of doubts are probably not coming from our heads. They're coming from our hearts. Our feelings. Our emotions. Our hurts.

John was not like "a reed swayed by the wind" (v. 24). Rather, he was a man of absolute conviction. That's exactly what faith means. *Pistis,* the Greek word translated "faith," means "firm persuasion, conviction." For our purposes today, firm persuasion or conviction represents head-faith! Perhaps John had questions, but they weren't enough to sway the reed! Had John really harbored deeply embedded questions about Christ's authenticity, I don't believe Jesus would have hesitated to rebuke him. He certainly didn't hesitate with some others. Christ was very gentle with John. He simply reminded John that He was fulfilling His job description to a T and not to "fall away" on account of Him.

I believe the root of John's question was why was John sitting in prison while Jesus was going about His business all over the countryside. Surely John was wondering how he was supposed to prepare the way from prison. If Jesus were meeting all the criteria of messiahship, He was supposed to be proclaiming freedom for the prisoners (see Luke 4:18). John knew a prisoner who could use a little freedom.

John's ministry had lasted only about a year. The baptizer could not have imagined that his purposes had been so quickly fulfilled. John couldn't have foreseen that he was a shooting star leading the way in the night until the dawn would rise.

Our discussion raises an important question: If a real difference exists between head-doubt and heart-doubt, is heart-doubt "no big deal"? When our emotions begin to override what our minds know is true, can we just surrender to our heart-doubts? I don't think so. Our heart-doubts can be very dangerous if we remain in them. But, if we wrestle through them with the Lord Jesus, when we get to the other side of our crisis, we will find ourselves spilled into a place of spacious faith!

Our challenge is to work through our doubts and not let them imprison us like John's were threatening to imprison him! Christ stated the biggest risk of doubt in verse 23: "Blessed is the man who does not fall away on account of me."

The original word for "blessed" is *makarios.* Revel in the definition: "Biblically, one is pronounced blessed when God is present and involved in his life. The Hand of God is at work directing all his affairs for a divine purpose, and thus, in a sense, such a person lives *coram Deo,* before the face of God."[1] Luke 7:23 tells us these words apply to the person who doesn't fall away on account of Christ.

What does "falling away" mean? The Greek word, *skandalon,* means "a cause of stumbling." Add the meanings of these two definitions and we arrive at the following sum total in Luke 7:23: *The Hand of God is at work directing divine purpose, or blessing, in all the affairs of the one who doesn't let the perceived activity or inactivity of Christ trap him or make him stumble.* It's a mouthful, but chew on it awhile!

I don't think Luke 7:23 is talking about falling away from Christ. It's talking about falling over a stumbling block into a trap. One of Satan's most effective devices for causing a devout believer to stumble is to trap him over a matter of faith. Satan even tries to use Christ, Himself, against us. The most effective faith-trap Satan could set for a Christian is to tempt him or her to doubt the goodness, rightness, or mightiness of Christ.

Note that Christ held John in highest esteem even after being questioned. John was under a terrible strain, and his martyrdom was imminent. Christ knew that! He could handle John's questions because He knew the heart and mind from which they came. After proclaiming that no one born of women was greater than John, Jesus said the "least in the kingdom of God is greater than" John (v. 28).

Please understand that this statement in no way diminished John. Christ simply meant that a new era was unfolding in the kingdom calendar and to be a part of it would be greater than being a prophet

213

under the old Covenant. Thank God every day that you live this side of Calvary!

Luke adds a parenthetical statement to tell us of two radically different reactions to the words of Jesus. Pharisees and scholars "rejected God's purpose for themselves, because they had not been baptized by John" (Luke 7:30). But those who had been baptized by John acknowledged that God was right.

God's way is always right. God's way was also right for John the Baptizer, but he would not fully realize it until heaven. I don't believe the timing of John's incarceration was an accident. It immediately followed Christ's introduction into public ministry. John's task was to prepare the people for Jesus, and he fulfilled his job description faithfully. Now John's work was complete. For him to continue in ministry might actually cause some to miss the very salvation the forerunner came to announce. Earlier John had so clearly stated the principle: "He must become greater; I must become less" (John 3:30).

Sometimes we can understand the purpose of our callings without fully understanding God's means. John's imprisonment and the events to follow were part of preparing the way for Jesus Christ. I think you can be certain of one thing about John the Baptizer: when he got to heaven, he wouldn't have traded his place in the kingdom plan for anything. Among billions of people to live on this planet, he alone was chosen to prepare the way for the Messiah. How could such a calling not have been costly?

Chapter 21

Loving Much

Luke 7:36–50

"Therefore, I tell you, her many sins have been forgiven — for she loved much. But he who has been forgiven little loves little." (Luke 7:47)

I'm about to teach one of my own lessons. I have been the sinful woman in this chapter. I am still so deeply moved by the infinite grace God has poured out on my life that my eyes burn with tears as I pen these words. I'm going to ask you to indulge me in a few moments of personal testimony to prepare for our lesson.

During the writing of *Breaking Free*, the enemy used every trick in the book to break me. He is our accuser (see Rev. 12:10) and a shameless opportunist (see Luke 4:13). He knew that *Breaking Free* necessitated very deep scrutiny of my history because the study is based on my journey to liberty. My whole life has forever been laid bare before God, but it had never been so vividly laid bare before me. At the taunting of the enemy, I found myself at one point so grieved over the "yuck" in my history that I could not imagine how God could possibly use me. I literally questioned my own calling.

During this painful time, I had a speaking engagement in Louisiana. Customarily someone from the host church delivers a devotional to the team before the conference begins. That day a woman who did not know me, had never heard me speak, had never read a single word I'd written, walked in the door and pulled up a chair in front of me. The entire group could hear her, but the devotional she delivered was for me.

She sat only inches away and never took her eyes off mine. With obvious anointing, she told the story we're about to study, then she said, "I don't know you, Beth. I have no idea why God sent me with such a message to give you, but He told me clearly to say these words to you: 'Tell her that her many sins have been forgiven — for she loved much.' " I cannot describe my feelings then or my feelings now.

This Scripture is the only one framed on my desk. It sits only inches from my computer. As I sit at my desk, I stare at the reminder of God's unreasonable grace, and I'm reminded that I'm forgiven. Indeed, how could someone like me not love Him much?

Allow me the privilege of narrating the passage from Luke chapter 7. Our scene unfolds in the dining area of one of the more prestigious homes in the village. The Pharisee's home was large enough to accommodate Jesus and an undisclosed number of other guests (see v. 49). The Pharisee's wife and any other women involved probably ate separately. They would not have considered this a slight since the men customarily practiced segregated fellowship in many social settings. Incidentally, their manly discussions often turned into passionate theological debates that they thoroughly enjoyed. Such conflict tends to make me nervous, so I would happily have stayed in the kitchen with the dessert and coffee.

Do you have difficulty picturing Christ in this scene? Do you imagine Him never fitting into a Pharisee's home? I think God desires to broaden our understanding and fine-tune some of our mental footage of Christ. The more I study His earthly life, the more I'm grasping that He could fit in anywhere . . . and nowhere.

Remember, Christ is void of all prejudice. He was no more likely to stereotype all Pharisees than He was to stereotype all who were poor, blind, or ill. Furthermore, He was just as anxious to save them from their sins. The obvious difference was how anxious the individual was to be saved.

Sometimes the blessing in being destitute or depraved is a greater awareness of sin and need. Before we are too harsh in our view of the Pharisees, we are wise to remember that their negative tendencies resemble those of anyone who values religion and ritual over relationship with the Savior. Interestingly, in the Gospels not once do we see a Pharisee who is confronted in the stronghold of legalism and self-righteousness ever admit to seeing it in himself. My point is that no one is likely to see him or herself as pharisaical without an honest and courageous look inside. In fact, our story never indicates that Christ's host received the message delivered to him through these events.

Someone else, however, got the message. While the respectable women were eating in another room and the men were enjoying hearty fellowship at the table, in walked a woman who had lived a sinful life in that town. As Jesus and the others reclined at the table, this woman stood by His feet and wept. "She began to wet his feet with her tears. Then she wiped them with her hair, kissed them and poured perfume on them" (v. 38).

Let's attempt to grasp the magnitude of the situation. The original word for "sinful life" is *hamartolos,* which "frequently denotes a heinous and habitual sinner."[1] Based on this definition, think what this woman's life must have been like.

Compassion stirs my heart as I look at the phrase "in that town"(v. 37). Any of us who have sinned habitually in a small town may grasp the added shame of publicity versus anonymity. A small community increases the risk of feeling so shamed that you can hardly go out in public. Church communities in a large city can create the same kind of atmosphere.

Destructive cycles of sin are hard enough to deal with in private. The shame others heap on the "sinner" magnifies the hurt and often tightens the chains of bondage. I've had the joy of working with several people who were breaking free from habitual sin. Without exception, a primary obstacle was the judgment of others. They seemed better able to break free from the behavior than the disapproval. In this instance, the publicity of the woman's sinful life is obvious by how much the Pharisee knew about her. He thought with a mental sneer: "If this man were a prophet, he would know who is touching him and what kind of woman she is — that she is a sinner" (v. 39).

I can't help but think that her desperation to be different and determination to show gratitude made her gloriously vulnerable to new life in Jesus Christ. She did not ask for Christ to come outside. She walked right through the door into the middle of the festivities. Talk about crashing a party! I imagine the party she crashed on earth gave way to a much grander one in heaven. Her sudden intrusion probably caused every single recliner to recoil into its upright position. No doubt, all but One were horrified.

She brought an alabaster jar of perfume to anoint Christ's feet, but she could not even open the jar before she began to anoint His feet with her tears. Picture it clearly. The word used for her tears in verse 38 indicates that she was sobbing.

For some, this scene has already grown far too personal and demonstrative. You may not be at all comfortable with the outpouring of this woman's heart. Believe it or not, I feel just as much compassion for the person who is uncomfortable with this scene as I do the hurting woman. You see, this woman was no longer in bondage. She had been loosed. Anything that holds us back from pouring our lives and our hearts out upon Jesus is a bond. Some bonds may look like angry ropes. Others like pretty ribbons. But if they keep us from the One who frees us, they are bonds just the same.

The spotlight momentarily shifts to the Pharisee. The Pharisee "said to himself . . ." This phrase and Christ's response have great importance because they force us to realize that He holds us responsible for the things we say to ourselves. Ouch. Yes, He reads our minds — and sometimes our thoughts need a viewer rating.

I am learning so much in my journey with Christ Jesus — lessons I wish I had learned long ago. I am learning that my heart and mind are of greater importance to Him than my words and deeds. Our innermost places desperately need daily purification. Part of the process is recognizing and confessing the judgmental, impure, or critical thoughts before they can make their way to our mouths and our actions. God really can change our negative thought processes, attitudes, and motives. The process takes time and cooperation, however, because these thought patterns are just as much habitual sin as the transgressions of the woman of ill repute.

Don't overlook the fact that Christ's willingness to allow the woman to wash His feet caused the Pharisee to question whether or not Jesus was a prophet. The Pharisee implied that Jesus obviously did not know what kind of woman she was. The original wording is quite interesting. The English "what kind" is derived from two Greek words: *poios,* meaning "what," and *dapedon,* meaning "soil." The Pharisee's comment that Christ did not know where she came from literally meant "He has no idea the dirt she comes from."

You know what, beloved? Dirt is dirt, and we've all got it no matter where we come from. I'm not sure Christ sees one kind of dirt as dirtier than another. One thing is for sure: His blood is able to bleach any stain left by any kind of dirt. Oh, thank You, Lord.

I like the King James Version of Christ's first response after He read the Pharisee's thoughts: "Simon, I have somewhat to say unto thee" (v. 40). Lest you think I'm feeling pious in my deep compassion for the habitual sinner, please know I'm presently shuddering over the times Christ has had somewhat to say unto me!

I also love the King James Version response of the Pharisee: "Master, say on" (v. 40) makes me grin. I wonder what he was expecting the Master to say on? I have a feeling it wasn't what Christ said. Christ told a parable of canceled debts. Two men owed money to a moneylender. One owed much, the other only a little, but neither had the money to pay what he owed, so the moneylender canceled the debts of both. Then Jesus asked Simon to summarize which debtor loved the moneylender most. The answer was obvious, but Simon's words "I suppose" revealed his reluctance to acknowledge it. After Simon pinpointed the one with the bigger debt canceled, Christ said, "You have judged correctly"(v. 43). Interestingly, Simon had been judging throughout the whole ordeal. It was just the first time he had judged correctly.

Christ then brought the parable to life. He compared their responses to Him. All three times Christ's description of the Pharisee's actions began with the unsettling words, "You did not." How poignant. You see, one of the surest signs of an ancient or modern-day "Pharisee" is a life characterized far more by what he or she does *not* do than what he or she does. "No, Simon. You did not sleep around. You did not take bribes. You did not externalize your depravity. But as well, you did not give Me any water for My feet. You did not give Me a kiss. You did not put oil on My head. You did not see yourself as a sinner, and you did not receive My gift of grace, but she did."

He packs the punch into the living parable in verse 47: "Therefore, I tell you, her many sins have been forgiven — for she loved much. But he who has been forgiven little loves little." Not because that's the way it has to be, but because that's the reality of our human tendency.

A couple of additional truths strike a chord in me. First, I see that Christ never downplayed nor minimized her sin. Human sympathy makes excuses like, "What you did wasn't that bad" or "After all you've been through, no wonder . . ." Christ never calls sin less than it is. To picture Christ minimizing the woman's sinful past is to miss the entire point of the encounter. The point is that even though her sins had been many, heinous, and habitual, she had been forgiven (see v. 48), saved (see v. 50), and liberated to love lavishly (see v. 47). Of all the commandments the Pharisee had kept, she rather than he observed the most important one. "Love the Lord your God with all your heart and with all your soul and with all your mind and with all your strength" (Mark 12:30).

The exquisite beauty of loving Christ is that it makes it impossible to keep only one commandment. The Word tells us that the person who truly loves God will pursue the obedient life (see John 14:21) and be far more likely to persevere in trials (see James 1:12). No other commandment has the vital lifeline to all others that loving God does.

Christ never preached the annihilation of affection. He taught the redirection of affection. Human affection first directed to God and filtered through His hands returns to us far healthier and fit for others. Love that goes through Him first is filtered.

The curtain draws on the scene with Christ's pointed words: "Your faith has saved you; go in peace" (v. 50). Notice that her faith is in His grace; it was not that her love had saved her. She was saved by His love, not hers. His last words to her represent far more than the common Hebrew benediction, shalom. Christ's intention for this woman who had committed such sin and suffered such shame was a very literal peace.

Perhaps, as it did for me, this passage has

caused you to picture yourself in her place. If you, too, have been in this scene with Jesus, perhaps you know the inner struggle of a sinful past. When I began the chapter, I shared my testimony of how Satan accused me. During that difficult period, not once did Christ say, "What you did wasn't that bad" or "After all you've been through, no wonder . . ." He simply sent a woman to deliver His Word — that I was forgiven. He whispered to my spirit, "Now, My child, be at peace." Oh, how I would love to be that woman to you today. Allow me to pull up my chair right in front of you, look you in the eye, and tell you what He told me to say: "Your many sins have been forgiven — for you love much." Go in peace.

Chapter 22

His True Brothers and Sisters

Luke 8:1–3

He replied, "My mother and brothers are those who hear God's word and put it into practice." (Luke 8:21)

One of my chief goals in this journey is for us to feel as if our feet have felt the warmth of the sand in every place where Jesus stood. As Luke's eighth chapter unfolds, we have a fresh opportunity to adjust our mental images to include a few new people on the scene. In addition to the Twelve, Jesus had other companions. "Women who had been cured of evil spirits and diseases: Mary (called Magdalene) . . . Joanna . . . Susanna; and many others" followed Him.

Jesus actively summoned the twelve disciples to follow Him. Whether or not the others received a verbal invitation, a powerful force drew them. After all Christ had done for them, these women could not help but follow Christ and serve Him. You don't have to talk many captives who've been set free into serving Christ. Like Paul in 2 Corinthians 5:14, the love of Christ compels them.

Jesus told the parable of the sower, and then we get a glimpse of a sudden development in family dynamics. His mother and brothers came to see Him but could not get to Him because of the crowd. When someone told Jesus that His family was there, He declared, "My mother and brothers are those who hear God's word and put it into practice" (Luke 8:21).

Jesus was not rejecting as much as redefining His family. His statement reflected inclusion more than exclusion. Christ's physical family probably came to take Him home to keep Him from appearing foolish. They surely weren't there to encourage Him. John tells us that "his own brothers did not believe in him" at this time (John 7:5).

Of course, we know that Mary certainly believed Jesus was the Son of God, but the pressure of family members can be quite forceful. Perhaps her other sons were intent on confronting Jesus, and she came along to act as a peacemaker. Sound familiar, moms? You don't have to be a mother to imagine how she felt in her present position.

As Christ redefined the family dynamics, I believe He meant for His words to be revolutionary. They are as critical for us today as they were for those who heard them then. Don't miss the profound importance of God's Word. Based on Luke 8:21, our kinship to Jesus Christ is directly revealed through what we do with the Word of God. What you are doing right now — studying God's Word — is not just a good idea. It is the very warmth and vitality of the family bloodline — proof that we are family to Jesus Christ.

Christ's priority is not how much we study the Word, enjoy attending Bible study, or discuss Scripture in small groups. His priority is for us to hear it and do it. Receive it internally. Express it externally. Both the verb tenses reflected in the words *hear* and *do* in verse 21 indicate continuous or repeated action. The context of Christ's statement about His family is the parable of the sower. His redefinition of family was to be understood in the relation to His teaching on the Word. Thankfully, Christ did not leave His disciples to decipher the meaning of this parable.

Luke 8:10 tells us that Christ's disciples were given "the knowledge of the secrets of the kingdom of God." All of us love to know a wonderful secret, not only because we enjoy the information, but because we enjoy the trust a shared secret implies! The word for secret in Luke 8:10 is *musterion,* meaning "some sacred thing hidden or secret which is naturally unknown to human reason and is only known by the revelation of God." Beloved, I want you to understand that the deep things of God were not limited to Christ's first twelve disciples. In John 8:31, Christ said, "If you hold to my teaching, you are really my disciples."

Think how our lives might be different if we should become people with whom Christ could share the deep things of God. Oh, friend, there is so much more to this journey. So much more to this divine relationship. So much more to the Word. We have scratched only the surface. Our lives with Christ were meant to be nothing less than the great adventure. Oh, God, make us people with whom You can share the deep things of Your heart.

The parable of the sower helps us to understand the obstacles that limit us and the elements that would free the Spirit to teach us the deep things of God. Consider

Christ's interpretation of the parable in Luke 8:11–15. He identified the seed as the Word of God. In the parable the seed falls on four types of soil.

The seed that falls along the path "are the ones who hear, and then the devil comes and takes away the word from their hearts, so that they may not believe and be saved" (v. 12). The seed on the rock "are the ones who receive the word with joy when they hear it, but they have no root. They believe for a while, but in the time of testing they fall away"(v. 13). The seed that fell among thorns "stands for those who hear, but as they go on their way they are choked by life's worries, riches and pleasures, and they do not mature" (v. 14). The seed on good soil "stands for those with a noble and good heart, who hear the word, retain it, and by persevering produce a crop" (v. 15).

Before we study the differences in each of the above, let's address a critical common denominator. All four had the same relationship with the Word: they heard it.

We cannot overemphasize the importance of applying and obeying the Word of God. You see, all four types of soil heard the Word, yet only one produced a harvest. It is not enough to hear the Word! We have just stumbled on my greatest burden for the body of Christ. How many people sit in church services where Scripture is never taught? They're not even hearing the Word of God! Furthermore, what masses of believers hear the Word but continue to live in defeat because they don't apply it?

I was one of them. I desperately wanted to change. I was miserable in my captivity. I just didn't understand that the power to be transformed was in the authentic application of Scripture. Our obedience is not to make God feel like the boss. Trust me. He's the boss and He knows it. Our obedience to apply the Word of God is so we can live victorious lives that glorify our Father in heaven. Hearing it is simply not enough.

Now let's consider each of the types of soil the seed of God's Word fell on.

The seed along the path. Note the activity of Satan. Jesus pictured him as a bird of the air. Ephesians 2:2 calls him "the ruler of the kingdom of the air." Luke 8:12 tells us Satan possesses the ability to come and take away the word from a hearer's heart. The Greek word for "take away" gives the image of an owl swooping down, snatching its prey in its claws, and soaring back victoriously to its perch. Scripture implies countless reasons Satan desires to snatch the Word from us before we've internalized it. Contrary to the hopes of some, hell won't be an eternal party. No one will be glad they came. Eternity is a long time for regrets. Imagine the evil nature of one who seeks to keep people from being saved.

The seed on the rock. The rocky soil represents the shallow hearers of the Word. These go a step further than those along the path. They do actually receive the Word. Perhaps you are troubled by the thought of Satan's ability to come and snatch the Word. Understand that Satan can't take anything the believing hearer claims. Once we've received the Word, it's out of his reach. He can try to distort our understanding of it, but he cannot steal it. As we'll soon see, however, we can give it up by our own volition.

The rocky soil didn't just receive the Word. It received the Word with joy! How eye-opening to realize that we can hear the Word and receive it joyfully, yet never let it penetrate the depths. Listen, some of the words of God are hard! I think He'd rather see us receive a Word, wrestle over it with tears, then let it take root, than to jump up and down with ecstatic joy for only a while.

The shallow hearer believes . . . until the time of testing (v. 13). What a terrible shame! We miss one of life's most awesome experiences if we don't see God's Word stand up under our trial. He wants to show us it works. He wants to show us He works! If we stop believing, we will never know the power and faithfulness of God. If you've developed a few deep roots of faith, you probably remember stages of superficiality and shallowness. You have probably had times in your life that, in retrospect, you recognize were shallow, but at the time you were oblivious to your lack of maturity. Just think: in several years, if we cooperate with God and keep growing, we're probably going to shake our heads over a few things that characterize us now!

The seed that fell among thorns. We've seen hearers of the Word confront demonic thievery and life's adversity. As influential as these two can be, the thorns are probably a greater daily threat. These hearers are defeated by the distractions of the world: worries, riches, and pleasures. We will deal with anxiety in a future chapter so we won't labor the point here. None, however, will argue with the fact that it's a constant battle.

The word for "riches" is *ploutos,* meaning "material goods, . . . abundance." We don't have to be rich to be distracted by riches. You don't have to have much to want more. Working ourselves into the ground to afford more things is symptomatic of this distraction.

The word for "pleasures" is *hedone,* from which we get our term *hedonism.* Hedonism views "pleasure, gratification, and enjoyment" as the chief goals of life. Please take caution before you view all forms of pleasure as an enemy of the faithful believer. Few things frustrate me more than people who picture the Christian life as entirely sacrificial and for martyrs only. Walking with Christ is the greatest pleasure of my life. But even this sacred pleasure cannot be my goal. Knowing and pleasing Christ must be my goal. Distraction of all kinds is my biggest challenge in this pursuit. The distracted hearer chokes on his or her own worldly appetites. Luke 8:14 says they also don't mature, which is far more than unfortunate. It is a tragedy. The word *mature* comes from two Greek words: *telos,* meaning "end, goal, perfection," and *phero,* meaning "to bring, bear." The hearers of the Word who are distracted by the constant call of the world will never fulfill God's awesome plan for their lives. According to 1 Corinthians 2:9, distracted individuals miss life's greatest treasure. No mind has even "conceived what God has prepared for those who love him."

The seed on good soil. The good soil represents the one who hears the Word and retains it. "Retains" pictures chewing the Word up and swallowing it until it occupies a place in us. When God's Word is deliberately internalized, it will be authentically externalized because it's no longer what we do — it's part of who we are.

Isaiah 55:11 declares God's Word will not return void. It will accomplish the purposes for which He sent it. That's a fact. But I want it to accomplish and achieve in me, don't you? When this generation asks who Christ's brothers and sisters are, I want Him to point us out joyfully. For our kinship to be obvious, we've got to hear God's Word and do it. When He sends forth His Word, may He find fertile soil in each of us.

Then, when we've reached our lives' intended goals, we will go out in joy and be led forth in peace, the mountains and hills will burst into song before us, and all the trees of the field will clap their hands. Persevere, doer of the Word. A harvest is coming.

Part 5

The Christ of God

At the conclusion of this portion of our study, we'll be at the halfway point of our journey. Can you believe it? Let me applaud you for walking with me on this path. God does not take your commitment lightly. I particularly encourage you to read the Scripture portion that goes with each chapter. His Word guarantees that you will inherit a blessing. He is changing you through the power of His Word. Not one moment you spend with Him is trivial. So tighten the straps on your sandals and take another deep swig of Living Water from your canteen. Next up we have some exciting miles to trek. We'll watch Christ deal with everything from demons to the dead. We'll also stand close by as He entrusts some of His power and authority to the disciples. You and I will receive a brisk reminder that His original disciples were privy to some of the same blunders that plague us. On the heels of Peter's bright and shining moment, he'll receive a reprimand that will make him want to hide behind the nearest bush. Thank goodness, the disciples weren't perfect. Christ's willingness to use them anyway is hope for us!

Enjoy Christ through this portion of our study, dear disciple. Allow His truth to penetrate the inmost places of your heart and mind. Ask God to imprint His name on every cell. That's your safety and your satisfaction.

Chapter 23

The Other Side

Luke 8:26–33

Jesus asked him, "What is your name?"
"Legion," he replied, because many demons had gone into him. (Luke 8:30)

Space prevents detailed study of Jesus' eventful trip across the sea to the other side. Tired from a hard day of ministry, Jesus slept on the boat ride until a sudden storm threatened the boat — and the disciples' faith. After rebuking the waves — and a boatload of disciples — Jesus arrived in the territory of the Gerasenes where they promptly encountered a memorable individual. The man they met was naked, lived among the tombs, possessed superhuman strength, and — did I mention — provided rent-free housing for a legion of demons. This demon-possessed man not only had the power to break ropes and chains; he also supernaturally recognized Jesus as the Son of God. We want to consider several points coming from the encounter.

Our God is even God over the godless. First notice that the second Christ stepped His foot on their "turf," the demons knew He carried His authority with Him. As hard as the demonic world tries to keep Him out, no one can keep Christ out of any place He is determined to go. Verse 28 tells us that when the demoniac saw Jesus, he cried out and fell at his feet. While I certainly wouldn't confuse the demoniac's trip to His knees with worship, it definitely was a sign of the demon's acknowledgment that Christ was the Son of the Most High God. Our second consideration is food for thought rather than doctrine for digestion.

The demons may have anticipated Christ's coming. Even my most conservative commentaries entertained the idea that the storm on the way could have been an attempt by the kingdom of darkness to discourage Christ's arrival. We see a hint toward the possibility of this idea in the way Christ rebuked the wind and waters as if they were disobedient. Could they have been temporarily acting under the instruction of the god of the air (see Eph. 2:2)? Just food for thought, but it would help to explain why the demoniac met Christ on the shore, knowing for certain who He was.

Before we proceed to the next point, consider a fact revealed in verse 27. The demoniac didn't live in a house. He resided in the tombs. I wonder how many people today are living "in the tombs"? I know a woman who is still so oppressed by despair that decades after the loss of a loved one, she still lives "in the tombs." In no way do I minimize the horror of her loss, but I despise how the evil one has used it to minimize her life.

The demons know their time is limited. Luke focused on only one of the demoniacs, but Matthew tells us that there were actually two. He also tells us that they begged Jesus not to torture them "before the appointed time." The demons knew something we may sometimes forget. According to Revelation 12:12, Satan is filled with fury because he also knows "that his time is short."

The devil hated to see the Word wrapped in flesh because he knew his time allotment was getting shorter and shorter. I don't believe the plan for the Son of God to come to earth was any secret. I believe Satan knew what was going to happen. I just don't think he knew when. The demons controlling the man on the Gerasene shore also knew a day of reckoning had been appointed for them.

Demons can enact supernatural strength. Matthew tells us that "they were so violent that no one could pass that way" (Matt. 8:28). Luke tells us that the demons enabled the man to break chains (see Luke 8:29). I feel the need to stress something about supernatural power: not all of it comes from God! I have felt chills run down my spine when I've heard someone say: "It had to be God! It was totally supernatural!" At times Satan is able to display signs and wonders.

I confess that I find great humor in another demon story — the seven sons of Sceva in Acts 19:13–16. The seven were exorcists who tried to cast out demons from a man in the name of Jesus. The demons replied, "Jesus I know, and I know about Paul, but who are you?" (v. 15). Then the demons beat the stuffing out of the seven exorcists.

Did you notice the presence of violence in both demonic encounters? While Satan certainly "masquerades as an angel of light" (2 Cor. 11:14), he also enjoys coming out of his shell. Violence is one of the most obvious fingerprints of Satan. We don't even have to wonder if the constant surge in societal violence is his activity. Unthinkable crimes are now commonplace. We can underscore two truths from this point:

- Not all supernatural power comes from God.
- While not all demonic activity appears violent, virtually all violence originates with the power of darkness.

Remember, ours is the Prince of Peace. All conflict He ordains is for the ultimate purpose of peace under His righteous rule. Oh, for the government that will be on His shoulders (see Isa. 9:6–7)!

Solitary places can be used by God or Satan. The man "had been driven by the demon into solitary places" (v. 29). Jesus also valued solitary places. In Mark 6:31 Christ said to the disciples, "Come with me by yourselves to a quiet place and get some rest." We all need times of solitude to spend with God, but our times of isolation can be used by the enemy as well. If we isolate ourselves from the support of others Satan can have a field day.

Only Christ can defeat demonic powers. Without Christ a "legion" of humans cannot take authority over a single demon. However, Jesus the One and Only can instantly take authority over legions of demons. The climactic point of the story reveals an almost laughable irony. The demons begged to be cast into the swine rather than into the abyss. (If you think I'm going to say a word about deviled ham, you're mistaken!)

The villagers came out of the woodwork only to find the talk of the region sitting at Jesus' feet, dressed, and in his right mind. The people allowed fear to eclipse the life-changing facts, and they begged Jesus to leave. He could have healed them, saved them, taught them, sanctified them, and, for heaven's sake, delighted them. But all they wanted Him to do was to leave them.

Jesus left the Gerasenes, all right. But not without a vivid reminder of who He was and what He could do. Long after they recovered from the swine-at-sea incident, there would still be a man about town with a restored mind and real dignity who couldn't seem to hush. Christ told him, "Return home and tell how much God has done for you" (v. 39). How long do you think it had been since he had been home? Not back to the tombs, but home. Clothes on his back. Roof over his head. Soundness in his mind. A message on his tongue. So the man went and told all over town how much Jesus had done for him. All the demons in the air couldn't stop him, for his knees had bowed to a new authority.

Chapter 24

Interwoven Wonders

Luke 8:40–56

Then the woman, seeing that she could not go unnoticed, came trembling and fell at his feet. In the presence of all the people, she told why she had touched him and how she had been instantly healed. (Luke 8:47)

I long to sit at Jesus' feet in heaven and hear Him describe personally His earthly experience. I want to hear all the missing details and what He was thinking when certain things happened. I think He will have plenty to say about our next text. In it we see two interwoven wonders. Jesus healed a woman who had been bleeding for twelve years and raised a preteen girl from the dead.

Upon Jesus' return from across the lake a crowd greeted Him. Luke 8:40 says they were all expecting Him. I do dearly love surprise encounters with Jesus, but I think He is pleased when we live our lives in expectancy. Verse 41 introduces a major player who didn't come just to welcome Jesus. He came desperate for Jesus. In his must-read book *Fresh Wind, Fresh Fire* Jim Cymbala wrote, "I discovered an astonishing truth: God is attracted to weakness. He can't resist those who humbly and honestly admit how desperately they need him."[1]

Jairus was a ruler of the synagogue, but this day no ritual dignity stood in his way. His daughter lay dying, and he threw himself at the feet of Jesus pleading for her life.

Jairus reminds me of the centurion in Luke 7. He seemed to understand the concept of authority because of his authoritative position. Likewise, the ruler of the synagogue seemed to grasp that one ruler existed before whom all others should bow. The events that follow weave two scenes together in such a way that I am compelled to offer thoughts involving both. The following observations strike me as I consider the healing of the bleeding woman and the raising of Jairus's daughter.

The Depth of Need

For both Jairus and the woman in the crowd, Jesus was literally their last hope. Who else could heal from the throes of death? And who else could cure what countless doctors had failed to cure, especially without pay? Indeed, Jesus was their only hope. Whom do you know that is possibly down to his or her very last hope? Perhaps, like me, you even know several people. Think of those people and keep them in your peripheral vision throughout our chapter. Next I want you to notice another detail of these two wonders.

The Length of Need

Don't you think it's interesting that the woman suffered her infirmity for the same length of time that Jairus' child had been alive? Ask anyone who has suffered with a chronic ailment how much focus it commands, and she'll tell you she struggles to focus on anything else. Ask any set of parents how much they focus on their one and only child, and they'll likely tell you the same thing. Have you struggled for a long time with some difficulty? I absolutely do not want to minimize your suffering when I tell you that Jesus specializes in the long-term and the hopeless.

Christ's Depth of Discernment

We read in verse 42 that the crowd pressed so closely to Jesus they were almost crushing Him. Yet a woman behind Him touched only the edge of His cloak, and He discerned the difference. Please keep in mind, she never even touched His skin. Amazing! Notice that when Christ asked, "Who touched me?" they all denied it. Odd, isn't it? The people were so close they were nearly crushing Him, but no one admitted to touching Him. Their response reminds me of children too afraid of getting into trouble to admit to something. Did they not realize He wanted few things more than for them to reach out to Him?

When the woman realized that she "could not go unnoticed," she "came trembling and fell at his feet" (v. 47). Beloved, no one goes unnoticed by Christ, least of all, a person acting on faith. I love the fact that the woman came trembling, even though she had exercised enough faith to draw forth the healing power of Jesus. It's good to know that the faithful still come trembling. In fact, their reverence is a critical part of their faith. The truly believing will most certainly also be the bowing.

Why do you think Christ asked her to identify herself? I think one reason might have been so she could enjoy the healing she had received. The New International Version doesn't record one phrase found in the King James Version of verse 48: "Daughter, *be of good comfort:* thy faith hath made thee whole; go in peace" (emphasis mine). In this way I believe Christ was saying, "Do not go forth as someone who feels they have stolen a gift! Be of good cheer! I freely give it to you!"

The Breadth of Jesus' Power

Verse 42 tells us Jesus was on His way to heal the dying child when the woman in the crowd touched the edge of His cloak. Christ Himself described what happened: "Someone touched me; I know that power has gone out from me" (v. 46). The primary point I want to make is that Christ released enough power to heal a woman of a twelve-year hemorrhage but still had plenty to raise Jairus's daughter from the dead! Let that sink in! I know you know it with your head, but I want you to receive it in your heart. Christ's power supply is limitless. He's not the Wizard of Oz with a limited number of wishes to grant. His power and mercy are infinite. He can take you much farther than Kansas, Dorothy.

One night at Bible study I asked the entire group to come to their feet for a time of intercessory prayer. I then asked anyone with an "overwhelming need" that seemed absolutely "insurmountable" to sit down. I don't mind telling you, few people were left standing, and based on their tears, I don't think they were just being dramatic. I had anticipated having enough intercessors left standing to lay hands on all those who sat down. Boy, was I mistaken! For a split second I didn't know how to proceed, then the Spirit of God seemed to speak to my heart. What joy flooded my soul that very moment as God called upon me to come boldly before His throne and ask for a miracle for every life because He had plenty of power to go around. That's exactly what I did. The testimonies written to me the next week were unforgettable. Virtually everyone witnessed some type of wonder that week.

Now hear this: Jesus has more than enough power! Does He seem to be on His way to another need, one that you perceive may be more important than yours? More a matter of life and death? No problem! Reach out and grab that hem! You are not going unnoticed — not even if He's on His way to raise the dead!

Right this moment, I'd like for you to stop for a moment. Get something to write with and on. Write a few sentences of intercessory prayer for the person or people you recognized earlier as being at their last hope.

Now, beloved, what is your greatest need, the deepest desire of your heart? Write them down. Two or three? Write them all. Don't tell me how trivial they seem in comparison! Write them! After you've written them all, I want you to consider your list carefully. Now I want you to say out loud: "Jesus, You have enough power."

Oh, friend, would you dare to believe that He is completely able? If He doesn't grant you what you ask in faith, it is never because He lacks the power. I believe it's because He wants to release an all-surpassing power and reveal an even greater glory through another answer. Will we laugh at the thought like the foolish mourners outside Jairus's home? Or will we be invited into the house to behold a miracle?

Chapter 25

Extended Authority

Luke 9:1–9

When Jesus had called the Twelve together, he gave them power and authority to drive out all demons and to cure diseases, and he sent them out to preach the kingdom of God and to heal the sick. (Luke 9:1–2)

Thus far in Luke's Gospel the Twelve have watched Christ at work and have witnessed His miracles, but they have not yet been empowered to exercise those wonders. I don't imagine the disciples expected to do anything but watch. They were about to receive a very special welcome to the wild world of Jesus Christ. Jesus called the disciples together and gave them "power and authority to drive out all demons and to cure diseases" (9:1). Then He sent them out to preach and heal. He told them to take along no provisions but to stay where the people welcomed them.

Wouldn't you love to eavesdrop on the conversations between the disciples as they prepared to go out? What kinds of emotions do you think they experienced after Christ told them what He was equipping them to do? Let's walk through these verses together, concept by concept.

The Extension of Power and Authority

Christ had a very good reason for giving His disciples such power and authority. The time would come when Christ would depart from them and work through them rather than beside them. He wisely gave the disciples power and authority while He was still tutoring and policing them personally and visibly. They would be "in charge" of the kingdom message from an earthly standpoint long before they wanted to be.

The Distinction of Calling

Christ's instruction to go and minister was for a specific mission or task. I believe the concepts of calling and task are often confused in the body of Christ. I know that I confused the concepts in the early years of my surrender to ministry.

When I was in my mid-twenties, my wonderful ministry mentor, Marge Caldwell, helped me to see that God had equipped me with some of the speaking gifts. Once I began to exercise those gifts, I assumed that speaking was my calling. God soon made very clear that my calling was to surrender my life every day to His will, to be His woman, and to do what He asked, whatever that was. I remember sensing Him speak to my heart saying, "Beth, I do not want you surrendered to an assignment. I want you surrendered to Me." I realized that God did not want me "hung up" on the kind of assignment He would give me. He didn't want it to matter to me whether He asked me to teach the Word of God to a hundred people or to rock one baby in the church nursery. My calling was to be abandoned to Him.

The Twelve were called to be Christ's learners or pupils. They also were designated apostles, meaning they would be sent forth. What would His pupils be sent forth to do? Whatever He told them. In our human need for the security of sameness, we tend to want one job assignment from

God that we can do for the rest of our lives. He's far more creative than that!

You may ask, "Isn't it possible for God to assign a lifelong task such as preaching at one church for forty years?" Absolutely! But we are wise not to make assumptions by surrendering to the assignment! Our calling is to surrender to God. Think of the pitfalls we could avoid if we were more abandoned to God than to a particular kind of service.

Remember the meaning of *disciple:* pupil, learner! We can't keep skipping class (our time with God in Scripture and prayer) and expect to know when He's scheduled a field trip!

The Motivation for Giving

Like us, I'm not sure the disciples had a clue what they had been given. They had the privilege to be the closest earthly companions to the Son of God. They were chosen to witness the most remarkable phenomenon in all human history: the Word made flesh and dwelling among us. They broke bread with Him, laughed with Him, and talked Scripture with Him. They knew the sound of His breathing when He slept. They knew His favorite foods. They watched Him heal the sick, deliver the demon-possessed, and raise the dead. If they had never received another thing, they had been granted a privilege beyond all others. However, Christ didn't stop there. He also gave them power and authority.

Christ's words in Matthew 10:8 should inspire us to pour out our lives like drink offerings for the rest of our days. "Heal the sick, raise the dead, cleanse those who have leprosy, drive out demons. Freely you have received, freely give." The word for "freely" is *dorean,* meaning "freely, gratis, as a free gift." I think you might be very interested to see another way this same Greek word is translated into English.

In John 15:25 Jesus said, "They hated me without reason." The phrase "without reason" is translated from the same word, *dorean.* What does that tell you about the things we've received from Christ? Unreasonable grace! Nothing is reasonable about the love of God or the gifts He so freely gives! Like me, I know you've received freely from God in ways you can't begin to count, but has that unreasonable grace caused you to freely give of yourself to others recently?

The Balance of Receiving

Jesus told the disciples to depend entirely on those who would welcome them to provide for needs such as food and shelter. The concept of God's people assuming responsibility for the needs of those who serve them vocationally is delightfully consistent throughout the Word. You will find that passages as diverse as Deuteronomy 10:8; 12:10–12, 18–19; and 1 Timothy 5:17–18 speak with a single voice. We who receive ministry are to care for the needs of those who minister the gospel to us.

The Wisdom of Awareness

Last, let's consider Christ's instruction to His disciples in Matthew 10:16. He told them, "I am sending you out like sheep among wolves. Therefore be as shrewd as snakes and as innocent as doves." I believe this word is just as applicable for all Christ's modern disciples as for the original Twelve. We, too, must "be as shrewd as snakes and as innocent as doves." The Greek word for "shrewd" is *phronimos,* meaning "prudent, sensible, practically wise in relationships with others." I had no idea when I entered ministry how prudent I would have to become about relationships.

The Greek word for "innocent" is *akeraios,* meaning "without any mixture of deceit, without any defiling material." I don't care who we are or what we do, all of us meet challenges when, momentarily, a lie would seem to serve us better than the truth.

Finally, let's look at the wisdom of possessing both biblical shrewdness and innocence because, between them, we will discover a vital balance. God doesn't want us to know we're being conned because we're master con artists ourselves. He doesn't want us to recognize deception because we know how to twist the truth. God deeply desires to develop godly integrity in each of us. He wants us to recognize the counterfeit because we're so familiar with the true article. He wants us to be smart without being suspicious — innocent without being naïve. The challenge is great, so take it seriously. We, too, are sheep among wolves. I've been eaten alive a few times, and I have some "scars" to prove it. What I'd give to save you some!

It's dangerous out there. My best advice, dear sheep, is to stick to your Shepherd.

Chapter 26

Baskets of Blessing

Luke 9:10–17

They all ate and were satisfied, and the disciples picked up twelve basketfuls of broken pieces that were left over. (Luke 9:17)

Any of us who have ever been exhausted by an intense time of ministry can deeply appreciate the opening scene in Luke 9:10. The apostles returned from their preaching and healing mission. Mark pictures the Twelve gathered around Jesus reporting all they had done and taught. What affection floods this setting! We can assume He omnisciently knew everything they had done and taught, yet I love how He celebrated their news with the excitement of someone at a surprise party.

Sometimes I'll be busy telling God every

detail of something exciting that happened, a thousand words a minute, when suddenly I will stop and say, "But I guess You already knew that." Every single time I sense Him saying, "Don't let that stop you, child! Tell on!" Beloved, I so much hope that you feel free to talk to Him with the excitement of a friend.

Christ not only sees our excitement, He sees our exhaustion. I love the way the King James Version says it: "They had no leisure so much as to eat" (Mark 6:31). He saw their need for leisure over a refreshing meal. His invitation to them is so warm and intimate that my affection for Him swells every time I read it: "Come with me by yourselves to a quiet place and get some rest."

Wouldn't you know it? In the middle of their private getaway, the public showed up. Christ's response to the crowd touches me: "He welcomed them" (Luke 9:11); "They were like sheep without a shepherd" (Mark 6:34). Desperate, vulnerable, without direction, without protection, and He had compassion on them. According to Matthew 14:21, we are safe to picture at least ten thousand people gathering all over the countryside. Christ "healed those who needed healing" (Luke 9:11). The day wore on, and the sun rested again on a western hill. About that time, some interesting things began to happen. Consider the following observations with me.

Christ sometimes provokes a question so that He can be the answer. I love how John's version tells us Christ prompted the question, "Where shall we buy bread for these people to eat?" (John 6:5). Verse 6 tells us, "He asked this only to test him." I think Christ might have been testing His disciples to surface what they had learned, or, like me, what they had yet to learn! Think of the miracles they had seen Christ perform by this time. Yet they couldn't imagine how they were going to feed all these hungry people. I think Jesus may have been testing them to see if they were beginning to think in a "faith mode." Their response proved they still practiced fragmented faith. While they had seen Christ cast out demons and heal the sick, it had not yet occurred to them He could feed the masses. They still had much to learn about Christ's complete jurisdiction. He can meet our spiritual needs, our emotional needs, and our physical needs. He is both deeply spiritual and entirely practical. Christ was teaching them to see Him, His power, and His authority in every area of life.

Christ wants us to be open to what He

can do through us. I love the way He tossed the responsibility for feeding the crowd right into His disciples' laps. "You give them something to eat" (Luke 9:13). Mind you, they had received power and authority to heal the sick and cast out demons, yet they looked helplessly at two fish and five loaves as the totality of their resources.

I believe Christ was saying, "Think bigger, boys!" This time, not only about what He could do, but also what they could do in His name. Where the disciples were concerned, I believe this event was all about stretching their thinking. His words are entirely absent of rebuke. Don't miss the fact that He used the disciples to distribute the meal. He wanted them to feel the weight of the baskets and see the hands of those reaching to be fed. Real power in real forms in real life. I wrote a few lines of verse in an attempt to capture what I think Jesus was saying to the disciples — and to us.

> Think bigger, boys!
> You've yet to find
> I've got all the power
> All of the time
>
> Think bigger, boys!
> While it is day

Watch what I do
Do what I say

Think bigger, boys!
See every scene
With Me in the middle
Reigning as King

Think bigger, boys!
For one day you'll see
Me in my glory
Then you'll say to Me . . .

We should've thought bigger.

Christ can perform astounding wonders when we bring Him all we have. Matthew 14:17 records the disciples saying, "We have here only five loaves of bread and two fish." Christ responded, "Bring them here to me." Beloved, I want you to hear something loud and clear: no matter what your "only" is, when you bring all of your "only" to Jesus, it's huge! When we bring Him everything we have, He multiplies it beyond our wildest imagination. On the other hand, we can surrender Him "some" of our lot, and it can dwindle to virtually nothing.

Christ saved a basket-load of leftovers for each disciple. The disciples picked up twelve baskets of leftovers. I just can't make myself think that was a coincidence. I'm no mathematician, but the numbers work for me. The people were fed. The disciples each wound up with a basketful of leftovers. That's what happens when you take part in God's provision.

At the age of twenty, my older daughter was asked to speak to a group of teenage girls in Oklahoma. Of my two children she is the shy one. With horror on her face, she told me she was certain God was telling her to say yes. I cannot express to you how far outside her comfort zone this was at the time.

The butterflies never left her stomach from the time of the invitation until the day of the conference. What emotion flooded my heart as I put her on that plane to go speak — instead of the other way around. Contrary to her worst fears, she lived through it! And the young women received a sound message from the Word . . . even if the voice was a little shaky here and there.

The next morning she called me with such a tender heart, her voice cracking, and said, "Mom, I just had my time with the Lord . . . and He was so . . . sweet."

I knew exactly what she was talking about. I said, "Oh, my precious child, you have just experienced that which would be worth selling all your earthly possessions to gain, and yet it's a gift of grace: divine approval. The smiling nod of God. Nothing like it."

With the slightest whisper, my very humble, gentle child said, "Yes."

I'm fighting back tears at the thought. You see, this act of obedience was terribly difficult for her. She could have provided a list of other students, but she didn't. In effect she said, "All I have is this pitiful handful of fish and loaves," and Jesus said, "Bring them to me." When all was said and done, she wasn't sure what the girls had received, but God had given her bread from His Word and she had distributed it the best she knew how.

Amanda was glad to have survived . . . but imagine her surprise when she didn't just survive. The next morning as she sat before the Lord, He handed her a basketful of leftovers. She had been willing to be a disciple. A learner. A novice. He would not have dreamed of leaving her empty-handed. You either, my friend. It's not His style.

Chapter 27

Confessions of the Heart

Luke 9:18–21

"But what about you?" he asked. "Who do you say I am?" Peter answered, "The Christ of God." (Luke 9:20)

Next we come to one of the most crucial points in Christ's earthly ministry. We see a chain of critically important conversations that are best understood when linked together. We will look at four segments of Scripture in this chapter.

Part One: Peter's Confession

Luke tells us that as Jesus was praying, He asked the disciples, "Who do the crowds say I am?" (Luke 9:18). They said people thought Jesus was John the Baptist, Elijah, or some other of the prophets come back to life. Then Jesus asked, "Who do you say I am?" and Peter answered, "The Christ of God" (v. 20).

In all probability, Herod's determination to know Christ's identity (Luke 9:9) helped heighten the talk among the crowds. We need not doubt that all who knew about Christ were trying to figure out who He was. Considering the nearness of the crucifixion on Christ's earthly timetable, it was not critical for the crowds to know Christ's full identity at that time, but it was of utmost importance that the disciples know. They would desperately need to know who He was, even when they couldn't understand what He was doing. "Who do you say I am?"

Peter stepped up to the plate: "The Christ of God" (Luke 9:20). The *Christos.* The Anointed One. The Messiah. Matthew's Gospel records the divine approval of Christ over Peter's inspired response: "Blessed are you, Simon son of Jonah, for this was not revealed to you by man, but by my Father in heaven" (Matt. 16:17). Do you realize that if you know the true identity of Jesus Christ, no preacher or teacher revealed it to you? The Father of all creation, the God who sits on the throne of the universe, pursued you and chose to reveal

His Son to you. Remember that the next time you feel insignificant.

I don't think Peter was the only one of the Twelve who knew Christ was the Lord's Messiah. He was no doubt a leader among them, however, and he did not hesitate to answer the question. Christ's response to him is a play on words: "I tell you that you are Peter, and on this rock I will build my church" (Matt. 16:18). The name Peter is the original word *petros,* meaning "a stone, . . . a large stone, a piece or fragment of a rock such as a man might throw."

After reconfirming Peter's Christ-given name, Jesus then said, "On this rock I will build my church." Stay with me here! In this use of the word *rock,* the word switches to *petra,* meaning "a projecting rock, cliff . . . Distinguished from the masculine *petros* in that *petra* is a mass of rock while *petros* is a detached stone or boulder."

When Jesus referred to the rock upon which He would build His church, I believe Christ was talking about the unchangeable, immovable testimony of Jesus Christ that Peter had just delivered. He was saying, "Peter, the testimony of My identity is the immovable rock upon which I will build My church. A cliff on which all of eternity hangs. You are a chip off this immovable rock whom I will greatly empower." Peter was a stone Christ would throw from place to place to give the testimony about the Rock from which he was hewn. How beautifully Isaiah 51:1 speaks to Peter and certainly to us: "Look to the rock from which you were cut and to the quarry from which you were hewn."

Notice that Christ said specifically that the gates of hades will not overcome His church. The thought often occurs to me that Satan can do nothing to overcome the church from the outside. No amount of perversity, depravity, or even persecution will ever overcome the church. Satan can't tear us down from the outside; that's why he seeks to do an inside job using division, bitterness among believers, infighting, and denominational elitism. Local church bodies don't die because of the world's influence; they die from internal diseases. Let's be on the lookout for inside jobs. Keep Satan out, and the very gates of hades cannot prevail against us.

Part Two: Christ's Prediction

Jesus made two radical predictions. One spoke to His future, one speaks to ours. In

Luke 9:22 Jesus clearly predicted His suffering and death. He followed those words with the eternal declaration, "If anyone would come after me, he must deny himself and take up his cross daily and follow me." In God's plan not only was Christ to suffer the cross, but we too must die daily. Does a fresh look at these verses astonish you as much as it does me? Christ didn't talk in parables here! No veiled truths. No innuendoes. Not a single mixed message. I am awed again by Christ's awareness of every detail of what He would face. "The Son of Man must suffer many things . . . and he must be killed."

Part Three: Peter's Reaction

Once again Peter takes the lead, but this time his mouth gets him into trouble. When Jesus said He must be killed, Peter took Jesus aside and told Him this must never happen. For all practical purposes, Peter shook his finger in the face of the Son of the living God. Try to picture Peter saying something like, "Jesus, can I see You just a minute right over here? Excuse me, brothers. We'll be right back." Then he commenced his rebuke. In my opinion,

Peter the rock was pretty fortunate he didn't get "thrown" into the nearest lake! Several thoughts surface as I look at this interchange:

1. One minute we can be so "on target" and the next minute so "off"! Without a doubt, some of my better moments preceded my worst disasters. How about you? I keep looking at those words: "This shall never happen to you!" (Matt. 16:22). I wonder, based on Christ's response to Peter, if in his heart he might have been thinking more readily: *This shall never happen to me! I've given up everything and followed You! You can't die on us here! We've got a kingdom to build!* Peter didn't understand that Christ's suffering and death were the means by which He would indeed secure the kingdom.

Peter understood Christ's *identity,* but he didn't understand Christ's *destiny:* the cross, the grave, the right hand of God. He might have been wiser to have asked a question such as, "Why must You die?" than to rebuke. However, Peter was not cast away — nor are we in our moments of outlandish foolishness. Glory to God! Christ did not retract Peter's calling, but He certainly told him a thing or two.

2. All Satan needs to have momentary

victory over a disciple is for us to have in mind the things of men. Satan doesn't have to get us thinking blatantly satanic thoughts to have victory over us. All he needs is to get us looking at life from man's perspective rather than God's. If we surrender our minds to the things of God, we are safe! We don't have to constantly look out for our own best interests, because He's constantly looking out for them. What Peter didn't understand is that what may have seemed best in the short run would have been disastrous in the long run. Had Jesus saved His disciples the anxiety of His betrayal, trials, and death, He wouldn't have saved them at all.

On this earth I don't know that we will ever perpetually have in mind the things of God rather than the things of man. If we don't make the deliberate choice to have in mind the things of God when faced with our biggest challenges, most of us will probably default back to our natural instinct — the things of man.

In comparing the Gospels of Luke and Matthew, all these events appear to have happened in a solitary scene. One moment Peter made a statement that Christ said could only have been revealed to him by the Father. The next thing we know he's made a statement Christ attributed to the devil.

One minute a rock — the next minute a stumbling block. Whew! What a frightening thought! How on guard we must be.

Part Four: Christ's Invitation

In light of Peter's performance and subsequent rebuke, we see an amazing response from our Lord. Don't miss the fact that Peter was still invited to "follow" after his horrible faux pas. I am intrigued that Peter actually heard the invitation to follow three times before Christ ascended to the right hand of the Father: Matthew 4:19, this passage, and John 21:19. Almost as if he were getting a crash course in Follow 101, Follow 202, and Follow 303. The first one was to follow Him as a disciple. The second one was to follow Him with a cross. The third one was to follow Him to death. Not coincidentally, tradition teaches that Peter indeed ended up following Christ to the death . . . on a cross.

Developing the mind-set of one who is continually taking up his cross and following Christ is the heart of having "in mind the things of God" (Matt. 16:23) rather than man. Don't forget that the issue that prompted this discourse was the identity of Christ. When we surrender to carrying our crosses and following Him, we identify with Him.

In Christ's invitation I see two other concepts: denying self and taking up the cross daily. Those who accept this invitation are called to deny themselves. I don't believe Christ was talking about the things we typically consider self-denial. The issue here wasn't fasting from food, nor was it denying self a single extra. It wasn't about self-loathing, for Christ commanded us to love our neighbor as ourselves. I believe the primary issue involved in this kind of self-denial is denying our right to be our own authority.

This passage brings us to the sobering realization that what we might think is our own authority — having in mind the things of men — could easily be transferred to Satan's authority. I've learned the hard way that denying my right to be my own boss is what keeps me from getting slaughtered by Satan in warfare. Let's face it: this "be-your-own-boss" stuff is nothing but a myth.

The key to true "follow-ship" with Christ is the recommitment to take up the cross daily. One reason I am drawn to Luke's version of this invitation over Matthew's is because he includes an all-important word — *daily.*

In my opinion, Dr. Luke wrote the prescription for the victorious life, and he wrote it for all of us who would desire to become Christ's disciple: live life one surrendered day at a time. Eyes to the East. Hands to the cross. Feet to the path.

Part 6

The Necessity

I love the portion of the journey waiting just ahead! Because our subject matter is biographical rather than topical, God is dealing with our hearts and minds on countless issues, isn't He? We're simply going wherever Jesus goes. And does He ever go! Have I told you lately how much fun I'm having on this trip with you? Together we get to be disciples #13 and #14. If we really assimilate and apply what we encounter in this part of our study, our discipleship will be transformed. God will challenge us to overcome unbelief, pride, and any misplaced motivation for serving Him. Christ has just as much to say to us as He said to those who stood face-to-face with Him in each encounter. We won't have to look for creative ways to apply these encounters to our lives. These sandals will instantly fit if we're willing to wear them. They will also keep our feet from slipping as we walk the ministry miles ahead. Let's ask God to help us be completely willing to relate.

Chapter 28

Who Is This Man?

Luke 9:28–36

And while He was praying, the appearance of His face became different, and His clothing became white and gleaming. (Luke 9:29 NASB)

OK, I'm crying my eyeliner off again. We are halfway through our journey together. I can hardly believe it. I want you to know something that I find so special about the body of Christ. My heart at this moment is overwhelmed with love for you. I don't know how that's possible.

As I've traveled to different places around the country and met lots of people who have participated in the Bible studies, they've said, "Beth, we feel like we know you, but I guess you don't feel that way do you?" The answer is "Yes, I do! Yes, I do!"

I don't even know how that's possible. I sit at the computer and think continually about the people I've met along the way. I will sometimes just weep. I just stop in the middle of a lesson God is giving me, and just weep with an overwhelming sense of love for you in the body of Christ.

I don't understand how God gives such love. I think in some ways it has come as an answer to prayer.

Early on as a serious believer, I began to try to recognize my spiritual gifts. After a while I figured that my gift was not shopping at the mall, which I originally thought. At first I had figured I had the spiritual gift of fashion or something. When I found out that fashion wasn't on the list in any of the passages of Scripture, my theory was blown. I had to go back to truth.

When I began to realize what my spiritual gifts were, I saw in 1 Corinthians 13 that God says He doesn't care if we speak with the tongues of angels, if we don't have love, we may as well be clanging brass to Him. He won't even hear us.

That truth hit me with a wave of conviction. I realized that any time I came before a group and was not filled with love for that group, what I had to say might matter to the group, but God couldn't even hear it.

Love in the body of Christ is a gift of the Spirit. Without love, we'll never see God's glory, and that brings us to our subject for this chapter.

God has often chosen to unveil His glory on the top of a mountain. In Exodus, He beckoned His servant Moses to climb the mount and see His glory. Elijah also had a mountaintop view of the greatness of God. When Christ summoned Peter, James, and John to the top of a certain mountain, they could never have imagined what awaited them. I think we can rest assured it was worth the climb.

God also calls us to hike some steep trails and to sometimes mount the insurmountable. If we are willing to climb, we too may see Him transfigured before our eyes.

Remember the question the disciples asked when Jesus rebuked the storm: "Who then is this, that He commands even the winds and the water, and they obey Him?" (Luke 8:25 NASB). Jesus took Peter, James, and John up on the mountain to show them the answer to that question.

"Some eight days after these sayings, it came about that He took along Peter and John and James, and went up to the mountain to pray. And while He was praying, the appearance of His face became different, and His clothing became white and gleaming. And behold, two men were talking with Him; and they were Moses and Elijah, who, appearing in glory, were speaking of His departure which He was about to accomplish at Jerusalem" (Luke 9:28–31 NASB).

Peter and his companions were very sleepy (Luke 9:32). Now try to take that in. Elijah and Moses were standing there chatting with Christ, but boy, it's been a long day and eyes are getting heavy! Then God shook up their nap. "But when they were fully awake, they saw His glory and the two men standing with Him" (v. 32 NASB).

They saw His glory.

When was the last time you saw Christ transfigured before you? You see, we grow comfortable with the Christ we know. Then suddenly He will shatter the box we've put Him in, leaving us asking again, "Who is this man?"

Perhaps you remember I earlier made the statement that Christ will reserve the right to bring us to places that force us to ask the question again. At those times, if we're willing, Christ will show us a glimpse of His glory. We are changed when Christ transfigures Himself before us. We see that change in several ways.

First we see that Christ seeks to readjust

our vision of Him. I believe the more we are willing to receive from Him, the more He is willing to reveal to us. I think the reason Jesus took Peter, James, and John to the mountain was because they were willing to receive greater revelation. How blessed we truly are when we have eyes that are willing to see and ears that are willing to hear. In the words of Jesus: "Whoever has will be given more, and he will have an abundance. Whoever does not have, even what he has will be taken from him" (Matt. 13:12).

How blessed we are when we want to see Him. When we begin to make it our chief cry to Him, "Lord, I want to know you. I want to know the reality of you. I want to know who you really are. Shatter my present perspective and show me the reality of you."

We are a direct by-product of who we believe or see Christ to be. I believe He blesses the prayer "Father, daily show me the reality, the greater reality of your Son Jesus Christ. Transfigure Him before my very eyes and then give me the courage to adjust my life to what I see." He continually seeks to readjust our vision of Him.

Let me show you an example. Paul wrote, "My purpose is that they may be encouraged in heart and united in love, so that they may have the full riches of complete understanding, in order that they may know the mystery of God, namely, Christ, in whom are hidden all the treasures of wisdom and knowledge" (Col. 2:2–3). He referred to Christ being the revealed mystery of God.

I want you to consider two words for knowing or knowledge in those verses. Verse 2 says, "that they may *know* . . . Christ." The word *know* comes from a wonderful word in the Greek language, *epiginostos.* It means a recognition of who Christ is. It designates a relationship with Christ based on participation on the part of the learner. It defines somewhat of a security of relationship. Paul is saying, "I want them to be secure, to have full assurance, in that relationship."

Now let me point you to the second word for knowledge. It appears in Colossians 2:3. "In whom are hidden all the treasures of wisdom and knowledge." This word for "knowledge" is a different word entirely. It is a word that means "present and fragmentary knowledge." Now hang with me a second because I think this will thrill you.

What Paul is saying is that God is the fullness of all security and mystery. He meets all our emotional needs as well as our mental needs.

Something in all of us loves a relationship that we can find to be both secure and mysterious. Are you with me here? Let me give you a very personal example.

My relationship with Keith is my most personal earthly relationship. I love knowing that I have security — full assurance — in my relationship with my husband. I believe I can tell you, after more than twenty-two years of marriage, that I know the man.

I remember a time when a friend of mine saw my husband having lunch with another woman. She saw that Keith was fairly affectionate to her. He often touched her in an affectionate way. He even put his arm around her as they walked out of the restaurant.

This sight troubled my friend. But when I found out that he had been seen with another woman, I said, "I want to tell you something. I don't know what the explanation is, but I can tell you right now, it isn't what you're thinking."

How fun it was for me when Keith came in after that and said, "You know I had lunch with Tina the other day, and we had the neatest time together." Tina is my husband's little sister.

Now I'm not telling you that something bad could not happen to my marriage. However, at that particular point in our marriage, I just felt that I had an assurance. For Keith to cheat on me would be so out of character for him. I have assurance there.

I don't know how in the world I could be this blessed, but even on difficult days I do not think I have lived a day of my married life that my husband has not told me at least once, and maybe two or three times, how much he loves me. He will pick up the phone in the course of a very busy day and make sure that I know that, even if he only has fifteen seconds, and then hangs up the phone without saying good-bye. I know at this point today that I have security in my relationship with my husband.

Yet, not too long ago, I was sitting in the company of some of our friends, and my husband began telling them a story. I watched his almost childlike face. He was so animated when he told the story. It was about a fish fry he had given for his fraternity in college. We had gone to the same college; that's where we fell in love.

Keith said, "I told them all that I was going to have a big fish fry. We'd have all the fish we could eat." But he said he ran out of time. So he went to the federal game reserve on that campus. A game reserve that was well guarded. He fished those fish out of the federal reserve.

Now I realize that was illegal, but it was twenty-two years ago and fortunately the statue of limitations has expired.

I want to tell you something. I was just watching Keith tell that story, and I had never heard it before. I just fell in love with him all over again. When we got in the car to drive home, I said: "You have never told me that!"

You know what thrilled me? I am still discovering things about my man. I have security in him, but if I had security and no mystery, that's no fun. Now if all I had was mystery, where would the security be? But in my husband, for right now, I have both security and mystery. That's what the Word of God is telling us we have in Christ.

Don't you love how Jesus meets our emotional and mental needs? He said, "You have the knowledge with security, with full assurance, in relationship with who I am. You also have a constant mystery as I will give you these little fragments of knowledge one at a time to open your eyes to My greatness." We will never learn it all while we're here. As much as we will seek Him, when we see Him, we will be stunned by His greatness.

Meanwhile, back to the mount of transfiguration. I want you to notice a second fact. Christ may choose to rearrange our surroundings. Did you notice that Jesus took them up on what Matthew says was a high mountain apart?

Has He rearranged your surroundings? It could be a move, a job, or different kinds of circumstances you didn't ask for. God rearranges our surroundings, perhaps for many reasons. Not the least of the reasons is to readjust our vision. Somehow from that new arrangement, whether you asked for it or not, He shows you a new perspective of the One who saved you.

Amanda was telling me some time ago that she had just begun dating a young man. They were getting to know one another; that's such an exciting stage of dating life.

They were walking through a shopping mall together, and he just wanted to tell her so much about himself. He said, "I want so much to know you, and I want you to know me. I want you to know what I love."

He began describing to her how much he loved mountain climbing, and camping, and just being out in the wild far from anything that is the norm to us in everyday life. He just went on and on about how much it meant to him, to just really be in the middle of nowhere and sense nature around him.

He said, "Amanda, I want to know you too. What is your element?" And Amanda looked around the mall and motioned all around her. "This is my element."

When she told me that, she wasn't even laughing. I had to push the hold button, go in my room, shut the door, and fall out on the bed laughing. I thought, *Yes, that's her element. Her mother raised her in that element.*

God chooses to pull us out of our element so He can adjust our vision. That's what He did with Peter, James, and John, and that brings me to a third observation.

No matter how God adjusts our earthly perception, the immortal reality still greatly exceeds any mortal revelation. As we continue to know Him more and more, to see a readjusted reality, that immortal reality continues to be far beyond anything we'll capture here.

In Luke 9:29 we find that "As he was praying, the appearance of his face changed, and his clothes became as bright as a flash of lightning." Can you imagine?

I'm not sure, but what I picture happening was for just that moment, Christ, the fullness of the Godhead bodily, who had been imprisoned in this body of flesh, suddenly just lowered it as if it were a coat — almost as if to just drop it to the ground — and for that moment stood there in His

Godness. For just that moment He became a little bit more of who He really was. He took off some of the human costume and stood there in a greater revelation of His glory.

That's what I want. That's what I wish for you also. I want daily to see more of His glory. I want Him transfigured before me, not so I can gloat or experience some thrill. I want Him transfigured so I can know Him better and love Him more.

Even so, Lord Jesus, show us Your glory.

Chapter 29

Everything Is Possible

Luke 9:37–45

" 'If you can'?" said Jesus. "Everything is possible for him who believes." (Mark 9:23)

As Christ, Peter, James, and John came down from the mountain after the transfiguration, they found the other disciples attempting unsuccessfully to cast out a demon. Luke's Gospel sets the time frame as "the next day," while Matthew and Mark imply the time immediately following the transfiguration. This might indicate that the transfiguration happened during the night. When Christ and the three returned, the other disciples were engaged in an argument with the teachers of the law. At first glance, the dispute seems to have little bearing on the events surrounding the demon-possessed boy, yet God purposely wanted us to know about it. I'd like to suggest that the argument may have greatly affected the disciples' failure. This statement ushers in our first point:

More Power

We are often empowered to do far more than we exercise. In Luke 9:1 we read that Jesus gave the disciples "power and authority to drive out all demons." Do you think He had taken it back? They still possessed the power but were unable to exercise it for some reason. What in the world happened to disable them? Let's explore a few possibilities.

1. Their most positive influences were absent. Keep in mind that not only was Christ out of sight but also the three leaders of the disciples. In moments like these, we learn where our confidence is. Is it in the presence of other believers with stronger faith? If we have boldness when certain empowered believers are close by but lose it in their absence, could it be that we've been sipping out of their power shaker of faith instead of filling our own?

I'm not taking anything away from the

power of the Spirit when many believers gather, but we don't ordinarily operate, day in and day out, in that kind of corporate atmosphere. Furthermore, we'll never discover what God has empowered us to do personally if we're dependent on the presence of our leadership. We'll never discover our strengths in the power of God if we keep drawing off another's.

2. Not only were their positive influences absent, but also some of their strongest negative influences were present. Nothing compares to trying to do your job when surrounded by people who would rather debate than eat! The presence of the teachers of the law must have been terribly intimidating to these comparatively uneducated men. You and I aren't always surrounded by faith-encouragers either. We can't afford to wait for all the right atmospheric conditions to act on the power of God.

I think God is teaching us that the worst conditions can provide the best atmosphere to act in faith. He doesn't want our confidence regulated by our audience. In fact, if faith-discouragers can shake our confidence badly enough to disable us, our confidence may be in ourselves instead of God. God's strength is unaffected by His audience.

I remember a recent time when a critical

letter from a seminary graduate shook my confidence. As I read the letter, my confidence drained like someone had pulled a plug. I started thinking: She's right! What in the world do I think I'm doing? I have no formal theological education. I looked over some mistakes she pointed out and thought: *I'm so stupid! I shouldn't even be doing this!*

God nearly snatched me baldheaded. He reminded me during the following days that I was exactly right: I shouldn't be doing this at all. This ministry is God's. If my confidence is in myself, I'm in big trouble. God also assured me that I will always make mistakes, but they will serve as reminders to my readers never to think more highly of this teacher than they ought. Only One can be taken at His every word. What counts most to God is that our hearts are right. He will forever be more interested in our fellowship than our scholarship. I believe the presence of those more educated than the disciples may have undermined their ability to exercise the right and might God had given them.

More Prayer

Prayer is the critical element of faith. I

asked why the disciples could not cast out the demon. Matthew's Gospel says it was their little faith. Mark's Gospel says it was their lack of prayer. Do these two answers represent a discrepancy? Hardly! Their little faith was the result of their lack of prayer. You see, without prayer, we return to our own ability rather than to God.

The disciples were arguing with the teachers of the law when they should have been rehearsing the greatness and power of God through prayer and asking Him to demonstrate His authority. True prayer, not just mindless, halfhearted petitions, is what digs the well God wants to fill with faith.

More Faith

Christ strongly reproves faithlessness. Christ responded strongly to the disciples' failure to exercise the power He gave them. All three synoptic Gospels record Him saying, "O unbelieving generation, . . . how long shall I stay with you? How long shall I put up with you?" (Mark 9:19). I sense Him saying, "How long are you going to take to get this together, boys? I won't be visible in your presence much longer!"

After nearly four decades of knowing

Christ, I am only beginning to realize the magnitude of the sin of unbelief. The word *unbelieving* means "not worthy of confidence, untrustworthy." The definition implies that when we are faithless, we are concluding that Christ is not worthy of our confidence and that He is . . . I can hardly bring myself to write the word . . . untrustworthy. The disciples' unbelief was their willingness to let the temperature of their faith rise and fall according to the surrounding dynamics rather than His steadfast Word. The characteristic cause of all spiritual failure is lack of faith in God.

The disciples weren't the only ones in the scene having a faith crisis. Let's spend the remainder of this chapter focusing on the faith of the boy's father. The father frequently feared for his boy's life. Only the son was possessed by a demon, but we don't have to wonder if his father was suffering. Try to imagine what this father had been through. Unfortunately, like many people, he was far more familiar with the power of the devil than the power of the Son of God.

Even in our churches, many are learning more about the power of the devil than the omnipotence of the living God! Like the father in the passage, many do not understand that surrounding dynamics like the length and depth of defeat have absolutely no bearing on Christ's ability to perform a miracle. Hear it again: no bearing. Consider the dynamics of length and depth in our text. The son had suffered since childhood (Mark 9:21).

Christ did not ask how long the boy had been in his present state because the answer had a bearing on His ability to free him; He asked the question for the purpose of framing a miracle against the backdrop of hopelessness. The father stated the hopelessness of the boy's state, then made a statement that probably provokes a host of emotions in each of us: "But if you can do anything, take pity on us and help us" (Mark 9:22). I'd like to break down the phrase into several pieces, then consider Christ's response.

"But . . ." This one little word suggests the tiniest mustard seed of faith in the father — a seed Christ compassionately watered. I am continually moved by Christ's willingness, not just to meet us halfway, but, like the father of the prodigal, to run the entire distance once we take the first step in His direction. The Word of God is filled with accounts of hopeless situations followed by the wonderful little word: "but . . ."! Because of His great compassion, sometimes

that little whisper is all the invitation Christ Jesus needs to show His power.

"If you can." Christ took exception to the father's use of the word *if.* When the action is consistent with the Word of God, the question is never if He *can.* It may be if He *wills,* but never if He can. The father was actually saying, "If You have enough power or ability . . ." Oh, He has enough all right. We who know Christ must always answer with a resounding *nothing* is too hard for Him!

Long-term defeat in the lives of those with access to Christ is often wrapped up in a continued "if You can" mentality. In at least one way, you and I can't claim the ignorance of the father in this story. We assume he didn't know Christ personally. Jesus didn't reprove the father the same way He reproved the disciples. Like them, you and I know Christ Jesus as far more than a teacher rumored to possess supernatural power. We call Him Lord. Consider the irony of addressing Him as Master of the universe, then asking Him to come to our aid — if He can. Notice the next words from this distraught dad:

"Do anything." Contrast the two words from Mark 9 for a moment: *anything* (v. 22) and *everything* (v. 23). Dear one, Christ can't just do anything. Christ can do every-

thing! I may have to shout hallelujah! Stop wondering if Christ can do anything in your situation and start believing Him to do everything glorious!

Immediately the father exclaimed, "I do believe; help me overcome my unbelief!" (v. 24). I can't describe the encouragement this father's honesty has given me through the years. First he cried out, "I do believe!" Then he confessed his unbelief. I believe the father changed his tune because he was looking straight into the face of truth. The closer we get to Jesus, the more difficult it is to stretch the truth.

The wonderful part of the father's exclamation is his realization that, although he lacked faith, he wanted to believe! Then he did exactly what he should have: he asked for help to overcome his unbelief. I can't count the times I've imitated this father's actions. In my earlier days with God, I viewed faith as my willingness to make a believing statement with my mouth rather than face the questions of my heart. If only I had understood how Romans 10:10 reverses that order: "For it is with your heart that you believe and are justified, and it is with your mouth that you confess and are saved."

It's time for a dramatic change of approach. If we don't have bold faith, let's start asking boldly for the faith we lack. Imagine the love of a God who says, "It's true that without faith it is impossible to please Me, but I am so anxious to reward you with blessing, I'm even willing to supply the faith you lack. Ask Me, My child! Ask Me for what you lack! I am the only One who can help you overcome your unbelief!"

Chapter 30

The Road to Greatness

Luke 9:43–56

"For he who is least among you all — he is the greatest." (Luke 9:48)

Luke 9:43–56 contains several seemingly disjointed snapshots of the disciples. First we see Jesus attempting to penetrate their thick skulls with the message of His soon-coming suffering and death. "Listen carefully to what I am about to tell you: The Son of Man is going to be betrayed into the hands of men" (Luke 9:44). Hard to make it much clearer than that, wouldn't you say? But we read that the Twelve didn't understand and were afraid to ask Jesus' meaning. Instead, an argument broke out among them about which of them would be greatest. Can you imagine? Jesus had to call a child to illustrate kingdom greatness.

Next, John said, "Master, . . . we saw a man driving out demons in your name and we tried to stop him, because he is not one of us" (v. 49). Jesus told John not to stop the man because "for whoever is not against you is for you" (v. 50).

Then as "Jesus resolutely set out for Jerusalem" (v. 51) a Samaritan village did not welcome the disciples, so James and John wanted to call down fire on the place. Probably tired of trying to explain, Jesus simply rebuked the "J" boys and went on to the next village.

Forgive me if this seems harsh, but we can be so full of ourselves at times, can't we? We are not so unlike Christ's original disciples. Let's look at each segment individually, then we'll draw some conclusions based on the attitudes propelling all three.

The Greatness Question (Luke 9:46–48)

The disciples had argued privately, they thought, but Christ knew their thoughts. We may never have argued with someone openly about our greatness, but Christ knows our thoughts, and the attitudes that inhabit them. Our society thrives on ambition, and if we're not extremely discerning, we bring our ambitions into the church. Our biggest hindrance to greatness may be the desire to be great. Don't miss the contrast of Christ and His disciples at this point in His earthly tenure.

Christ was on the road to greatness, but His road would take Him through betrayal, rejection, suffering, and death. Philippians 2:6–8 tells us that Jesus "did not consider equality with God something to be grasped, / but made himself nothing, / taking the very nature of a servant" and "humbled himself" becoming "obedient to death — even death on a cross!"

Hebrews 12:2–3 urges us not to grow weary and lose heart because Jesus "endured the cross, scorning its shame" for the joy set before him. Hebrews 2:9–10 makes the remarkable statements that Jesus "tasted death" on our behalf and says it was fitting for God to "make the author of [our] salvation perfect through suffering."

Don't be confused by the idea that the author of our salvation became perfect through suffering. Christ was always perfect in terms of sinlessness. The word *perfect* in this verse is *teleioo,* meaning "to complete, make perfect by reaching the intended goal." Christ reached the goal (our salvation and His exaltation) through suffering. His road to greatness was a rocky one. A painful one. He knew it in advance, and yet He set His face resolutely toward the goal and accomplished it. Simply put, we were worth it to Him.

No matter how resistant we may be to the call, our road to true greatness is also the highway of humility. At times it too will involve suffering, rejection, betrayal, and, yes, even death — to self. The question becomes, "Is He worth it to us?"

Without a doubt, one of the primary works God has sought to accomplish in me is to help me get over myself. The process has been excruciating and will no doubt be lifelong, but I have never been more thankful for any work in my life. I know no other way to say it: God finally got me to a place where I made myself sick. Oh, I still get plenty of glances at my self-centeredness, but never without a good wave of nausea. God and I now have a term for it in our prayer time. Don't expect something deeply intellectual or theological. We just call it my "self-stuff." Almost every day I ask God to help me address any active "self-stuff" and nail it to the cross. I literally name anything He brings to mind and look it straight in the face even if it makes me cry.

The following terms fall under the category of "self-stuff." Give them a good look: self-exaltation, self-protection, self-righteousness, self-will, self-loathing, self-worship, self-serving, self-promotion, self-indulgence, self-absorption, self-delusion, self-pity, and self-sufficiency. Did I leave anything out? Is that some stuff, or what? If you think of others, by all means, add them to my list. Self, self, self! May it be enough to make a "self" sick! Here's the big lie: Satan has convinced us that laying down our self-stuff is some huge sacrifice. Oh, beloved, what deception! Our self-stuff is what makes us most miserable! What an albatross our self-absorption is.

I cannot stress strongly enough that getting over the self-stuff is a daily challenge. As long as we inhabit this tent of flesh, it will rise up in us. We must choose to "deny [ourselves] and take up [our] cross daily" (Luke 9:23). The challenge demands total honesty before God. Remember, God never convicts us to condemn us. He wants to liberate us. Oh, God, so deal with self in each of us that when You read our thoughts You will find stronger and stronger evidences of Your own. The disciples asked a greatness question, but they asked more.

The Exclusivity Question (Luke 9:49–50)

John said they saw a man driving out demons in Jesus' name and tried to stop him. I don't believe John was concerned simply about the validity of the other man's actions. You see, Scripture tells us that unlike the unfortunate sons of Sceva in Acts 19:13–16, this man actually was driving out demons in Christ's name.

Remember, the twelve apostles were chosen from among a much greater number of disciples. Soon we will see Christ send out seventy-two that He will empower with immense authority. Many others believed, and, if God saw fit, their faith could have enabled them to exercise a certain amount of authority in Christ's name. The man described in Luke 9:49 was bearing good fruit! I don't think John had a problem with the man's results. He had a problem with his rivalry. John took issue with the fact that the man wasn't one of them.

Don't you think Christ sometimes looks at us and says, "Who do you think you are?" Few things probably raise Christ's ire like our versions of "Tick, tock, the game's locked, and nobody else can play." We make the outrageous assumption that if someone else is not like us or among us, he or she isn't one of us.

I remember the moment I realized God was changing my thinking and sickening my stomach over similar attitudes. We were having a women's banquet at my church, and I went to the sign-up table to buy my ticket. One of the ladies at the registration table said, "We'll be sure and seat you with good people, Beth!" I turned around and said, "You don't have to do that. I'll enjoy whoever I sit by." I couldn't get it out of my mind for days. I was not offended by her. How could I have been? I thought like that for years! I was offended by our pitifully selfish sin nature. I knew that moment that I never wanted God to let me get away with elitist attitudes again. Next notice that James and John raised a third question.

The Judgment Question (Luke 9:51–56)

James and John remind me of two little boys holding their popguns, jumping up and down pleading: "Let me shoot! Let me! Let me!" The difference is, this was no game. They wanted to call down the fire of God. They were eagerly asking for permission to be agents of massive, irreversible destruction. Nothing is more permanent or terrifying than the destruction of the lost. We ought to be scared to death to wish such a thing on anyone. Eternity is a long time. Even when punishment comes to the terribly wicked, we are wise to remember with deep sobriety, humility, and thankfulness that only grace saves us from a like sentence.

We know this world is filled with wickedness. As Christ's present-day disciples, we will no doubt be offended when people reject the Savior as the Samaritan village did that day. God's desire, however, is for us to pray for His mercy, His Spirit's conviction, and their repentance rather than their judgment. Christ said even of those who hammered the nails into His flesh, "Father, forgive them, for they do not know what they are doing" (Luke 23:34).

God is indeed the righteous Judge. When Christ returns, those who rejected Him will literally cry to the mountains, " 'Fall on us!' and to the hills, 'Cover us!' " (Luke 23:30). Judgment is coming, but may the thought of it cause us to weep, plead, and pray. Never boast or feel satisfaction. Only one thing stands between us and the lost: a blood-stained cross.

Dear one, I know I've seemed harsh in this chapter, but even when I wanted to cry,

God would not seem to ease up. Please know this message was written with such love. I have been the worst of transgressors in so many ways. No matter how common these attitudes are, they are terribly offensive to Christ. May we humble ourselves before Him, repent, and daily choose to lay down the albatross of our own egos.

Oh, God, give us a longing — not for the sin of this world to be judged — but for the sinners of this world to be forgiven.

Chapter 31

The Seventy-two

Luke 10:1–24

At that time Jesus, full of joy through the Holy Spirit, said, "I praise you, Father, Lord of heaven and earth, because you have hidden these things from the wise and learned, and revealed them to little children." (Luke 10:21)

Part of what I love about God's Word is that it reaches us in every way. I don't have an emotion that God hasn't quickened through His Word. I have laughed and cried. I've been offended. Amazed. Shocked. Frightened. Delighted. Changed. I absolutely love it. I appreciate even the uncomfortable feelings God's Word raises in me because they are proof the Word is working. If you are "face-to-the-carpet" after our previous chapter, then prepare to get up off of that floor and dance. Luke 10 is so full of "teachables," I hardly know where to start and what to prioritize! Let's highlight the following elements in this passage:

The "Two by Two"

Jesus sent out seventy-two disciples to teach and heal. He instructed them to "ask the Lord of the harvest . . . to send out workers into his harvest field" (v. 2). He sent them out "two by two." The original language phrase is *ana duo.* I love the fact that Christ sanctions companionship in the work of the gospel! The point is not the magic number of "two" as opposed to three or four. The point is togetherness.

Exceptions exist when we are called to stand alone, but the "rule" of our lives in Christ is far more often the fellowship, protection, accountability, and double dividends of joint service. I can hardly describe the joy my coworkers in the gospel bring me. My best friend and I met each other by serving together in Mothers' Day Out over twenty years ago. God called us to work *ana duo,* and we've been a duo ever since! Few things can add to life like the fellowship of serving together. Also I encourage you to notice a second principle in the passage.

The Transfer of Rejection

Jesus taught another great truth in Luke 10:1–24. In verse 16 He said, "He who listens to you listens to me; he who rejects you rejects me; but he who rejects me rejects him who sent me." This concept represents something else I love so much about Christ. In many ways, He says to those who belong to Him and seek to do His will: "Don't take rejection personally. Let me take it for you."

We see this principle at work in Acts 9. Saul set out to persecute Christians, but Jesus came along and knocked him off his donkey. Saul "fell to the ground and heard a voice say to him, 'Saul, Saul, why do you persecute me?' " (Acts 9:4). Beloved, can you accept that Christ takes very personally the unfair things that happen to you? Consider a few reasons we are wise to let Christ assume our rejections.

- *Only Christ can take rejection without being personally incapacitated or hindered by it.* Who can begin to estimate the mileage Satan gets from rejection?

314

We have an overwhelming tendency to take it personally. From a bit of rejection Satan can get anything from a mile of discouragement to a thousand miles of despair. Christ says to us, "Let Me take it personally for you. It can hurt Me, but it can't hinder Me." David had it right when he wrote, "Contend, O Lord, with those who contend with me; / fight against those who fight against me" (Ps. 35:1).

- *Only Christ can properly respond to rejection.* We are often powerless to do anything about it. Our attempts often make the situation worse. We don't fully understand what lies at the heart of rejection. We cannot judge another person's heart or motive but Romans 2:2 assures us that "God's judgment against those who do such things is based on truth."

I love to hear Keith say, "Elizabeth, let me worry about that." In essence, Christ says the same thing to us. If we suffer rejection, let Him worry about it. Let Him take it personally so we don't have to. Now take one last look at Luke 10:16. "He who listens to you listens to me; he who rejects you rejects me; but he who rejects me rejects him who sent me." Did you catch who takes it personally for Christ? In this wonderful passage notice another facet.

The Ecstatic Joy of Effectiveness

The seventy-two returned, rejoicing with something that resembled amazement. In verse 17 they essentially said, "Wow! It happened just like You said it would. Even the demons were subject to us in Your name! What a rush!"

Sandwiched between expressions of jubilation, Christ took a quick moment to remind them they had a greater motivation to rejoice because their names were written in heaven. Though we see Him celebrate their victories, we also see Him teach them to base their joy on something far more reliable than accomplishments and abilities. He wants us to understand that the greatest cause we have for joy is not what we do but who we are. We are children of the eternal *El Elyon*. Our names are recorded in heaven. We are very wise to find our joy in who we are because of Him, rather than what we can do because of Him.

Now let's enjoy these two awesome moments of celebration. Verse 21 tells us Jesus was "full of joy through the Holy Spirit."

Here's a place where the original language is so much fun. In verse 17, the word for the joy of the disciples is *chara,* meaning essentially what you'd assume: "rejoicing" and "gladness." The word switches in verse 21 to a far more intense original word. The word for Jesus' joy is *agalliao,* meaning "to exult, leap for joy, to show one's joy by leaping and skipping, denoting excessive or ecstatic joy and delight." In the Septuagint of the Psalms, it was "often spoken of rejoicing with song and dance."

Someone may ask, "Do you expect me to believe Christ jumped up and down with ecstatic joy?" I don't have one bit of trouble believing it!

Could the word simply mean He rejoiced in His heart? Possibly, but the essence of the word *agalliao* is when *chara* gets physical! You may apply it either way, but I prefer to jump up and down with Jesus. With all my heart, I believe Christ Jesus was and is demonstrative. What would cause Jesus to leap with ecstatic joy in this scene (whether physically or internally)? At least two catalysts for colossal joy appear in these verses:

Satan's defeat. "I saw Satan fall like lightning from heaven" (v. 18). According to Revelation 12:10–12, Satan was cast out of heaven for pride, rebellion, and his desire to usurp the Most High (see also Ezek. 28:16–17; Isa. 14:12–13). At the risk of oversimplification, Satan has attempted to get back at God ever since by targeting those He loves.

We who are in Christ possess the power through God's Word and His Spirit to avoid being defeated by the evil one. Problem is, we don't always exercise that power. In Luke 10, the disciples exercised the authority He had given them, and Christ was ecstatic! At the end of the contest recorded in verses 1–16, the scoreboard read: Believers 72, Satan 0. That was a score Jesus could have spilled His popcorn over! When was the last time you got excited over the defeat of the devil? Then notice the other side of the equation.

The servants' victory. "I praise you, Father, Lord of heaven and earth, because you have hidden these things from the wise and learned, and revealed them to little children" (v. 21). You see, the wise and learned of this world are often too sophisticated to throw caution to the wind and believe they're capable of doing something they've never thought possible. If we stay in our neat little perimeters of safe sophistication where we walk by sight and not by faith, we'll never

318

have room to leap and skip with Jesus in ecstatic joy.

Oh, beloved, give Him a chance to leap and dance over you! Dare to do what He's calling you to do! And don't always be so reasonable. I have a feeling there's one thing Christ likes better than leaping and skipping and dancing over you. How about *with* you? When you hear that victory music playing, get up out of that chair and shake a leg!

Chapter 32

The Heart of a Neighbor

Luke 10:25–37

But a Samaritan, as he traveled, came where the man was; and when he saw him, he took pity on him. (Luke 10:33)

I hope you have your Bible at hand to read Luke 10:25–37. Take it slowly. Picture every moment of it as if you were an eyewitness hiding behind a boulder on the Jericho road. This is the story of the good Samaritan.

First see Christ's overconfident opponent in a match of the minds. We read that a man sought to test Jesus. Scripture describes him as an expert in the law. His job was to interpret the law of Moses the way modern lawyers interpret the constitution. He considered himself such an expert that he intended to make Jesus look foolish. The problem is, you can't find a subject on which Christ isn't the ultimate expert. The expert in the law didn't know that Christ knew the drill better than he did.

Jesus responded with a question that means little to us but was very familiar to the lawyer. He asked, "How do you read it?" The question was used constantly among scribes and lawyers. One would ask the other his interpretation on a certain matter. Before he would give his answer, he would say, "How do you read it?" The one who asked the question ended up having to "go first."

Of course, you and I know what the scribe didn't know. Christ not only wrote the law, He came to fulfill it. The resident expert in the law was way over his head when he threw a pop quiz at the author of the Book.

The expert, being forced to "go first," delivered the correct answer according to Old Testament law: " 'Love the Lord your God with all your heart and with all your soul and with all your strength and with all your mind'; and, 'Love your neighbor as yourself' " (Luke 10:27).

The conversation could have stopped at Christ's "Do this and you will live" (v. 28). Instead, the lawyer had to ask one more question: "And who is my neighbor?" (v. 29).

Do you hear a change in tone? The man wanted to justify himself — to show himself righteous — but why? Who said he wasn't? Christ didn't say a single condemning word to him. Jesus simply told him his answer was correct and to go live his answer.

The man couldn't let the matter go. In Christ's presence, the lawyer felt condemned by his own words. He knew God intended for His people to help those in need. The lawyer attempted to justify himself by splitting hairs with his definition of a neighbor.

God demands compassionate action no matter how we try to hide in loopholes of terminology. The lawyer's immediate defense mechanism was to try to start an argument. Not an unfamiliar tactic, is it? We've all been experts at that one!

Jesus answered the question "Who is my neighbor?" with one of the most repeated stories in the New Testament. A man was beaten and robbed. The crime scene was a spot on a fifteen-mile road between Jerusalem and Jericho. The road was so treacherous it became known as Adummim or The Pass of Blood. As many as twelve thousand priests lived in Jericho, commuting to Jerusalem when they were chosen by lot for temple service.[1]

Jesus spoke of a priest and a Levite who

both ignored the injured man. Christ's terminology suggests they were each on their way home to Jericho from Jerusalem. He described each as going down the road; it was quite a sharp descent in terrain. The irony in the unwillingness of the priest and Levite to help would have been more obvious to the lawyer than to us. He would have quickly understood that they were on their way home from the most important life work they would ever do — performing their brief tenure of service in the temple. We would expect that at no time would they have been more humbled, grateful, or willing to meet someone's needs. That's not what happened. In fact, both the priest and the Levite passed by on the other side.

The words of the law in Exodus 23:4–5 make the actions of the priest and Levite even more incriminating. Moses wrote, "If you come across your enemy's ox or donkey wandering off, be sure to take it back to him. If you see the donkey of someone who hates you fallen down under its load, do not leave it there; be sure you help him with it."

Matthew 22:34–40 records a conversation on the same topic with a different lawyer. In verse 40 Jesus declared that "all the Law and the Prophets hang on these two commandments." God's law was always far more about relationship than ritual! That's how Jesus could offer Himself as the fulfillment of the entire law. The ultimate point of obedience to the law was never about human goodness.

Don't you praise God for the third passerby in the scene? Our common name for this parable would have been an oxymoron to many Jews of that era. Most would have believed there was no such thing as a good Samaritan. They were considered little more than mongrels. Half-breed dogs. That's precisely why Christ interjected the Samaritan into the play.

Scripture tells us the Samaritan saw the man and took pity on him. You would think that at least the priest and the Levite would have done the right thing because of their positions, even if they felt the wrong thing. In sharp contrast, the Samaritan came upon the scene with no obligation whatsoever, and everything within him was deeply moved with compassion. He didn't just do what was right. He felt it.

Here's the shocker: the traveler left half-dead was almost certainly a Jew. The route was used almost entirely by Jews, and virtually all of Christ's parables centered on the experiences of Jewish people. I love the way one commentary explains it: "Jesus introduced a Samaritan as the only one on that lonely, dangerous Jericho road willing to befriend a helpless Jew. The very man from whom no needy Jew could expect the least relief, was the one who gave it."[2]

The Samaritan had the perfect opportunity to exact a little revenge on behalf of his people, but he didn't. Why? Because sometimes good at its best is when the law of the heart eclipses the law of the land. Stepping across a boundary to help is sometimes our first introduction to the commonality of humanity on the other side. Offering help in a time of need can be the first step to overcoming God-dishonoring prejudice.

Don't forget the reason Jesus told the story. Whom did He say was our neighbor? I am reminded of an Old Testament verse that describes a neighbor at Passover. Because all of the lamb must be consumed at the Passover observance, Exodus 12 explains that a family must share with their nearest neighbor if their household was too small for a whole lamb.

From Jesus' parable we can see that our neighbor is the person with a need — the broken one. In terms of Exodus 12, our neighbor is one with whom we can share the Lamb. As a people passed over by the angel of death, we are called to share the Lamb.

Chapter 33

A True Tale of Two Sisters

Luke 10:38–42

"Martha, Martha," the Lord answered, "you are worried and upset about many things, but only one thing is needed. Mary has chosen what is better." (Luke 10:41–42)

I'm already grinning, and we haven't even started. I love women. I have a great appreciation for men, too, but I don't share their psyche. I get a huge kick out of women. We're just so . . . woman-y. With the exception of my best buddy who lives out-of-state, most of my closest friends work or volunteer at Living Proof Ministries. One reason I'm so crazy about them is because we are so hilariously different. I guess we represent almost every conceivable dimension of womanhood.

Among all of us, we're in the throes of young motherhood, menopause, and memory pause. We've got a healthy population of Marys and Marthas. Marys never get to drive or plan our luncheons. Marthas never get to lead prayer time — except when we're hungry. They tend to give the quickest blessing. I hope you have such a group in your life. They are a blast! Fight isolation and independence. It's no fun.

Mary would want us to stop here and meditate on all the relationships we share in Christ, but I hear Martha chiding, "Get busy! There's study to do!" Since I'm more intimidated by Martha than Mary, we'd better get busy.

While I was in Israel taping the video for the workbook series, I learned that many believe Mary's and Martha's tombs are identifiable in Bethany. Supposedly their names are actually on them. I wanted so badly to go look for the tombs, then suddenly it occurred to me their names would be in Hebrew. Another "duh moment" with Beth Moore.

Before we get to the heart of our chapter, let's allow John 11:5 to help us establish a critical fact: "Jesus loved Martha and her sister and Lazarus." This passage is not a contrast between good and bad. It's a contrast between good and better. Martha was a good woman. Jesus loved her very much, apron and all. Her joy and satisfaction, however, were sacrificed on the altar of self-appointed service. Recognizing Martha's positives and negatives, let's go back to Luke 10 and explore some applications together.

1. Martha opened her home, but Mary opened her heart (vv. 38–39). Don't miss the fact that Martha opened her home to Jesus. Not Lazarus, the head of the house. Nor Mary, the depth of the house. It was the hands of the house that invited Jesus in. Otherwise, Mary wouldn't have had a set of feet at which to sit, nor would Lazarus have had a friend with which to recline. Martha's hospitality brought Him there. If only Martha had understood that Christ wanted her heart more than He wanted her home.

Here's a place where we who are not Marthas must fall under a little conviction. Although I force myself to keep an orderly home, I am so far from a "Martha" that I rarely ever open my home to others. I have a very public ministry, and I view my home as my sanctuary with my family. Not a bad idea, but I fear I've taken it too far. Although our home is open constantly to our daughters' friends, I almost never have anyone over for a bite to eat, a few moments of prayer, or a look at the Word. I save those things for the office. Ouch! I have an idea God is saying to some of us non-Marthas, "It's best to open your heart, but it's also good to open your home." Next notice another lesson we can glean from Martha.

2. Distraction is the noble person's biggest hindrance to listening (vv. 39–40). Martha wasn't stopping her ears and refusing to listen. She simply "was distracted." In this way, we've all been Marthas! How many times have we reached the car after a church service only to realize that we missed half the message due to a distraction?

Now imagine that the church service was meeting in your den while you were preparing lunch! Talk about distracting? Listen, I have to turn off every television and radio in the house and make my family go outside just to read a recipe. Even then, I read it aloud; and if anyone interrupts me, I have to start over. In Luke 10:40, the Greek word for "distracted" is *perispao,* meaning "to draw different ways at the same time, hence to distract with cares and responsibilities." Can we relate? You see, our culture may be entirely different, but women have had the same challenges since the beginning of time.

3. Sometimes ministry can be the biggest distraction to the pursuit of true intimacy with God (v. 40). "Martha was distracted by all the preparations that had to be made." You may faint when you see the Greek word for "preparations." The word is *diakonia.* It means "service, attendance, ministry." We are more familiar with the word *diakonos,* meaning "servant." God's Word is saying that if we're not careful, even our need-meeting, well-meaning ministries can distract us from what is most important. My dad would tell you that he served his church tirelessly, doing all sorts of good for many years, while remaining unchanged by a heart-to-heart relationship with Jesus Christ.

I've heard the saying many times, "If Satan can't make us bad, he'll make us busy." Actually, he can't make us anything, but he gets a lot of cooperation. I am reminded of our study on the good Samaritan. How wise of our God to place these two accounts back-to-back in Scripture. First we saw an incriminating look at servants of God who ministered in the temple but refused to help a dying man. Now we catch a look at a servant far too busy helping to hear from the heart of God. Notice another fact about our friend Martha.

4. Martha forgot to keep the "pre" in prep-

aration (v. 40). Let's not overlook a very important little point. "Martha was distracted by all the preparations that had to be made." Understand that these preparations were not frivolous. They were important! By doing them, Martha served Christ appropriately and enhanced the atmosphere in which He taught. Very likely she served a meal and made sure all the arrangements were made for His comfort and the exercise of His own ministry.

I wish to make absolutely no inappropriate comparison to Jesus' ministry. But if I'm going to stay in someone's home when I travel and speak, I want to stay with a Martha! You could starve to death at Mary's! Martha's preparations were important. They just weren't limited to the "pre." The issue is that she continued all her duties when the time came to sit at Christ's feet and listen.

I speak at many conferences during which the event's leadership either never makes it into the sanctuary or, when they do, they never lose that harried and distracted look. Recently I spoke at a conference where the leadership was the most participatory, involved group during Bible study. When I inquired later, they said, "Oh, we worked really hard in advance to get everything finished so we could relax when the time came." They made all the preparations, but when the time came, the men of the church and several hired caterers served while they attended. What wisdom we find in keeping the "pre" in preparation!

You see, their preparations were critical. What if they hadn't planned for all those women? What if they hadn't taken registration and made no arrangements for an adequate sound system for the praise team? I don't believe God would have been honored by the lack of preparation. But God was doubly honored because they prepared in advance, yet didn't miss the most important part by immersing themselves in further preparations.

5. Those distracted by service are often those who miss how much Jesus cares (v. 40). Martha came to Christ and asked, "Lord, don't you care?" I have a feeling if someone had asked Mary at the end of the day if Christ cared about her, she would have answered affirmatively without hesitation. Mind you, John 11:5 has already assured us Jesus loved both of them very much. I don't think it's unreasonable to assume that at times Mary probably sensed His love and care more readily than Martha. Why? I believe John 15:9 holds the key.

Jesus told the disciples, "As the Father has loved me, so have I loved you. Now remain in my love."

Beloved, the more we cultivate a keener awareness of Christ's presence, the more we will abide or remain in the sense of His love. Christ's love for us never changes. However, our sense of His loving care changes dramatically from time to time. I think we'd all agree the difference is not hardship. I may sense the loving care of God more readily when I'm going through difficulty than when I'm not. I believe the determining factor is our willingness to abide in Him or to seek to practice a relationship in which we develop a keener awareness of His presence.

Sometimes we are so shocked when a seasoned servant of God confesses that he or she is struggling with belief and awareness of God's loving care. We might think, *You of all people! You are such a wonderful servant of God. How can you doubt for a moment how much He cares for you?* Could it be that somehow service has distracted from the abundant, life-giving intimacy? Don't neglect to give Him ample opportunities to lavish you with the love He always feels for you.

6. *Many things are important, but only*

one thing is necessary (v. 42). In our fight for right priorities, many things vie for the top of the heap, but only one is necessary. Ultimately, our relationship with Christ is the one thing we cannot do without.

Christ's message is not that we should neglect family and responsibilities to pray and to study the Bible. His message is that many things are important, but one thing is essential: Him. Incidentally, Mary turned out to be one of the greatest servants of all, lavishing Christ with her most expensive offerings (see John 12).

As we conclude, look at three simple words from Luke 10:42: "Mary has chosen." That's how it will always be. Right priorities will never choose us. They are a choice — in the midst of many other good ones. The word *chosen* comes from the Greek word *eklego,* meaning "to choose, select, choose for oneself." We can't choose what is necessary for anyone else, but we can certainly set an example. The remainder of the definition reads: "not necessarily implying the rejection of what is not chosen, but giving favor to the chosen subject, keeping in view a relationship to be established between the one choosing and the object chosen. It involves preference and selection from among many choices." That's what I love most about Mary and Martha. Their story started us laughing but ended with us really thinking. Shall we allow good to become the enemy of our best? The choice is ours.

Part 7

The Infinite Treasure

Can you believe we've made it this far? I realize countless things are vying for your attention and that the evil one has performed no few feats to distract you. I am so thankful you're hanging in there. I want to encourage you again to read the entire Scripture passages from your Bible and to keep resisting the temptation to put aside your study — even with the intention of returning to it "later." "Later" has a strange way of getting later and later, doesn't it? Here's a little fresh motivation: Deuteronomy 29:29 says that the truths God reveals to you are yours forever! You are allowing God to inscribe His words on the tablets of your heart. Scripture is literally becoming part of you. That's what Christ meant when He instructed us to let His word "abide" in us (John

15:7 KJV). The same passage also tells us that His abiding Word transforms our prayer lives. Beloved, the intense study of God's Word has mammoth effects. You may be the last to notice them in yourself, but I assure you, Scripture never returns void! God has a specific purpose for this study in your life. Let Him have His awesome way.

Chapter 34

Someone Stronger

Luke 11:14–28

"But when someone stronger attacks and overpowers him, he takes away the armor in which the man trusted and divides up the spoils." (Luke 11:22)

In Luke 11:15 some of the observers accused Jesus of driving out demons by Beelzebub, the prince of demons. Christ responded to the accusation by making three primary points about the kingdoms of God and Satan. Let's explore each of them together.

A Divided Kingdom (Luke 11:17–20)

In essence Christ responded to His accusers, "Think this through with Me. If I were part of the kingdom of darkness, why would I work against Myself by driving out demons?" He then made a statement that may have turned the religious leaders inside out: "But if I drive out demons by the finger of God, then the kingdom of God has come to you" (v. 20).

Christ's brief discourse suggests two origins of supernatural power: the kingdom of God and the kingdom of Satan. If Christ's power didn't originate with Satan, it obviously came from God. If Christ was performing all those signs and wonders through the power of God, the revolutionary implication could only be that the kingdom of God had come to them — they were staring the Messiah in the face (see Luke 7:20, 22).

The phrase "the finger of God" is used only a few times in Scripture. One of them appears in the Book of Exodus. We find that Pharaoh's magicians were able to imitate some of the miracles wrought through Moses. However, when the magicians could not duplicate the plague of gnats, they declared to Pharaoh that "this is the finger of God" (Exod. 8:19). In essence they said, "Nobody but the living God could have done that!"

I love the reference to the finger of God. It

says to me God is so powerful, all He has to do is point and His intended work is accomplished. Allow me to say with a grin that I know a few things I wish God would point at today, don't you? We have to trust that God not only knows what to point at but also when.

I would be remiss if I failed to also emphasize the implications of division in Christ's words. Satan knows he can hinder God's kingdom by provoking division among Christ's people. We desperately need to make unity in the body of Christ an ongoing pursuit.

A Strong Man (Luke 11:21–22)

Jesus said when a strong man guards his house his possessions are safe unless someone stronger comes along. Assuming the strong man in Luke 11:21 is Satan, we can make a few important observations. The first one seems obvious, but it needs emphasizing: Satan is strong. We are wise neither to overestimate nor underestimate Satan's power. He is no match for God, but we are no match for him. As Paul taught, we can take our stand against Satan only when we are strong in God's might. Second, we

341

observe that not only is Satan strong according to Luke 11:21, but also he is "fully armed."

Could you give testimony of a few weapons you believe are in Satan's arsenal? I personally have encountered the weapons of shame, secrecy, and deception. Based on this short parable, a third observation is that Satan guards his own house. Just as God is possessive over His holy house, you can be sure Satan is possessive over his unholy house. Second Corinthians 4:4 describes just one way he attempts to guard his house or protect his interests. Paul said Satan "has blinded the minds of unbelievers, so that they cannot see the light of the gospel."

Luke 11:21 would be pretty frightening without the verse that follows: "But when someone stronger attacks and overpowers him, he takes away the armor in which the men trusted and divides up the spoils." Let's move to Luke 11:22 and make a few observations about Christ.

1. Satan may be strong, but Christ is "someone stronger." Count on it. We may be at war with a very powerful enemy, but we who are in Christ are at peace with a far more powerful God.

2. Christ will attack and overcome Satan. Satan is a defeated foe. The defeating blows actually came through a hammer on the nails of the cross. Christ finished the work when He willingly gave His life for our sins. God is busily biding His time until His kingdom calendar has been accomplished and all who will accept His offer are redeemed. Then one day, God's finger is going to point right at the strong man, and he's going to wish he'd never existed.

3. *Our someone stronger is going to take away Satan's armor.* I believe the representation of the armor is anything Satan "wears" to keep from being defeated.

4. *Christ is going to divide up the spoils.* Do you know what this means to us? Jesus Christ is going to steal back what Satan has stolen from us! Do you want to hear some even better news? Not all the spoils have to wait until we're in heaven!

I can readily cite a personal example. Even though Satan stole many things from me through my childhood victimization, I am finally ready to say that God has given me back more than my enemy took. The spoils or plunder that finally tipped the scale has come to me in the form of response letters to *Breaking Free: Making Liberty in Christ a Reality in Life.* I believe I can now say that the grace gift of seeing others helped through the power of the Holy Spirit has begun to outweigh the many years of pain that resulted from the abuse. Finally, note with me the third point about the kingdoms of God and Satan.

A Vacant Place (Luke 11:24–26)

Christ's third response to the accusation that His power originated with the prince of demons had to do with filling our lives with God. Jesus spoke of a man who somehow was rid of a demon. The man cleaned and swept his figurative "house." When the demon came again, he found the accommodations so appealing that he brought seven worse demons to move in. "And the final condition of that man is worse than the first" (v. 26). Bummer. I see three principles from Jesus' words and the total teaching of Scripture.

1. Demons seem to be more at home where they've previously dwelled.
2. Those of us who are believers in Christ cannot be demon-possessed, but we can certainly be demon-oppressed.
3. I tend to believe Satan would rather return to a previous job on an individual than find a new one.

Satan is a lot of things, but creative is not often one of them. He ordinarily sticks to what has worked in the past. I've experienced this personally when he has attempted to return to an area in my life where he held a previous stronghold — even though he's already been forced to leave.

Lives swept clean and put in order are vulnerable to demonic defeat. Beloved, listen carefully. We were created by God to be inhabited by His Spirit. We were not created to be empty. The vacuum in every human life does not yearn to be fixed. It yearns to be filled. God can deliver us from a terribly oppressive stronghold, and we can truly clean up our lives and put them in order; but if we don't fill the void with Him, we are terribly susceptible to a relapse.

My Sunday school class has what we call VIPs — Victors in Process. Every quarter, members who need extra prayer and accountability come before our class for special notice. Throughout the quarter, they can hardly get through the door without lots of hugs and direct questions about how they are doing. We also give reports of their progress to the entire class. Presently one of our VIPs is a beautiful young woman recovering from a fierce cocaine addiction. How wise she is to realize that she can't just "get clean." If she's going to be safe, she's got to fill the cavernous void left by the cocaine with the satisfying, liberating filling of the Holy Spirit.

A second round of the same demonic stronghold can be more powerful than the first. What a frightening prospect for someone who isn't sealed by the Holy Spirit (see Eph. 1:13; 4:30)! Most of us are at higher risk of oppression than possession, but the principle still applies: once we've been delivered from a stronghold, if we make ourselves vulnerable to it again, our second encounter may be far worse.

I can think of several reasons for the above principle. Satan hates to lose. If he was defeated once, given the opportunity, he'll try harder the next time. Furthermore, a second onslaught can cause such discouragement and feelings of hopelessness that the victim is weaker than ever. And, finally, the empty space — if left uninhabited by Christ — leaves the victim with a voracious appetite. The greatest tragedy is that all the defeat was unnecessary. Yes, Satan is strong, but Christ is far stronger! We'll repeat this concept until it's engraved in our cranium: victory is not determined as much by what we've been delivered *from* as by what we've been delivered *to*. The only safe house for every former captive is our "someone stronger." When Satan comes prowling, may we "be found in him" (Phil. 3:9).

Chapter 35

His Treasure, Your Treasure

Luke 12:1–34

"How much more valuable you are than birds!" (Luke 12:24)

Sometimes in this study, we have to bypass some wonderful segments of Scripture to prioritize others. From the beginning, I felt that the midportion of Luke (where most of the parables appear) was the wisest place to bridge and accelerate. Keep in mind that we are accelerating now so that we can slow down later. We will bridge ten chapters of Luke in parts 7 and 8, so that we can spend the entirety of our final two sections on Luke's climactic conclusion. With this in mind, let's look at chapter 12 of the Gospel.

The events of the chapter follow a common thread. Jesus warned the disciples about "the yeast of the Pharisees" which was hypocrisy(v. 1). The Pharisees valued honor from men over the pleasure of God. But Jesus warned His followers to fear "him who, after the killing of the body, has power to throw you into hell" (v. 5).

Someone in the crowd asked Jesus to settle an inheritance dispute (v. 13). Jesus took the moment to teach them about greed and told them the parable of the rich fool. The farmer had a bumper crop, so rather than consider himself as a steward of the blessings of God the rich fool said to himself: "I will tear down my barns and build bigger ones. . . . And I'll say to myself, 'You have plenty of good things laid up for many years. Take life easy; eat, drink and be merry' " (vv. 18–19). God called the man a fool and said, "This very night your life will be demanded from you. Then who will get what you have prepared for yourself?"(v. 20).

This lesson is about value — what God values and what we value. Luke 12:34 reveals that you can find someone's heart if you discover what he or she truly values. One of the best ways to become more acquainted with the heart of God is to search the Scriptures and study the things He values most. The next question may seem very obvious and basic, but too much hinges on it to make any false assumptions.

In terms of earthly things, what does God appear to value most according to Luke 12:24? "Consider the ravens: They do not sow or reap, they have no storeroom or barn; yet God feeds them. And how much more valuable you are than birds!"

No matter how much value everything else represents, you are more valuable to God. A good friend, who is a speaker and a Bible-based counselor, has said, "We act out what we believe, not what we know." Our actions, our lifestyles, and our decisions are all reflections of our belief systems. We may say otherwise, and, intellectually, we may know better, but we will live out what we truly believe.

I'd like to emphasize one precept: if we truly believe what God says about our value to Him, our lives will be dramatically altered. Based on this segment of Scripture, I want to suggest five ways such a belief makes a difference.

1. Believing our great value to God frees us from much hypocrisy. Christ opened the bold declarations in Luke 12 with a warning against hypocrisy. The primary meaning of the word is "pretending." Please give special attention to His specific audience. Although He was surrounded by crowds of unbelievers and religious leaders, "Jesus began to speak first to his disciples" (Luke 12:1). True disciples who follow Christ and lead others to do likewise face great temptation to be hypocritical. Christ warned, "Be on your guard" (v. 1). In other words, if we're going to live free of hypocrisy, we must proactively guard against it. The bottom line of hypocrisy is the need for people to think more highly of us than we really are. Let's face it. It's easier to act than to clean up our act.

Hypocrisy has so much to prove. Ironically, it seeks to prove what is not even true. When we accept our real value to God, we don't have anything to prove. We can be real because we are of great value to the only True Judge.

2. Believing our great value to God frees us from unnecessary fear. Luke 12:4 comes like a shock wave to our systems: "I tell you, my friends, do not be afraid of those who kill the body and after that can do no more." Why do we have such difficulty grasping Jesus' point of view? Because we are far more convinced of the "here and now" than the "after that." Eternity is a far greater reality than this short breath of time. If we are in His fold and are called His friends, Christ's word to us is don't be afraid; you are worth more.

Keith and I keep a bird feeder on the back porch. I watch the sparrows scatter the seed and flutter their wings. They are not beautiful like other birds that grace our yard. They are plain and ordinary; but I love knowing that God never forgets a single one of them. When fear seeks to assail me, I go to the window and am reminded again — if He cares for them, He most assuredly cherishes me. After this short breath is a long after that.

3. *Believing our great value to God frees us to acknowledge Him shamelessly.* Verse 8 assures us that Christ Jesus can hardly wait to acknowledge us before the very "angels of God"! Even after all our frailties and failures! (Check out Jude 24.) If He is unashamed of us, in all our imperfections, how can we be ashamed of Him, our Redeemer and our Deliverer? Don't duck your head in shame under your coffee table. Listen, Satan is the breeder of all shame. At one time or another, all of us have faced the temptation to shrink away from openly acknowledging Christ.

I've learned one of the best ways to get over our attacks of shame. Do it over and over until it loses its intimidation! The more we practice, the easier it gets! Tell Him if you're afraid and all the reasons why; then ask for the power of the Holy Spirit to come upon you and make you a powerful witness (see Acts 1:8). He will! Then one day, He'll acknowledge you before the angels!

4. Believing our great value to God frees us from the need for riches. In verse 15, Christ also warns us to "be on [our] guard against all kinds of greed." Then He reminds us of a powerful truth: "a man's life does not consist in the abundance of his possessions." Aren't you thankful it doesn't? However, once again I'm reminded of my friend's statement. We act out what we believe, not what we know. If we believe our value to God and believe our life does not consist in the abundance of our possessions, why do we have such an abundance of possessions? Perhaps we know Luke 12:15 with our heads, but we really don't believe it with our hearts.

James 1:17 tells us our Father is the giver of all good gifts. Throughout all of eternity, we will be lavished in the limitless wealth of the CEO of the universe. Until then, we show ourselves to be sons and daughters of the one true God when we give, give, and give. Let's keep shoving that abundance out the door to help others in need, and God will lay up treasures for us in His own divine storage lot.

5. Believing our great value to God frees us from much worry. "Life is more than food" (v. 23)? I need a needlepoint of that for my kitchen! The issue of food, however, is not the point. The point is worry. I'm not sure many things compare to the challenge of ceasing to worry.

Why do you think worry is so difficult to control? Maybe one reason is because we have so many prime opportunities! We're never going to overcome worry by eliminating reasons to worry. Rest assured, life isn't going to suddenly fix itself. God wills that we overcome worry even when overwhelmed by reasons to worry.

Christ summed up the futility of worry in verses 25 and 26. We can't add a minute to our life by worrying. Simply put, worry is useless. Luke 12:25 has helped me with a much greater issue than my own life. It has helped me with the lives of my children. I am prone to worry somewhat about myself but endlessly over them. All our worry in the name of love can accomplish absolutely nothing. But all our praying in the name of Jesus could entreat God to accomplish anything. When will we learn to turn our worry effort into prayer?

Christ's remedy for worry is to be like the ravens and lilies — trust God to do His job.

The prescription for worry is trust. Trust comes to those who take God at His Word. Make a list of all your reasons to worry. Then write the word TRUST in big, bold letters on top of your list. Then seek Him and seek His kingdom with everything you've got . . . and all the right things will be given to you as well (see Matt. 6:33).

As we conclude, please feast your eyes on verse 32: "Do not be afraid, little flock, for your Father has been pleased to give you the kingdom." What tender words. Do you hear the love? Do you sense the care? With one glance in the nearest mirror, you can see a reflection of the heart of God. For where His treasure is, His heart is also.

"For you are a people holy to the Lord your God. The Lord your God has chosen you out of all the peoples on the face of the earth to be his people, his treasured possession" (Deut. 7:6).

Chapter 36

Keep Your Lamps Burning

Luke 12:35–48

"Be dressed and ready for service and keep your lamps burning, like men waiting for their master to return from a wedding banquet." (Luke 12:35–36)

Jesus told the disciples a set of interlaced parables about being ready for His return. The point of each dealt with watchfulness and doing what Christ assigns us to do. Christ wants His people to be ready and waiting. No matter whether you're a pretribulationalist, a post-tribulationalist, an amillennialist, a dispensationalist, or have no clue what any of those mean, Christ is coming back. Every eye will see Him. Some things about God's ways make me grin . . . like the way He knows our tendency to play amateur prophet. He puts all of us in our date-setting places by basically saying, "The only thing I'll tell you about My next visit is that you won't be expecting Me." The urgency is to be ready at all times.

Christ told us to "keep your lamps burning" (Luke 12:35). Our version of keeping our lamps burning is leaving a light on at night for someone out late. One of the shocks of the empty nest is no longer having someone to "wait up for" at night. Those of us who have older children have experienced the late-night difficulty of falling into a deep sleep before they get home. We can doze perhaps, but we don't fully sleep until they're safe inside. Even though waiting up is exhausting, it's a reminder of close family relationships and responsibility.

At this particular season in my life, my heart is encouraged to know that we have Someone for whom to "leave the light on." Five years ago a precious friend of mine lost her only son, a young adult. Last week she lost her husband. I have ached for her aloneness. I am so grateful that those of us in Christ always have Someone for whom we can wait expectantly at all times. Christ calls on us to be watching for Him when He returns, not inactively, mind you, but as servants (v. 35). Luke 12:37 tells us, "It will be good for those servants whose master finds them watching when he comes."

Christ's desire is that we live in such close involvement with Him that all we lack is seeing Him face-to-face. Oh, that God would create in each of us such an acute awareness and belief of His presence that we won't be caught off guard! That our faith will simply be made sight! That we'll be gloriously shocked but unashamed!

God, create in us a longing for Your appearing so our lamps will be ever burning. I can't imagine what Christ meant when He said that those He finds ready and waiting will recline at a table and He will wait on them (v. 37). My mind can't fathom such a thing.

For those with a knowledge of God, the cost of wickedness during the wait is astronomical. I'm not sure we ever hear stronger words out of the mouth of Christ than these in Luke 12:46: "He will cut him to pieces and assign him a place with the unbelievers." I believe Christ was most likely talking to people like those He described in Luke 11:52: "Woe to you experts in the law, because you have taken away the key to knowledge. You yourselves have not entered, and you have hindered those who were entering." These are people who were given knowledge, but they did not enter in. They had knowledge but no faith in the truth. The example of many of the Pharisees provides a reminder that we can have heads full of knowledge and souls full of death.

Please note the behavior of the servant in Luke 12:45. He came to believe the master was not returning, so he began beating his menservants and maidservants. I believe Christ addressed His remarks primarily to the religious leaders.

I'd like to suggest that the picture of the head servant beating the menservants and maidservants while the master was away could easily represent spiritual abuse. God will hold those of us who are leaders responsible for any spiritual abuse. Think through this concept.

I can think of many examples, but one instantly raises its ugly head in my mind — the preacher who beats and bangs hellfire and damnation on his pulpit, piously condemning his flock for all manner of evil, while abusing his wife and children at home. I wish I could tell you that I've only heard such a testimony once or twice. Let me stress that I still believe the far greater population of Christians resist that kind of hypocrisy, but spiritual abuse of this nature exists far more than we want to believe.

Another form of spiritual abuse is using Scripture or the name of God to manipulate others. I have very little doubt we will be called to account for the times we have used God's name to get what we want. Christ despises all forms of human oppression. A huge penalty awaits those who possess a knowledge of God yet persist in meanness and self-indulgence. Forgive me if my temperature on this matter is showing. If not for the authentic examples of godliness, I would despair over all the abuse I've seen in the religious community.

I also see another truth in these parables about being prepared for Jesus' return. The future punishment of the unfaithful will be fair. Let's conclude with a look at the last sentence in our focal passage: "From everyone who has been given much, much will be demanded; and from the one who has been entrusted with much, much more will be asked" (v. 48). That's fair. But that's serious.

I have been given so much. I must accept the fact that much is also required. Here is our joy and security in the midst of much required: Christ is never the author of spiritual abuse. Every single thing required of us will be amply rewarded far beyond our imagination. Until then, keep the porch light burning. Your Master will return.

Chapter 37

How Often Have I Longed?

Luke 13:1–35

"O Jerusalem, Jerusalem, you who kill the prophets and stone those sent to you, how often I have longed to gather your children together, as a hen gathers her chicks under her wings, but you were not willing!" (Luke 13:34)

In Luke 13:31–35 the light of God's Word illuminates a different dimension of Christ's character. Some Pharisees came to Jesus to deliver a warning that Herod wanted to kill Him. Their warning may or may not have been sincere. The surrounding Scriptures offer more to suggest their insincerity than their sincerity. Regardless of the motive for their warning, they could have saved their breath. Jesus replied, "Go tell that fox, 'I will drive out demons and heal people today and tomorrow, and on the third day I will reach my goal.' In any case, I must keep going today and tomorrow and the next day — for surely no prophet can die outside Jerusalem!"(vv. 32–33).

I love Christ's last five words in verse 32: "I will reach my goal." Not if all the conditions are right. Not if you cooperate. Not if I'm still alive. "I will reach my goal." Beloved, find security in the fact that nothing is haphazard about the activity of God. He has a goal, and He has a definitive plan that is to be executed precisely according to His will. You no doubt noticed Christ's symbolic phraseology.

In a sense, Christ spoke in the style of a parable. When He said "today and tomorrow," followed by "the third day" and "the next day," He spoke not in the immediate sense but in a future tense. Because of our hindsight advantage, we hear the unmistakable hint of the three days beginning with the cross and ending with His resurrection. In essence, Christ said, "I have a goal. I have work to do today toward that goal. I have work to do tomorrow toward that goal. But very soon that goal will be accomplished."

Perhaps Christ's use of the words *today, tomorrow,* and *the third day* suggest three segments of time in our lives as well. Today is our now. The third day could represent the fulfillment of God's goals for our lives through our heavenly completion. Tomorrow could represent every moment between now and then.

Christ's return message to Herod emphasized that nothing could turn Him from His goal. Neither Herod nor any other power posed a threat to the plan. They would be used only as puppets to fulfill it. When we live our lives according to God's will, no Herod in the world can thwart our efforts at reaching God's goal either. Not a Herod of sickness nor a Herod of crisis. Not even a Herod that seems to hand us over to death. Let me give you an intriguing example.

Revelation 11 tells of the two witnesses. John wrote, "I will give power to my two witnesses, and they will prophesy for 1,260 days. . . . If anyone tries to harm them, fire comes from their mouths and devours their enemies. . . . Now when they have finished their testimony, the beast that comes up from the Abyss will attack them, and overpower and kill them" (Rev. 11:3, 5, 7).

What happens to the two witnesses is a perfect example of the principle I call immunity — shelter from all evil imposition on God's plan. I chose the two witnesses as an example because the account is so dramatic; the elements of immunity are easy to identify:

1. The witnesses get their power from God (v. 3).
2. When they are opposed, God dramatically defends them (v. 5).
3. When they have finished their testimony, the beast kills them (v. 7).

The two witnesses cannot be killed until they have finished their testimony. Also note that their deaths are by no means a tragic end to their story. God raises them from the dead and makes a mockery of their enemy (see Rev. 11:11–12).

Although the prophecy of the two witnesses is far more dramatic than the story of our lives, they illustrate a principle God applies to us as well. When we live under the umbrella of God's authority and seek to obey His commands, the enemy may oppose us and even oppress us, but he cannot thwart the fulfillment of God's plan for our lives. Any permission he receives to oppose us will be issued only for the greater victory of God. Death cannot come to the obedient children of God until they have finished their testimony. When we surrender our wills to the will of our Father, we find a place of blessed immunity. Strengthened by His power and shielded by His protection, we will reach our goal.

The heart of God is beautifully illustrated in His Son as He cries out, "O Jerusalem, Jerusalem, you who kill the prophets and stone those sent to you, how often I have longed to gather your children together, as a hen gathers her chicks under her wings" (Luke 13:34). The Old Testament paints a similar portrait in Psalm 91. These words fall like a down comforter from heaven. The psalmist wrote: "He who dwells in the shelter of the Most High / will rest in the shadow of the Almighty" (Ps. 91:1). The implication of the verse is that a place of safety or a certain level of immunity from evil onslaughts exists for those who choose to dwell there. The concept of dwelling in Psalm 91:1 is virtually synonymous with the concept of obeying or remaining in John 15:10 where Jesus tells us we abide or remain in Him and His love through obedience.

Obedience to our Father's commands is the key to immunity from the enemy. Obedience is what positions us in the shadow of the Almighty; any evil that comes against us will have to go through God first. Christ lived for one purpose: to do the will of the One who sent Him (see John 6:38). Because

He was entirely surrendered to the will of His Father, Herod's threat had no power over Him. When the time came, the rulers and the chief priests could be used only as puppets by God in His pursuit of greater glory.

I am convinced the same is true for us. We gain the place of immunity through obedience to His will. This explains why Christ longed to gather the children of Israel into His arms like a hen gathers her chicks under her wings, but He did not. Why? Because they weren't willing. They chose their own will over Christ's, forfeiting the shelter of His wings. The result was desolation and defeat (see Luke 13:35; 19:43).

The same unwillingness can have similar results today. As believers in Christ, two different forms of immunity apply to us. All who personally receive the grace gift of God have immunity from eternal judgment. We stand in the shadow of the cross. The judgment that should have come to us came to Christ instead.

A second kind of immunity does not come automatically upon our salvation. It results when we surrender our will to the Father's will. When we bow to His authority, we become immune to defeat and all threats to the plan of God for our personal lives. I don't mean we're immune from trouble, tribulation, or even a certain amount of oppression, but they won't be able to defeat us. We will possess and practice the God-given power to overcome them, and God's plan will be uninterrupted.

I know these principles because I've experienced them. I have complete assurance of my salvation. I am convinced that the cross has immunized me against all judgment for sin. However, I have without a doubt been temporarily defeated by the enemy and done things that were not part of God's plan for my life. By surrendering to my own will in certain seasons, I stepped outside the shelter of the Most High and, although he could not have me, the enemy certainly had a field day with me.

I am a living, breathing, grace-filled Plan B. But I'm a Plan B who has learned some painful lessons that have changed my practices. I presently jump out of bed with one primary plan of attack for the day: ducking under the sheltering wing of the Most High so the enemy will have to get through Him to get to me. As we conclude our chapter, I want you to read Psalm 17:8–9.

Keep me as the apple of your eye;
 hide me in the shadow of your wings

from the wicked who assail me,
from my mortal enemies who
surround me.

Personalize these verses as if every word were written just to you. Pray the verses in your own words of faith and gratitude to the God who invites you to a blessed place of immunity.

Christ Jesus longs to draw us under the shelter of His wings — so close to His side that we can hear His tender heartbeat. He yearns to lavish us with His possessive, protective love. To cover us from so many unnecessary harms.

There is a secret place. Go, beloved, and hide.

Chapter 38

When God Runs

Luke 15:1–32

While he was still a long way off, his father saw him and was filled with compassion for him; he ran to his son, threw his arms around him and kissed him. (Luke 15:20)

Perhaps the most mind-boggling doctrine in the Word of God is that the Creator and Sustainer of the universe who dwells in unapproachable light pursues us. I will never comprehend why, but His Word assures us it is true. He rides the clouds like a chariot and chases after you. He has chosen you not out of obligation but out of love. His is a love that will not let you go.

In that vein, our next chapter is all about lost — and found — things. Be sure and note what prompted the three parables in

Luke 15. The tax collectors and "sinners" gathered to hear Jesus, "but the Pharisees and the teachers of the law muttered, 'This man welcomes sinners and eats with them' " (v. 2).

Jesus responded with three parables, one each about a lost coin, a lost sheep, and a lost son. I cannot think of a more pointed summation of this chapter of Scripture than Christ's words in Luke 19:10: "For the Son of Man came to seek and to save what was lost."

Christ didn't come to save the pious and perfect. He came to seek and to save the lost. At times I've descended from the place of appropriate repentance where I was sorry for my sins to the place of inappropriate self-loathing where I was sorry Christ was "forced" (as if He could be) to save me. I'd find myself wishing I had been a nicer sinner. More pleasant to save. Emotion washes over me today as I remember again: Christ came for sinners like me. He wanted to save me. Our Savior came to seek and to save the lost. The hopeless. The foolish. The weak. The depraved. In His own words: "It is not the healthy who need a doctor, but the sick. I have not come to call the righteous, but sinners to repentance" (Luke 5:31–32).

I have no idea how many times I've read

and even taught the story of the prodigal son, yet it still brings me to tears. I am such a product of this kind of father love. Perhaps you are too. If not, you may more readily identify with the older brother, and God's Word will speak riches to you. This parable offers a priceless inheritance to everyone. Rather than attempt to exhaust the entire segment and apply every applicable point, I'd rather center unhurriedly on just a few. Notice them with me.

A Son Sick of Home

As the curtain rises, the younger son asks his father for his share of the estate. Although his father was not obligated to give it to him, he did. The wise father knew that his son was unwise, but sometimes allowing a persistent young adult to do what is unwise leads to wisdom, albeit down a painful road. The son set off for a distant country. This was no mistreated son, and his was not a dysfunctional home.

Perhaps we prodigals distance ourselves from the good in an attempt to keep it from haunting us in the bad. Sometimes in our rebellion we foolishly long for a searing of conscience, having no idea it would be a fate

371

worse than death (see 1 Tim. 4:2). In the distant land the son squandered his wealth in wild living. The word *prodigal* comes from the definition of the Greek word for "wild." *Asotos* means "profligately, riotously, prodigally." An important element surfaces in the definition of *asotia,* the feminine noun of *asotos.* It describes the prodigal as "having no hope of safety."

Consider the words *having no hope of safety* in terms of our previous discussion of immunity. Keep in mind that the father represents God and the younger son represents every prodigal.

Psalm 91:1–4 tells us of God's desire to shelter us under His wings, but when the prodigal chose to step out from under the umbrella of his father's authority, he forfeited the protection of the umbrella as well. He did not lose his father's love, but he lost his father's shield. How many of us have been right there with him? The devil is so sly. He tempts us to think that God is somehow out to cheat us. Have you ever been tempted to think God just wants to imprison me and take away all my fun?

As we begin to grow up in Him and in His Word, we understand that nothing could be further from the truth. Our freedom, our abundant life, our dignity, our dreams come true — are all found in the glorious will of God. We finally learn that under God's umbrella, we are free to sing in the rain. Outside God's umbrella, we nearly drown in the flood.

A Prodigal Life in a Spiral

At first, it's so exciting, it's intoxicating. Soon its dizzying effects spiral downward, and truth gives way to consequences. We can see with each step of degeneration this boy faces a more painful harvest of the seeds he had sown. Keep in mind that he was a young man who was reared well. Imagine his feelings and responses based on his upbringing. In ways I'm not sure we Gentiles can understand, this Hebrew son hit rock bottom. He came from a home where pigs were considered unclean animals. I assure you his father did not bring home the bacon, and his mother didn't fry it up in the pan. Yet not only was he forced to take a job feeding swine, but also he longed to eat their food!

One of the most wonderful things God has taught me from my past is that we don't always have to hit the bottom. When tempted to wander, we can turn back to

Him early. God's most effective method for teaching me this principle is the memory of excruciating consequences from the past. I'd have to lose my mind before wanting to go back to some of the places I've been.

I've watched God take a young woman I love very much and restore her to the right road after a prodigal detour. She has cried out to me, "When will all these painful repercussions end?"

I have answered her, "Not until the very idea of straying causes you such painful flashbacks that you're hardly ever tempted to depart His will again." God wants to whisper to our hearts, "Are you sure you want to go back there again?" and hear us say, "No way do I want that kind of pain!"

God is far too faithful to allow the prodigal life to be cost-free. In fact, consider that if we can sin freely, we may have a far more serious problem. If we can remain outside the umbrella of God's authority for an extended period of time without feeling the negative effects of it, we may not be saved. The Holy Spirit never falls down on His job. To feel no conviction of sin for a length of time is a serious sign that the Holy Spirit may not reside in us. We can quench the Spirit, but we cannot disable Him. Now let's focus on the prodigal's about-face.

A Homesick Son

The words in verse 17, "When he came to his senses," introduce a turnaround. Few things force us to look up like being all the way down. The son realized that, considering where he came from, the way he was living didn't make sense.

The same is true for you and me. When we accept Christ, we are brought into a family of "more than conquerors" (Rom. 8:37). To live in defeat simply doesn't make sense! To be beaten down by the harsh elements of life when we could be shielded from so much is insane. Under the umbrella of God's authority, we are not immune to some hard winds and getting our faces wet in the rain, but we cannot be defeated by them. May we quickly come to our senses when living any other way!

Luke 15:17 tells us that the son considered the abundance of his father's hired hands and realized the insanity of starving to death. He waited to go home until his desperation exceeded his pride. That the prodigal planned what he would say hints at the difficulty of his return. He literally practiced what he would say when he got home. He planned to say, "Father, I have sinned against heaven and against you. I am no longer worthy to be called your son; make me like one of your hired men" (vv. 18–19), but notice the Father had other ideas.

A Father Homesick for His Son

Don't miss a single description of this father: "While he was still a long way off, his father saw him" (v. 20). The prodigal's father was looking for his son in the distance. I imagine that every day since his son's departure, his father had studied the horizon in search of his son's silhouette.

I wonder if the son was pacing. And pacing. And pacing. He could see his home in the distance, but perhaps he could not bring himself to walk that last mile. He looked at his father's vast estate and glanced down at his own poor estate. His clothes were worn and filthy. Dirt under every nail. His hair long and matted or shorn to the skin to defend against lice. All at once, he became aware of his own foul smell. He was destitute. Degraded.

But . . . "his father saw him and was filled with compassion for him" (v. 20). The Greek word for "compassion" in this verse means "to feel deeply or viscerally, to yearn, have compassion, pity." Just as the starving son had longed for food, his father had yearned for him. His was a kind of yearning so deep that no amount of work could assuage it. Family members could not replace it. No distraction could soothe it. Oh, friend, can you glimpse the heart of God? Do you realize that when you run from Him, He yearns for you every minute and cannot be distracted from His thoughts of you?

When God sees our poor estate and the ravaging effects of our foolish decisions, He doesn't just sit back and say, "She got what she deserved." He is filled with compassion and longs to bring us back home. Yes, we face consequences, but those consequences are a loving summons back to the Father.

In one of the most moving moments in all of Scripture, Luke 15:20 records that the father "ran to his son." Scripture often employs anthropomorphisms — descriptions of God as if He had a human body. We sometimes read that God walked (in the midst of His people) or that He rode (on the clouds like chariots), but this is the only time in the entire Word of God when He is described as running.

What makes God run? A prodigal child turning his face toward home! How can we resist Him? How can we not reciprocate such lavish love?

When was the last time you saw an older man, the father of adult children, run? Would you picture it now? Can you hear his heart pounding in his chest? Can you hear him catching his breath? Nothing could keep him from his son.

When he reached the son, the son tried his best to give the speech he planned but to no avail. In all his talk of unworthiness, he didn't realize he was unworthy even before he left. He was a son not because he earned the right to be, but because he was born of his father. He could exceed the realm of his father's shield, but he could not exceed the reach of his father's love. " 'Quick! Bring the best robe and put it on him. Put a ring on his finger and sandals on his feet. Bring the fattened calf and kill it. Let's have a feast and celebrate. For this son of mine was dead and is alive again; he was lost and is found' " (vv. 22–24). The father literally kissed the son's past away.

Merciful Savior! Graceful God! You have kissed this prodigal's past into forgetfulness! Though mockers may accuse me, though gossipers may make sport of me, though brothers may jealously despise me, I will celebrate! Let all hear music and dancing! For I once was dead and now I'm alive again. I once was lost and now I am found.

Part 8

The Answer

One of my favorite things about God's Word is that it is gloriously inexhaustible. While I am somewhat frustrated that we don't have the space to pore over every Scripture in the Gospel of Luke, I am reminded that we would still fall short of the definitive study of Christ's life. Colossians 2:3 says that in Christ "are hidden all the treasures of wisdom and knowledge." We'll never outsearch the treasures He's willing to reveal. May our present treasure hunt simply cause you to search for more.

The segment of study awaiting us is a bit confrontational. I hope we are beginning to think that's OK. I can't think of a radical change in my life that didn't find its catalyst in a radical confrontation by God. We can find much encouragement in trusting that our God never confronts to condemn, but to complete what is lacking. In the midst of some pretty straight talk from God, we will also share a few reprieving grins. We've got some tree climbing to do with a certain wee little man. Keep looking forward to it when the moments get heavy.

By the way, has anyone reminded you lately that Christ is coming back? It's a fact. And one we'll study together briefly before this part of our book concludes. Let's get started.

Chapter 39

Causing Others to Sin

Luke 17:1–5

Jesus said to his disciples: "Things that cause people to sin are bound to come, but woe to that person through whom they come." (Luke 17:1)

Let's state a serious fact based on Luke 17: events or situations can actually cause people to sin. Before we attempt to interpret Christ's statements, let's make sure we understand what He didn't mean. Christ didn't mean that in some cases people have no choice but to sin. He didn't absolve the one who sins from the responsibility to repent. He did mean that conditions can exist and things can happen that so greatly increase the tendency toward sin that a terrible woe is due the responsible party.

What are these offenses or "things that

cause people to sin"? The Greek word is *skandalon*. The idea of our English word *scandal* is present in the meaning of the Greek word. *Skandalon* is "the trigger of a trap on which the bait is placed, and which, when touched by the animal, springs and causes it to close causing entrapment. . . . *Skandalon* always denotes an enticement to conduct which could ruin the person in question."

If you apply the concept to Jesus' words, you see that the declaration of woe would apply to the one who set the trap or figuratively speaking "became" the trigger of a trap. Woe to the person who baits another person into entrapment.

Making a careful comparison between Luke 17:1 and the definition, we see a second person involved. Christ said the victim of the trap also sins, even though another designed the trap; therefore, let's identify these two figures as the trapper and the sinner. Without a doubt, I have experienced entrapment, but to be liberated I must not shift all responsibility to the trapper. Unfortunately, all too often I took the bait.

To live consistently outside a trap, I must recognize my own responsibility in at least three ways. I am responsible for (1) repenting of the sin of taking the bait; (2) learning why I took the bait; (3) asking God to mend and fortify the weak places in the fabric of my heart, soul, and mind so I will not continue life as a victim.

A critical part of my freedom has been asking God to help me search my heart, soul, and mind for vulnerabilities to foolish decisions. Taking responsibility in these areas produced one of the greatest harvests of my life. I learned to willingly lay my heart bare before Him, to invite Him to reveal my weaknesses and handicaps, and to be unashamed. I also developed daily dependency upon God because my old vulnerabilities had become such habits, practices, and ways of life.

We looked at the sin of the victim; now let's zero in on the sin of the trapper. The ramifications of the trapper's sin are so great that he or she becomes the object of woe, meaning "disaster, calamity."

Christ issued a woe to anyone who causes another person to sin, but He pronounced a particular indictment against anyone who causes "one of these little ones" to sin. The word Jesus used to refer to little ones certainly includes literal children because He actually "called a little child and had him stand among them" (Matt. 18:2). However, careful attention to the word He used suggests additional meaning. I believe Christ includes those who are childlike or inferior to the trapper in knowledge, experience, authority, or power — anyone of whom it might be easy to take advantage. A sixteen-year-old may have the body of an adult, but he or she most assuredly is not grown up. Seduction by an adult is entrapment even if the young person "sinned" in any level of willing participation. Similarly in adult life one person often wields authority over another in much the same way through rank or position.

That Christ holds the trapper greatly responsible is a gross understatement! He appears to be saying, "If you have entrapped a weaker, more vulnerable person in sin, you're going to wish you had drowned in the deepest sea rather than deal with Me."

Most of us have asked, "Why do these things happen?" Luke 17:1 tells us that these atrocities "are bound to come." "But why?" we ask. Matthew's version suggests one reason. Matthew 18:7 reads, "Woe to the world because of the things that cause people to sin! Such things must come, but woe to the man through whom they come."

The original word for "must" means "compelling force, as opposed to willingness . . . as a result of the depravity and wickedness of men, there is a moral inevitability that offenses should come." Add the kingdom of darkness to the depravity of humans, and you have a formula for exactly the evil we see in our world, but a day of reckoning is coming. No trapper gets away with entrapment — of the human kind or of the spirit kind. Neither can escape the eyes of *El Roi*, the God who sees.

Luke 17:3 suggests the trapper is not always the "other guy." Jesus said, "So watch yourselves." Christ wasn't just issuing an assurance of horrible consequences for the trapper. He was also issuing a warning that His disciples better not be among them. If Christ's temperature rises over the godless trapper, can you even imagine how His temperature rises over the trapper who bears His name? God forbid!

Most of us are not naïve enough to think that these kinds of offenses never happen in churchgoing families. I'd like to highlight one area that doesn't get much press but where people are at great risk for offense in the church.

New believers are so impressionable. Sometimes their zeal far exceeds their knowledge. They sometimes believe virtually anything a more experienced Christian tells them. Biblical doctrines can be twisted into false teaching to entrap immature believers in all sorts of sins. If God would judge those outside His own household, I think we can rest assured He would discipline His own.

Let's not start feeling guilty for some atrocity we may not have committed, but by all means let's be on our guard never to cause another person to sin. The Word is clear we have that potential.

Next, allow me to draw your attention to the forgiveness issue Christ addressed in Luke 17:3–4. He said, "If your brother sins, rebuke him, and if he repents, forgive him. If he sins against you seven times in a day, and seven times comes back to you and says, 'I repent,' forgive him."

Christ suddenly switched to a subject that seems to have no relationship to things that cause people to sin. However, I'd like to suggest a powerful connection between the two. Few things cause people to sin like unforgiveness. Difficult-to-forgive circumstances can set a trap. Satan uses unforgiveness as bait to entrap us in sin (2 Cor. 2:10–11).

Please note that Christ's specific prescriptive in Luke 17:3–4 is to fellow believers when we sin against one another. Someone might ask, "Does this mean I have to forgive only other Christians?" No, indeed. Luke 11:4 clearly tells us we are to forgive "everyone who sins against us."

The difference may not be in the forgiveness but in the rebuke. I believe Christ suggests a different method of dealing with a brother's or sister's sin. He issued a directive to rebuke a fellow believer. When dealing with the unsaved, we are still called to forgive — but not necessarily to rebuke. We were called to be different in the body of Christ. If we are functioning as a healthy body, ideally we should be able to bring issues that affect us to the table with one another and dialogue and, when appropriate, even rebuke or receive a rebuke. This type of approach demands the maturity expressed by Ephesians 4:14–15. Paul told us we are no longer to be infants but are to "speak the truth in love" to one another.

Needless to say, a tremendous burden of responsibility falls on the one giving the rebuke. An appropriate rebuke is speaking the truth in love "with great patience and careful instruction" (2 Tim. 4:2). We may not be off base in concluding that a rebuke that invites anger and bitterness might fall under the category of entrapment to sin. Obviously, a huge responsibility also falls on the recipient to rightly accept the rebuke. I am learning that an important part of maturing as a believer is knowing how to receive a rebuke.

Do you know what occurs to me as we wrap up this chapter? If we would learn the art of giving and receiving an appropriate rebuke in the early stages of wrongdoing, we would guard ourselves more effectively against offenses of millstone magnitude! I don't know about you, but I'll be chewing on this lesson long into the night.

Chapter 40

Where Are the Nine?

Luke 17:11–19

One of them, when he saw he was healed, came back, praising God in a loud voice. (Luke 17:15)

We have a family joke. When one of us compliments another, the recipient will tease, "Thank you. But after all, I cannot be less than who I am." It rarely fails to bring a laugh — or a pillow flying across the room. What makes the reply so preposterous is that all four of us are very aware that without Christ, we indeed could be less!

With Christ we are so much, but we often act like far less than who we are. Christ Jesus, on the other hand, really can't be less than who He is. No matter what was pending, He never set aside His position as Son of man, the deliverer and the healer.

Next we catch up with Him on His way to Jerusalem. Christ knew all that would come upon Him. I think even the best of us would be somewhat distracted by pending suffering and death. Who wouldn't have understood if Christ wanted to travel a remote path to Jerusalem, far from the tugs of the needy? Yet all the way to the city that would scorn Him, Jesus continued to minister, heal, teach, and warn. Why? Because He simply could not be less than who He was.

On the border between Samaria and Galilee, Jesus encountered ten lepers. In response to their pleas for healing, Christ instructed them to go show themselves to the priests. On the way they were healed, but only one returned to say thank you.

While I ministered in India, I was often stunned by what God empowered me to do. He seemed to raise me above my fleshly senses and allow me to minister in extreme circumstances. I was unable to do only one thing, and it has haunted me ever since. I had confidently planned to minister in a leper colony. The opportunity didn't readily arise, but after passing very close to several colonies, I deliberately did not pursue it.

The reason was not unconcern. Rather, I feared I would dishonor them by becoming physically ill. You see, I almost became ill just passing by. Nothing could have prepared me for the sight or the smell. I had been in one squalid village after another without hindrance, but the smell of diseased and decaying flesh was more than I could handle.

I don't know if God was upset with me, but I was definitely upset with myself. My experience helps me to appreciate this story. Let's highlight several significant pieces of information shared about the lepers in Luke 17.

1. The lepers were outside the city gate. What could be worse than forced isolation? I can hardly stand the thought of the emotional results of this dreadful disease, especially in an ancient society. The law of Moses said, "As long as he has the infection [leprosy] he remains unclean. He must live alone; he must live outside the camp" (Lev. 13:46).

Many of us still wear emotional scars as the result of being excluded from certain groups in our youth; yet, by comparison, that was nothing! Try to imagine what this was like. Presumably, the scene is the city gate. Christ met the lepers as he prepared to enter the village. We are told "they stood at a distance" (Luke 17:12). They were obeying the laws meant to control the spread of the infectious disease.

Oh, beloved, I'm so grateful we never have to stand at a distance from Christ. Not only is He incapable of catching our "disease," but also He is never reluctant to embrace us. Rejoice with me in the words of Psalm 34:18: "The Lord is close to the broken-hearted / and saves those who are crushed in spirit."

Who could be more brokenhearted, more crushed in spirit, than these outcasts? Even though Christ honored their respect for the law, His healing Spirit had to have drawn close while bathing them with soothing balm.

2. The lepers cried out in a loud voice. Don't miss the fact that every word attributed to the lepers is "in a loud voice" (vv. 13, 15). The distance explains their initial volume, but why did the one who returned and fell at Jesus' feet also cry out in a loud voice?

I'd like to suggest that they were accustomed to having to shout. Leviticus 13:45 is probably as hard for you to read as it is for me: "The person with such an infectious disease must wear torn clothes, let his hair be unkempt, cover the lower part of his face and cry out, 'Unclean! Unclean!'"

I was reared by my grandmother and mother to be a cheerleader for the underdog. At my house, a fate worse than death awaited the one who dared to look down on someone who couldn't help his condition. As I read this verse in the Old Testament, I can hardly bear the thought of the excruciating blend of exclusion and publicity. Imagine it. Outside the city gate, unable to work, entirely dependent on charity, yet while excluded they were forced to publicize themselves by crying out, "Unclean! Unclean!" Don't miss the description: they cried out. They were forced to cover their mouths yet shout continually so that no one would accidentally come near them.

Because of the nature of this ministry and my own testimony, I encounter many people who live like the ten lepers. They are in bondage either to sin or to the aftereffects of sin. Far too often I see actual believers in Christ wearing shame like a cloak, scarlet letters on their chests. Their voices may be silent, but their expressions cry out: "Unclean! Unclean!" They feel excluded from the pretty part of the body of Christ. Yet they feel their shame is displayed for all to see. My heart breaks every time.

In Luke 17:12, the lepers cried out, "Jesus, Master, have pity on us!" I discovered that the original word for "pity" included these words: "To show mercy, to show compassion, extend help for the consequence of sin . . . implying not merely a feeling for the misfortunes of others involving sympathy, but also an active desire to remove those miseries." These lepers were not just asking for sympathy. All the sympathy in the world could not change their miserable condition. They needed far more than people feeling sorry for them. They needed someone to change their lives! Jesus was the One and Only who could. Part of my horrible struggle about going to the leper colony in India was an awareness that I could do nothing to help their physical estate. Christ still overflows today with a pity that doesn't just sympathize but changes conditions. Often physically. Always spiritually.

3. *The common condition of the lepers eclipsed their differences.* The village in today's scene was located along the border between Samaria and Galilee. Both Samaritans and Jews, who actively despised each other, lived in this region. The lepers had to have been a mix of Samaritans and Jews. Christ never would have commented that only a "foreigner" returned with thanks if none of the ten had been Jews.

The tragic plight of the lepers gave them

far more in common than their differences as Jews and Gentiles. In reality, aren't we the same way? Before we are redeemed, not one of us is better than the other. We are all in the same sad state — lepers outside the city gate. Lost and isolated. Marred and unclean — whether we've lied or cheated, devalued another human being, or committed adultery. Lost is lost. Furthermore, found is found. All of us in Christ have received the free gift of salvation in one way only: grace. When we judge a brother's or sister's sin as so much worse than our own, we are like lepers counting spots. "She has more than I do."

Let's face it. We've all had leprosy, and our cure cost a life whether we had a dozen spots or a thousand. We separated ourselves in all sorts of ways, but our disease was really the same — as was our cure.

4. The lepers were cleansed during their faith-walk to the priest. Before Christ healed them, He told them to go and show themselves to the priests. The Old Testament directive for those healed of infectious skin diseases like leprosy appears in Leviticus 14:1–9. If a leper was healed, the priest was to come and examine him or her.

Instead of waiting for the priest to come and examine them, Christ told them to go to the priests. Mind you, the priests were inside the city gates. The lepers risked expulsion, ridicule, repulsion, and every other kind of human insult. The Word tells us, "As they went, they were cleansed" (Luke 17:14).

Picture them taking their walk of faith, step-by-step. They probably noticed the healing of their feet first because the disease is very disfiguring, making a simple walk awkward if not impossible. Perhaps they noticed their hands next. What a glorious sight! You see, their healing was not simply a matter of the skin clearing. They literally had fingers restored. The numbness in their appendages gave way to the sense of touch.

Can you picture them turning their palms up and down with amazement, running to one another, laughing and expressing their joy in stereo? When they clapped their hands with celebration, they felt the welcome sting of healthy flesh. What an exhibition passed through the simple village that day! Who could have missed it? Ten lepers made whole. Their hair still unkempt and their clothes still torn, but for once they were oblivious. Glad spectacles were they.

As I prepared for this passage by studying the life of a leper in the ancient Hebrew world, I learned something that really caused me to think. The Mosaic law was very specific about the proper methods of purification after someone with leprosy was cured. Oddly, "the Bible never implies that leprosy can be cured by non-miraculous means, even though it does contain guidelines for readmitting cured lepers into normal society."[1] Leprosy was incurable.

Only a handful of references in the Old Testament record lepers being healed, but not one was through natural means. Don't you find it a little odd that the Old Testament law provided such elaborate instructions for purification and reentry to society after healing, and yet it never happened apart from rare divine intervention?

Ah, but did Christ not say He had come to fulfill the law? All those centuries they had been waiting for the cure that the Old Testament law implied had to be possible. All ten of those lepers knew what to do after they were healed, yet they never could find a cure — until one day when their cure found them.

I love the way Scripture refers to their healing as being made clean. Oh, dear sister or brother, that's what healing has meant to me. Being made clean! Do you know why I recognize those who wear shame like a cloak? Scarlet letters on their chests? Because I did. But I don't anymore. Acts 10:15 tells us so clearly, "Do not call anything impure that God has made clean."

You can be fairly certain the village priest had never practiced the purification ritual to pronounce a leper clean. I can almost picture him reading the instructions in Leviticus 14 step by unfamiliar step — like we read a new recipe. What a story he had for the Mrs. that night! Then again, it wouldn't have been like a woman to miss the parade of ten former lepers dancing their way down Main Street. Then note the punch line of the event:

5. One leper returned to give praise to God. I wonder if he tried to get the other nine to come with him. Or if he suddenly stopped in his tracks realizing he hadn't said thanks, then darted impulsively from their presence to find Christ. The point is, his healing made him think of his healer, not just himself. Sadly, the rest of them never knew Christ except from a distance. When the one returned, he was unrestrained — falling at Christ's feet and thanking Him.

Just one last thought. I wonder if he was the one with the most spots?

Chapter 41

Lacking One Thing

Luke 18:18–30

When Jesus heard this, he said to him, "You still lack one thing. Sell everything you have and give to the poor, and you will have treasure in heaven. Then come, follow me." (Luke 18:22)

I know some real heroes of the faith. I'm sure you do too. Permit me to introduce one to you right now. Her name is Scotty Sanders. She is a beautiful and godly woman, several years my senior. We have the privilege of serving in the same church. Scotty has literally had it all — wealth, prestige, status. She knows celebrities from all over the world. People you and I only read about call her friend. Scotty's passion is inner-city missions. Day in and day out she pours her energy into lives without privilege.

"Why wouldn't she?" someone might ask. "After all, at night she can return to a mansion and her live-in maid." Nope. At night she parks her car in a dangerous area of Houston and returns home to a cracker-box apartment in a broken-down complex, right in the middle of the community she serves.

I am honored beyond description to call Scotty my friend. I know many wealthy people who serve God lavishly through their riches. Although I believe He always requires believers with wealth to be excellent stewards of what He's entrusted, He doesn't always require them to give up everything and live among the poor. But that's what my friend, Scotty, began to sense Him saying to her. The sacrifice has been tremendous, but you will never hear a hint of martyrdom in Scotty's tone. I want to be standing there in heaven when God presents her with the mansion He's prepared. It's going to be something. But if I know Scotty, she'll move everyone with a lesser mansion into hers.

Luke 18:18–30 tells the story many of us know as "the rich young ruler." The man came to Jesus asking what he must do to inherit eternal life. Jesus first directed him to the law, but the young man claimed to have kept that. Then Jesus told him to sell his possessions and give them to the poor, and the man went away sorrowful because he was excessively attached to his possessions. Mark's version contributes an additional insight: "Jesus looked at him and loved him" (Mark 10:21).

Keep in mind that this is an actual encounter, not a parable. Although the ruler possessed much of what earth had to offer, he was wise enough to know this life isn't all there is. How gracious is our God to create us with a spirit that somehow knows life must be more. That "knowing" was meant to compel a search for God who promises to make Himself "findable." Let's explore several dimensions of this interesting encounter.

"Why do you call me good?" (v. 19)

What an intriguing inquiry! The young man addressed Jesus as "good teacher." Why in the world would Christ respond with such a question? I believe He was testing the ruler's knowledge of His identity. When He said, "No one is good — except God alone," I think He was prompting the ruler to think about the root of Christ's goodness. The man may have considered the basis of Christ's goodness to be His good works. Aside from God, no human being is inherently good.

Sometimes I can be smack in the middle of seeking and serving God, living beyond all my "self-stuff," when suddenly something will happen to bring out a reaction in me that reminds me: O, Lord, I know nothing good lives in me, that is, in my sinful nature (Rom. 7:18). At times an experience like this makes me sob with frustration. Other times, I simply bend the knee and thank Christ again for humbling me and showing me that He alone is good, for He alone is God. Any good thing in me is Him.

The rich young ruler did not yet understand the imperative relationship between goodness and God-ness. Christ strongly hinted His deity in this encounter, wooing the man to a place of redefinition. Consider that many of the world religions consider Jesus to have been very good. They just don't consider Him to be God.

"You know the commandments." (v. 20)

After Christ redefined goodness, He made this statement to the young man's credit: Nothing is more dangerous than an earthly ruler who sees himself above all rule.

I think this ruler respected God as the real sovereign; I'm just not sure he had a very accurate regard for himself.

Christ began reminding the ruler of the commands he already knew. Interestingly, each one Christ named concerned man's relationship with man.

Without a hint of hesitation, the ruler said he had kept all these since he was a boy. Oh, brother. If I may say, this statement reflects the little piece of information shared by Matthew's version in Matthew 19:20: this rich ruler was young. If he were a rich old ruler, he still may not have given up his wealth, but I don't think he'd be quite as quick to give himself such high marks. When I recall some of the statements I made and thoughts I had in my early twenties, I could nearly die. Talk about self-righteous! And, friend, I didn't have anything to be self-righteous about!

No wonder God had to humble me! And I am so grateful He did. I would be sickening if I had the track record I wish I had. Perhaps others can handle a spotless track record, but I don't think I could do this ministry if I had one.

Actually, I'm not sure the young ruler was dealing with his track record very well either. Consider the abbreviated list of commandments Christ mentioned. Let's play a game together. The game is not meant to judge this man but to cause us to think about ourselves. Take a look at each command he claimed to have kept since boyhood, and give each a mental check mark for the ruler's probable obedience and a mental X for those that seem a little less probable.

"Do not commit adultery" (v. 20). OK, this one may have been a pretty easy check mark, that is, if he knew nothing about lust as committing adultery in our hearts (Matt. 5:27–28).

I am still willing to give the rich young ruler the benefit of the doubt. Perhaps he practiced a very disciplined life and did not feed his flesh with things that spur wrong thoughts. Let's give him a check mark here.

"Do not murder" (v. 20). Of course, there's that little "anger" issue that Christ discussed in Matthew 5:21–22, but let's go ahead and give him a check mark on this one, too.

"Do not steal" (v. 20). The kind of stealing intimated by the language in this verse is performed by a *kleptes* as opposed to a *lestes*. A *lestes* steals "by violence and openly." The *kleptes* steals "by fraud and in secret." Maybe we've never mugged someone on the street or even swiped candy from

the convenience store, but did we ever secretly defraud or steal anything of a less tangible nature from another person? Perhaps so. I'm still willing to give him a check mark, but let me just say I'm impressed!

"Do not give false testimony" (v. 20). This command is simple: never tell anything false or untrue. Any exaggeration would fall under the category of false testimony. Picture us at age seventeen, talking to our friends on the telephone, giving our version of this story and that. The rich young ruler's protection may have been that he had never been a seventeen-year-old girl nor owned a phone. Hopefully he never had time to fish, either. We can give him a check mark if he insists, but you better give me an X.

"Honor your father and mother" (v. 20). Let's see. I hardly ever dishonored mine to their faces, but does it count if, behind their backs, I did a few things they told me not to do? Oops. Go ahead and give the wonder boy a check mark, but I get another X.

How did you fare throughout our game? Shall we call you perfection personified? Or is your halo slipping a bit? If we get honest, most of us will have to say, "I was thrown out of the game in the first inning, quarter, or whatever."

Boy, am I thankful for a Savior! The rich

young ruler needed one too. His good track record had certainly fogged up his mirror. Don't get me wrong. I like him. I'm even impressed with him, but I'd rather be saved than be like him!

"You still lack one thing." (v. 22)

Christ's response to the rich young ruler's claim is best understood in Matthew 19:21: "Jesus answered, 'If you want to be perfect, go, sell your possessions and give to the poor, and you will have treasure in heaven. Then come, follow me.' "

If this were a game show, the bell indicating the mention of the secret word would have just sounded. Eternal life with God demands perfection. Someone has to be perfect. Either us or someone who stands in for us. This man wanted so badly for it to be him. As good as he had been and as hard as he had tried, he was still lacking. Christ then stuck a pin in the rich young ruler's Achilles' heel: his possessions.

One of the primary purposes of this divine pinprick was to show the man he wasn't perfect nor would he ever be. I really believe a second purpose may have been to offer an authentic invitation for the searching young man to follow Him. Remember, Jesus didn't have only twelve disciples. He had twelve apostles among a greater number of disciples. If the rich young ruler had done what Christ suggested, could he have followed Him? Certainly! He simply needed to lighten his load and be free of wealth's encumbrances. A truckful of possessions would have proved cumbersome.

I also believe Christ had a purely benevolent purpose for the seemingly harsh demand. Jesus looked at this young man and saw a prisoner. The man wasn't really the ruler. His possessions were. Jesus pointed him to the only path to freedom. Sometimes when our possessions have us, we have to get rid of them to be free.

Of course, Christ knew in advance what the young man would choose. When it comes right down to it, we all follow our "god." The ironic part about this story, however, is that the rich young ruler was grief stricken over his own choice. He walked away very sad or in Greek, *perilupos:* "severely grieved, very sorrowful." Unless his heart changed somewhere along the way, he lived the rest of his life with all that wealth and an empty heart. The question would have haunted him forever: "What do I still lack?" (Matt. 19:20).

Perfection or a perfect substitute. He had neither. He lacked Jesus.

I wonder if the man stuck around long enough to hear the rest of the conversation between Christ and His disciples. Christ said something like this: Yes, an eternal inheritance involves sacrifice here on earth, but whatever you lay down here for My sake, you will receive a hundred times as much in eternity (see Matt. 19:29).

Be advised that Jesus was not approving of His followers' neglecting their families. God has called me to make some sacrifices where my family is concerned, but He would never bless neglectfulness on my part as a mom or wife. He has given me the ministry of wife and mother. I can't turn my back on my ministry — in or outside my home. The challenges of both force me to continually seek His will. I certainly don't always get it right, but God keeps me close, and I believe the pure-hearted pursuit of His will is a large part of what God honors. When He sent me to Israel for the taping of this series, I cried over leaving my family. Then God reminded me of these verses. Had I been shirking my responsibility I don't think the verses would have been applicable.

"Who then can be saved?" (v. 26)

The scene draws to a close with a very strong reaction from the disciples: "Who then can be saved?" Do you hear their fear? I think they may have thought something like this: If a wealthy man who has done virtually everything right has no inheritance in heaven, what will happen to people like us? Jesus' reply is the glorious hope for every man, woman, and child, no matter how they score on the Ten Commandments: "What is impossible with men is possible with God" (Luke 18:27). Thank goodness!

Only God can change our value systems and truly show us what is lacking. Even when what is lacking is poverty, so that He might make us rich. Just ask my friend Scotty.

Chapter 42

A Wee Little Man

Luke 19:1–10

When Jesus reached the spot, he looked up and said to him, "Zacchaeus, come down immediately. I must stay at your house today." (Luke 19:5)

I love knowing we have a variety of backgrounds. Some of us grew up in Bible-teaching churches. Others went on Sundays but know very little Scripture. Some attended only on Easter and Christmas, and some may never have attended and have only recently begun to seek God through Scripture. So many different backgrounds, and yet here we are studying together. How awesome! At this moment, however, I wish we could all sit together in those baby-bear chairs and hear my preschool Sunday school teacher dramatize our next encounter. It is one of my favorite childhood Bible stories.

One reason I like this story so much is that it is equipped with a very theatrical theme song, passed from generation to generation. I taught the same tune to my little girls that my teachers taught to us. I can still see my daughters' tiny, fisted hands with thumb and pointer about one inch apart singing, "Zacchaeus was a wee little man, and a wee little man was he. He climbed up in a sycamore tree for the Lord he wanted to see." The dramatic part of the song began when the pointer finger would shake authoritatively while they sang, "Zacchaeus, you come down . . . for I'm going to your house today. I'm going to your house today!"

I'm not sure I'll tell the story as well as my Sunday school teacher, but I'll give it a try. Jesus traveled to Jericho. There the chief tax collector wanted to see Christ, but the man was very short. So he ran ahead and climbed a tree.

Can you imagine the desire that must have driven Zacchaeus to risk such humiliation? As Jesus came to the tree He called for Zacchaeus to come down, and amazingly, Christ declared Himself to be the guest of the tax collector.

This little visit caused quite a stir in the

community. Can you imagine what the title of the next day's headline would have been if there had been a newspaper called *The Jericho Chronicle*? As a means of creative exploration, let's try to capture a few of the newsiest statements that might have appeared in a newspaper article. Mind you, the bold statements that follow will be strictly fictitious stabs at what a journalist might have written, but the commentary will reflect on Scripture. The lead story might have read:

The renowned Jesus of Nazareth passes through Jericho yesterday. Jesus couldn't seem to pass through anywhere without getting involved. He seemed to attract the dust of every village in His sandals no matter how resolved He was to reach Jerusalem. I wonder if His disciples were ever frustrated that He couldn't go anywhere without getting involved in one way or another. By the time they reached each village, they most likely were tired, thirsty, and famished, yet they encountered one commotion after another. Earlier we saw that He couldn't get through the gate of a border town without healing ten lepers. I'm sure His followers were thrilled and amazed by all He did, but every now and then we sense a bit of impatience.

For example, in Luke 18:15–17 we read of the parents bringing their children to Jesus. I'm not sure which got on the disciples' last nerve: the parents or the babies! Their reactive rebuke earned them a sterner one. If Christ's disciples were like most of us, every now and then they probably tried to draw a few boundary lines for Him — lines that soon disappeared beneath His sandal prints as He walked right over them. He passed through, all right, but He couldn't seem to pass by.

Chief tax collector seen scurrying up a tree. Zacchaeus was no run-of-the-mill publican. He was their boss. He made a fortune at a business that provided no small opportunity to cheat citizens of their earnings. The locals were often at the mercy of the merciless. The only rule most publicans had to abide by was to make sure Rome got its due. Whatever the tax collectors could pilfer in the process was entirely up to them.

That particular day, something caused a greater stir than taxes. Zacchaeus wanted to see who Jesus was badly enough, in fact, that he went to considerable lengths for a grown man. Mainly because, for a grown man, he didn't have much length. I'm smiling because if my staff and I had attended that Jericho parade, I know exactly which one of us would have been forced to climb the tree. The one with a stool in her office. I have a feeling that Zacchaeus may have been even shorter than she. At least that's the way my Sunday school teacher portrayed him. She measured him right around her elbow, and I always saw her as an expert on those kinds of things.

Picture this grown man running ahead of the parade of people, looking for a tree with a view. Did he have to jump to reach a sturdy branch, or did the sycamore spare him a nice low rung? Either way, this was a scene to behold. The chief of publicans could not have been a young man. He had to work his way up the swindler's list.

Can you hear him huffing and puffing his way up that tree? Clad in a robe, no less? Nothing like climbing a tree in a long dress. How long has it been since you climbed your last tree? Mine was in '65. My older sister and her friend were in our tree house, and I was spying on them. Why do I remember it so well? The branch fell. Thankfully, Zacchaeus didn't perch himself smugly on dead wood during his spy detail.

One of my favorite Old Testament verses is Jeremiah 29:13: "You will seek me and find me when you seek me with all your heart." The verse proved true in our story. So maybe the headline would read:

Traveling man requests chief publican's hospitality. I love verse 5! "When Jesus reached the spot, he looked up and said to him . . ." (Luke 19:5). Isn't that just like Jesus? He came down to us, all right, but He didn't come to look down on us — not even the least worthy of us. I can almost picture Christ working His way through the crowd as if totally oblivious to the short man in a tall tree.

"Jesus reached the spot." What spot? The spot of His divine appointment. He suddenly looked up with complete familiarity. "Zacchaeus," He said. How in the world did Jesus know his name? Maybe the same way He knew Nathaniel's a few years earlier. We could be under a fig tree, in a fig tree, or up a creek without a paddle; Jesus can still spot us. In fact, Jeremiah 1:4 tells us, "Before I formed you in the womb I knew you." Psalm 139:15 says our frame was not hidden from Him when He wove us together in our mother's womb. God carefully knitted those short legs of a certain tax collector knowing that one day he'd use them to scurry up a sycamore to see His Son.

"Zacchaeus, come down immediately. I must stay at your house today" (Luke 19:5).

Why must He? Perhaps because the Son lived to do the will of His Father, and His Father simply could not resist a display of interest in His Son. The Father and Son have an unparalleled mutual admiration society. That day Zacchaeus may have had a pair of skinned knees and elbows that endeared a special dose of the Father's affections.

Luke 19:6 says, "So he came down at once and welcomed him gladly." At once. I'm not sure God honors anything more in a man than a timely response to His Son. Revelation 3:20 tells us that Christ "stands at the door and knocks."

When was the last time you stood at a door and knocked . . . and knocked . . . and knocked . . . and knocked? Isn't the repetition even more frustrating when you know someone is home? I praise God that Christ is often willing to knock repeatedly. But that day on Jericho Drive, He didn't have to. Zacchaeus opened the door of his heart. No doubt the chief tax collector had many regrets in life, but among them wasn't the time he wasted between Christ's invitation and his welcome.

Chief publican caught in the act of rejoicing. Luke 19:6 tells us Zacchaeus not only came down at once, but also he welcomed Christ "gladly" — and with rejoicing. I don't think we're off base to imagine that his sudden display of glee was slightly out of character. The Word doesn't paint tax collectors as campus favorites. Don't you love how Christ can change an entire personality! Not only can He make the blind man see, but also He can perform a much greater feat: He can make the grump rejoice! Our church pews might not have so many empty seats if we'd invite Him to display such a feat in us. The good news coming from people in a bad mood undermines the message a tad.

Don't you think Christ delights in our glad responses, when we rejoice to obey Him? Let me be clear that God honors obedience even when we're kicking and screaming. Can you imagine how blessed He is when we're eager to do His will?

Noted preacher goes to dinner with a sinner. I think you'll enjoy the definition of the Greek word for "guest" in Luke 19:7. The word means "to loose or unloose what was before bound or fastened. To refresh oneself, to lodge or be a guest. It properly refers to travelers loosening their own burdens or those of their animals when they stayed at a house on a journey." In effect, Zacchaeus's hospitality said to Jesus: Come to my house and take a load off. Lay Your burden down and be refreshed. I'd be honored to have You. What an awesome thought that at the same time, Christ was saying to Zacchaeus: Let Me come into your house and take your load. Lay your burden down and be refreshed. I'd be honored to have you.

Jericho's richest resident gives half his possessions to the poor and repays debts with heavy interest. Luke 19:8 says Zacchaeus stood up and said to the Lord, "Look, Lord! Here and now, I give . . . and . . . pay back." One short man had never been taller. I don't hear a single shred of resistance, do you? He almost seems anxious to get rid of some things. Perhaps the wealth had been less a blessing and more a curse.

Proverbs 15:27 tells us, "A greedy man brings trouble to his family, / but he who hates bribes will live." Maybe Zacchaeus had come to see the trouble of valuing wealth over God.

Luke 19:8 records that "Zacchaeus stood up and said to the Lord, 'Look, Lord! Here and now I give half of my possessions to the poor, and if I have cheated anybody out of anything, I will pay back four times the amount.' " Here and now! The moment the Holy Spirit moves, I often sense a greater empowerment to respond generously. The more time I allow to pass, the more my self-ishness is apt to well up.

Please realize that Zacchaeus did not receive salvation because he gave to the poor and paid back everyone he owed. Rather, his actions were evidences that a true turn had occurred — the essence of authentic repentance. Earlier we talked about the probable change in the chief publican's demeanor as he responded with gladness. What is the most marked difference you see that Christ has made in your life, whether in demeanor or life practice?

God is amazing, isn't He? I don't remember much about my life before salvation because I was very young, but I can tell you that Christ's authority over my life has dramatically changed both my demeanor and life practices. I was overly sensitive and very fearful, and I would ten times rather have watched television than studied His Word. My character showed it too. I have a long way to go; but change is not only possible, it's also gloriously inevitable! He who began a good work will complete it (see Phil. 1:6)!

Student of God's Word, I have waited until now to ask you to reflect on some words from the previous story of the rich young man. Please observe Luke 18:24–25: "Jesus looked at him and said, 'How hard it is for the rich to enter the kingdom of God! Indeed, it is easier for a camel to go through the eye of a needle than for a rich man to enter the kingdom of God.'"

A rich young ruler. A chief publican. Both wealthy men. One walked away lost. Salvation lodged at the other's home. Give this question some time: What do you think the difference or differences might have been?

Salvation was not impossible for either one of those rich men. Both had the Son of God standing right there in front of them . . . willing and able to deliver. The difference was that one saw how much he had to lose. The other saw how much he had to gain.

Notice, Christ did not ask Zacchaeus to sell everything he had and give to the poor. Maybe because once he regarded Christ as life's true treasure, his wealth didn't mean nearly as much to him — which I believe is probably God's primary point to the rich.

A cynic might say, "Why did he only give away half to the poor?" It may have taken every other shekel to pay back all the folks he cheated! Anyway, God isn't looking to take away our possessions. He is looking to make His Son our greatest possession.

Do you have a few scrapes and bruises

from trying your hardest to see Jesus? A few tears in your best robe? Have you looked pretty silly to onlookers in your pursuit of Christ at times? If so, good for you.

Let's keep climbing and stretching to places with a view. He'll never be too crowded to spot us in the tree.

Chapter 43

Signs of His Coming

Luke 17:20–36; 21:5–38

"When these things begin to take place, stand up and lift up your heads, because your redemption is drawing near." (Luke 21:28)

I love eschatology, a fancy word for end-time events. Few subjects are more exciting to study than the glorious future awaiting us. Just don't lose your head over it! Bible topics are not meant to become our focus — not even critical themes like holiness and service. Jesus is our focus.

Remember, the enemy's primary goal is to disconnect us from the Head. Colossians 2:19 describes the kind of person who becomes more interested in spiritual things than the Spirit of Christ: "He has lost connection with the Head." That's why we must be very careful when dealing with exciting subjects like eschatology.

We need to assemble some clear facts about Christ's return, beginning with the fact that it will be unmistakable. Two Scriptures explain why. Luke 17:24 says the "day will be like the lightning, which flashes and lights up the sky from one end to the other." Luke 21:27 tells us that people "will see the Son of Man coming in a cloud with power and great glory."

Revelation 1:7 makes it clear that Christ's return to this earth will be impossible to miss: "He is coming with the clouds, and every eye will see him, even those who pierced him; and all the peoples of the earth will mourn because of him."

If you carefully compare Luke 21:7 with Matthew 24:3, you will see that the disciples asked about two events. I believe the disciples thought they were asking only one question. In reality they asked about two events separated by millennia — the destruction of the temple and the return of Christ. The temple was destroyed in A.D. 70. We await Jesus' return today.

I confess that I would like to shake those disciples and tell them to ask better questions. Parts of Jesus' discourse fit the events surrounding the destruction of the temple.

Some of His words can apply only to the Second Coming. Some leave us wondering. Why do you suppose Jesus didn't choose to be more clear about these events? Wouldn't you like to have a clearer road map or time-table? Whether or not we can answer all the questions, you and I can be sure we are living in an era on the kingdom calendar that will climax with the visible return of Jesus Christ.

You can see the significance of the dual question in Jesus' words: "This generation will certainly not pass away until all these things have happened" (Luke 21:32). The destruction of Jerusalem took place in the generation of Jesus' immediate followers, but He obviously was not referring exclusively to that specific generation. Rather, I believe He referred to the generation they represented. The original word for "generation" includes the meaning "a descent or genealogical line of ancestors or descendants." Jesus' words apply equally to the genealogical line through which His witness continues — His spiritual descendants. He will raise up spiritual descendants as His witnesses in every generation until His return. Let's emphasize a few facts concerning the end of the age and Christ's return:

Christians will long for Christ's return be-

fore the world ever sees it. Luke 17:22 intimates that one of the signs of His return will be a heightened longing. Christ is most assuredly returning, but the Word suggests not as soon as believers may hope as they look upon the tragic state of the earth. I experience that longing every time I watch a documentary on a starving, suffering people or hear a horrific report of violence and victimization. My only answer is to pray, "O, Lord Jesus, come quickly!" I don't doubt that you also have overwhelming moments when you deeply long for Christ to return and right all wrongs.

Many will come claiming to be Christ. In both Luke 17:23 and Luke 21:8, Christ warned that as the end of time as we know it hastens, the incidence of false-messiah claims will increase. The visibility of Christ's return is one reason why believers should never be susceptible to that kind of deception. When Christ returns, people won't have to read about it in the paper. Every eye will see Him. Any rumor of His return is automatically false. The whole world will know it.

Based on your experience, you may think this particular sign has not yet come to fruition. But in fact, false claims of the Messiah occur continually in many different places in the world. One of the largest cults in the United States teaches that Christ's return has already taken place. Every day people are led astray by false-messiah claims.

The world will display dramatic increases in depravity. One key word characterizing the hastening conclusion of this age is *increase*. God's Word describes end-time events like birth pains (see Matt. 24:8), meaning the evidences increase in frequency and strength. Matthew's version plainly characterizes the end of the age as marked by the increase of wickedness. "Because of the increase of wickedness, the love of most will grow cold" (Matt. 24:12).

Luke 17:25–28 states that the time of Christ's return will be like that of Noah or Lot. The Old Testament lends some important insight into the condition of the societies surrounding both Noah and Lot. Much human depravity involves sexual sin. I believe the end of time will parallel the days of Noah and Lot in many ways, but among them will be dramatic increase in perversity. Can anyone deny that we are living at a time of dramatic escalation in sexual sin? I believe our society is presently being sexually assaulted by the devil. I am convinced based on multiple characteristics of the last days that they have already begun. However, I'm certainly not date-setting Christ's return. Luke 12:40 makes it plain that forecasting a time of Christ's return is a waste of time. Jesus said, "the Son of Man will come at an hour when you do not expect him."

Although Christ doesn't want us date-setting, He does want us prepared. Scripture doesn't tell us how long the latter days will last, but we must be primed, like Noah, to be righteous people surrounded by a sea of unrighteousness. Much of it will center on sexuality. We have no other recourse than to radically refuse to cooperate and proactively choose to fight back. If we're going to be victorious in a latter-day society, we must become far more defensive and offensive in our warfare. Peter learned the hard way that we must be ready for Satan to attack. He gave us both excellent defensive and offensive advice.

Defensive: Peter wrote, "Be self-controlled and alert. Your enemy the devil prowls around like a roaring lion looking for someone to devour" (1 Pet. 5:8). Offensive: 2 Peter 3:11 tells us we "ought to live holy and godly lives." Let's proactively guard ourselves and our families! The devil is sly and extremely seductive. I believe God is calling upon His church to proact rather than react.

Depravity won't be the only increase. God's Word is clear that *the latter days will show a notable increase in violence and cataclysmic events.* Luke 21:10 tells us "nation will rise against nation, and kingdom against kingdom." Luke 21:12, 16 and Matthew 24:9 warn of the escalation in the persecution and martyrdom of Christians. All you have to do is peruse an issue of *Voice of the Martyrs*[1] to see how many Christians are dying for their faith. Those of us who live in the United States like to think persecution and martyrdom are not characteristic of our generation of believers, but we are mistaken. Parts of our body are suffering terribly in many areas of the world.

Had enough bad news for now? Me too! How about some good news?

The worldwide witness of the gospel of Jesus Christ will increase. Jesus said, "This gospel of the kingdom will be preached in the whole world as a testimony to all nations, and then the end will come" (Matt. 24:14).

Ours is such a God of mercy! He will not judge the wickedness of the earth until the testimony of His Son has reached every nation. What kind of simultaneous increase does this prophecy necessitate? An increase in missionaries! Dr. Jerry Rankin of the Southern Baptist International Mission Board told me that the number of people surrendering to foreign missions is increasing so dramatically that it can be explained no other way than as God fulfilling prophesy. Rejoice in the fact that there will be a soul harvest that no man can count of every tribe, tongue, and nation (see Rev. 7:9)!

According to Acts 1:8, the power to witness with the kind of effectiveness the last days will demonstrate comes from the Holy Spirit. That brings us to the last increase we'll highlight before we conclude our lesson with a spirit of celebration:

The activity of the Holy Spirit will increase. Acts 2:17 proclaims, "In the last days, God says, / I will pour out my Spirit on all people. / Your sons and daughters will prophesy, / your young men will see visions, / your old men will dream dreams." I believe God was hinting at an insatiable appetite to know and share God's Word! Beloved, your love for Scripture is evidence of that harvest. We haven't simply "wised up" in this generation by getting into God's Word. It's the outpouring of the Holy Spirit! Unprecedented numbers of people are becoming armed with the sword of the Spirit because we're entering an unprecedented spiritual war!

I'm so grateful to live during this awesome season on the kingdom calendar. In some ways, we live in the worst of times to date. But in other ways, we live in the best of times. The winds of true worship are blowing. The Spirit of God is moving. I don't want to hold on to my church pew and sing, "I shall not be moved." I want to move with Him!

Behold, He is doing a new thing. Shall we not know it? He's going to make a way in the wilderness and streams in the desert (Isa. 43:19).

What's a believer to do? Look for a stream and splash in it.

Part 9

The Lamb of God

We can be so thankful that our previous section concluded with the reminder of Christ's certain return, because the next part of our study involves His violent departure. We've known it was coming. Most of us know this part of the story better than any other event in Christ's earthly life. Yet as we view the events from street level, they will seem more traumatic. After all, we've walked beside Him now. Perhaps we'll better understand some of the feelings and reactions of Christ's very human disciples. We may even wonder if we would have hung around as long as they did. John 1:11 is going to jump to life before our very eyes: "He came to that which was his own, but his own did not receive him." Not only will we see them reject Him, but also we'll watch as jealousy awakens an insatiable thirst for blood. Hang in there, dear student. If we are to know Christ, we must intimately know the way of His cross.

Ask God to give you a fresh encounter with Him as we enter the next portion of our study. Discover each encounter as if you've never read it before. Beloved, God has something new to show you.

Chapter 44

An Available Conspirator

Luke 21:1–6, 37–38

Then Satan entered Judas, called Iscariot, one of the Twelve. (Luke 22:3)

We have arrived at the most critical juncture in our journey. Having accelerated through the parables, we now slow to a crawl, with magnifying glass in hand, to move through the final three chapters of Luke's Gospel. We will spend every remaining moment attempting to become eyewitnesses to the events at the conclusion of this Gospel.

Luke 9:51 records that "Jesus resolutely set out for Jerusalem." He performed many miracles and delivered vital messages along the way. Luke 19:28–48 indicates that Christ's presence was suddenly more than His opposition could stand. In Bethany Christ raised a man who had been dead four days. To the religious establishment, this astounding work was the proverbial straw that broke the camel's back.

I wish we could all sit together on the Mount of Olives and look at the Holy City for a while. Picture this in your mind. The garden where Christ retreated was on the hill directly across from the altar of sacrifice on the temple mount. Jesus taught at the temple during the day, then at night He retreated to the Mount of Olives, which overlooked the temple.

I recently sat near the place Jesus retreated. I couldn't help wondering what went through Jesus' mind during the days. On that temple mount God had provided the substitutionary offering for Isaac (see Gen. 22:1–19; see also 2 Chron. 3:1). Paul wrote that through Abraham God provided an "advance showing" of the gospel of grace (Gal. 3:8). "Fast forward" two thousand years to the scene where Christ was camped on the mountain parallel to the place of sacrifice at the temple. He resolved to fulfill the gospel that had been preached to Abraham. The time was imminent.

Let's take one verse at a time and wind our way through Luke 22:1–6.

Verse 1: "The Passover . . . was approaching." God's timing is never coincidental, but it was perhaps never more deliberate than in the events that unfolded in Luke 22. A new year on Israel's sacred calendar had just begun. The most sacred and critical year in all of human history was beginning — "the year of the Lord's favor" (Luke 4:19). The age of the completed redemptive work of God was unfolding. Can you imagine the anticipation in the unseen places? The kingdom of God and the kingdom of darkness were rising to a climactic point on the divine calendar.

Verse 2: They "were looking for some way to get rid of Jesus." The same verse also tells us the chief priests and the teachers of the law "were afraid of the people." I think they suddenly felt out of control. They were quite content as long as they were controlling the people, but all of a sudden popular opinion had swung in the direction of One who threatened their self-exalted positions.

I find this thought interesting: when Christ is close by, He has an uncanny way of making those people who don't know Him as Lord feel out of control. Since they would rather maintain control over themselves and those around them, they would just as soon get rid of Him. However, people who are submitted to His authority experience just the opposite feelings — security and peace.

When circumstances suddenly seem out of our control, our reactions may define the nature of our relationship with Christ. Rest assured the chief priests and teachers were feeling very out of control as Christ captivated the attention of their constituency. They needed a plan to deal with their problem. Yet, those same chief priests and teachers would soon discover the hard way how difficult it would be to eliminate their problem.

Verse 3: "Then Satan entered Judas, called Iscariot, one of the Twelve." I wonder if Judas knew he was inhabited the moment it happened. Perhaps the entrance of the unholy spirit has counterfeit similarities to the entrance of the Holy Spirit. Most of us do not remember "feeling" the Holy Spirit take up residency within us the moment we trusted Christ as our Savior, yet He soon bore some sign of witness through the fruit in our lives. We have no way of knowing if Judas "felt" the unholy spirit take up residence within him, but it certainly wasn't long until the fruit of wickedness was revealed.

If you are new to the study of Scripture, the thought that Satan could enter a disciple might be terrifying. Please understand that just because a person appears to follow

Christ doesn't necessarily mean he has placed saving faith in Him. Keep in mind that Satan entered Judas as opposed to Peter, James, or John, even though at times each of them had certainly revealed weakness of character. Satan was able to enter Judas because he was available. Judas followed Christ for several years without ever giving his heart to Him. The authentic faith of the others protected them from demon possession, albeit not oppression, just as it protects us. Judas proved to be a fraud, whether or not his tenure began with better intentions.

Verse 4: "Judas . . . discussed . . . how he might betray Jesus." In other words, Judas had a plan. I'd like to suggest that it wasn't one he devised on his own. I believe the order of events in Luke 22:3–4 implies he had a little help from his new inhabitant.

Hear this in high volume: Satan has a plan. Ephesians 6:11–12 issues an emphatic "heads up" about the devil's schemes. The evil one methodically seeks to work in your life and mine. Satan's methodical planning counterfeits the awesome work of God. Just as our God has a holy plan that He executes in an orderly fashion, the enemy of our souls has an unholy plan he also executes in an orderly fashion.

Satan hasn't enjoyed success for centuries because he's stupid. When I recall the technical procedures he's enacted in my life, I am stunned at his working knowledge of my fairly well-disguised vulnerabilities. By disguised I don't mean just those vulnerabilities I hid from others; I mean some that were even hidden from me. Something new I learned about him is that he possesses a surprising amount of patience to weave seemingly harmless events into disasters while his subject often never sees it coming.

What is our defense? The Word tells us not to be ignorant! Wising up to what the Word has to say about Christ's authority and the devil's schemes has empowered me to throw some holy kinks into Satan's unholy plans for my life.

Verse 5: "They were delighted and agreed to give him money." These events not only demonstrate that Satan is a planner but also that he is a user. Observe how Satan used Judas. He convinced Judas that the betrayal was for the fraudulent disciple's own benefit. Judas had a weakness for money, so that's what Satan used.

One of Satan's most successful tricks is to convince his puppets that they have much to gain. In reality Satan makes no real friends. He never uses anyone that he does not ultimately betray. There won't be buddies in hell. Satan will have betrayed every inhabitant by using his or her own self-interest.

Judas is not the only person Satan used in this scene. Although we are not told that he "entered" the chief priests and teachers, he certainly used them. Again, he capitalized on their personal lusts. He used their appetite for power and control to make them willing parties in an unholy alliance.

Luke 22:5 records that the religious leaders "were delighted" with Judas's proposal and that they "agreed to give him money." They weren't just agreeing with a thief and a betrayer. They were cutting a deal with the devil. The thought sends chills down my spine. Please keep in mind we're talking about the leaders of the religious community. We who fill the church pews cannot afford to be ignorant about the devil's schemes. Hell's most effective attacks often are the result of deals religious people unknowingly make with the devil.

Verse 6: "He consented, and watched for an opportunity." Don't you think the concept of Judas's "consenting" is interesting? After all, it was his idea. Sometimes I think that's how Satan works. He tries to make us think the plan was our idea all along, and he's just doing what he can to help. Anything that betrays Jesus in our lives is Satan's idea. Anything. He doesn't have to inhabit people to tempt them to betray Christ. The religious leaders in this scene are proof. Remember, Satan capitalizes on our lusts — whether for greed, power, control, or sensual pleasure. Let's be careful not to sell out for personal gain, betraying the fact that we have been called to be Christ's disciples. Make sure Satan knows your cooperation can't be "bought."

The curtain drops on this troubling scene as Judas watched and waited for the perfect opportunity while the evil one plotted. Satan is a planner and a user. He seeks opportunities to use people to fulfill his plan. He puts on a coat and tie, slicks back his hair, and offers whatever he can to help humans make a personal profit. He's the consummate counterfeit wealth manager. People invest with the intention of drawing high interest, and Satan ends up extorting the profit. He's the betrayer's betrayer. Buyer beware.

Chapter 45

The Last Supper

Luke 22:7–23

He took bread, gave thanks and broke it, and gave it to them, saying, "This is my body given for you; do this in remembrance of me." (Luke 22:19)

On a fresh spring morning, the sun rose over the Mount of Olives and cast a spotlight on a city preparing for the most cherished celebration on the Jewish calendar. No other day held the same significance as the fourteenth of Nisan. The Passover feast had arrived.

Scripture assures us Christ knew everything that would happen to Him. I wonder if He closed His eyes a single time that Passover eve? Jesus' vantage point gave Him a bird's-eye view of the temple and all the pilgrims entering the city. In fact, when the sun

441

rose that morning, it appropriately rose right over His head. Malachi 4:2 (KJV) says, "the Sun of righteousness [would soon] arise with healing in his wings." On this day the Son of righteousness began His walk to the cross. Surely Christ's tent of flesh had never been less comfortable to wear.

As the last spoonfuls of sand slipped through the hourglass, surely the blood pumped harder through His veins, over-working His heart. Would God have allowed Him to forego the tightness of dreadful anticipation in His chest? Would He have interfered with His Son's experiencing the full gamut of the human body's involuntary anticipation? Did God allow His Son's hands to shake? Oh yes, I think Christ felt every bit of it.

Dread is not sin. Disobedience is. I believe Christ's humanity had never been more constricting or alarming. And it was only just beginning. The people of Israel had observed the Passover for approximately fifteen centuries. But that particular night, a change occurred. Christ not only observed the ancient memorial of the Passover, He instituted something new.

That Jesus had given much thought to the approaching feast is evident in Luke 22:15: "I have eagerly desired to eat this Passover with you before I suffer." If we were to read the statement with the strong double construction of the original language, it would more accurately be reflected by the words, "with desire I have desired."[1] Even if we never fully grasp the significance of the evening, our perception can be deeply marked by the fact that Jesus considered it to be enormously profound.

You probably remember the story. Christ sent Peter and John to prepare the Passover meal in the room He had chosen. He told them they would find the room by following a man who carried a water jar (see Luke 22:10–11). Nothing about the evening was trivial or accidental. With the same omniscience He exerted to arrange the circumstances of the chosen venue, Christ also chose His two ambassadors. Until now, we have rarely seen Peter and John as a pair. We have seen Christ encounter each of them individually, but when they were grouped apart from the Twelve, it was almost always as a threesome with James, John's brother.

I don't believe Christ simply glanced up, saw Peter and John, and decided they'd be as good a choice as anyone to prepare for the Passover. Quite the contrary, this profound work was prepared in advance for them to do (see Eph. 2:10). It's likely the two men may have wished someone else had been chosen for the tasks, some of which were usually assigned to women. The Passover involved a fairly elaborate meal with a very specific setting. They may have grumbled, as we often do. Why? Because we may have no idea as to the significance of the work God has called us to do. Give some thought to the preparations Peter and John made.

You can read about the original Passover in Exodus 12:1–14. The meal involved three symbolic foods to be eaten during every observance: "meat roasted over the fire, along with bitter herbs, and bread made without yeast" (Exod. 12:8).

The bitter herbs symbolized the bitterness of the suffering memorialized in the Passover observance: the bitterness of slavery, the bitterness of death, and the bitterness of an innocent lamb's substitution. The herbs, eaten intermittently during the meal, would intentionally bring tears to their eyes as a reminder of the associated grief.

While every part of the meal was highly symbolic, it had no meaning at all without the lamb. The most important preparation Peter and John made was the procuring and preparing of the Passover lamb. The detailed preparation involving the lamb would soon be fulfilled in Jesus Christ. They may not have grasped the significance of it at the time, but eventually they "got it."

Peter and John are the only two of the Twelve who were recorded referring to Jesus as the Lamb. Many years later Peter would write of Jesus that we were redeemed "with the precious blood of Christ, a lamb without blemish or defect. He was chosen before the creation of the world, but was revealed in these last times for your sake" (1 Pet. 1:19–20). For John's part, you can read Revelation 5 for what I think is the most majestic passage in Scripture about the Lamb of God.

Is it coincidence that only these two apostles wrote about Jesus as the Lamb? Not on your life. Christ's ultimate goal in any work He assigns to us is to reveal Himself, either through or to us. The Holy Spirit used the tasks He assigned them that day to reveal to them the Lamb of God. The images and remembrances were deeply engraved in John's mind. Many years later God inspired him to refer to Jesus as the Lamb at least thirty times in Revelation. Beloved, the tasks God gives you are never trivial. More than anything else, His desire is to reveal Himself to you and through you.

When the hour came, Jesus and His apostles reclined at the table. The Passover was a celebration for families and those closest to them. Christ was surrounded by His closest family. They may have been weak, self-centered, and full of unfounded pride, but they were His. He desired to spend this time with them.

Capture this meal with your imagination. I think we've inaccurately pictured the last meal as moments spent over the bread and the wine. Christ and His disciples observed the entire Passover meal together. Then He instituted the new covenant, represented by the bread and the wine.

As they gathered around the table at sundown, Christ took the father role in the observance. Soon after they gathered, He poured the first of four cups of wine and asked everyone to rise from the table. He then lifted His cup toward heaven and recited the Kiddush, or prayer of sanctification, which would have included these words or something very close: "Blessed art Thou, O Lord our God, King of the universe, Who createst the fruit of the vine. Blessed art Thou, O Lord our God, Who hast chosen us for Thy service from among the nations . . . Blessed art Thou, O Lord our God, King of the universe, Who hast kept us in life, Who hast preserved us, and hast enabled us to reach this season."[2] This is very likely the blessing He recited in Luke 22:17.

If Christ and His disciples followed tradition, they took the first cup of wine, asked the above blessing, observed a ceremonial washing, and broke the unleavened bread. These practices were immediately followed by an enactment of Exodus 12:26–27. The youngest child at the observance asks the traditional Passover questions, provoking the father to tell the story of the exodus. Early church tradition cited John as the youngest apostle.[3] In all likelihood, John assumed the role of the youngest child in the family, asking the traditional questions that provoked Christ to tell the story of the Passover. Many scholars believe John may have been the one who asked the questions at the last supper because of his position at the table. John 13:23 tells us John was reclining next to Christ.

The four cups of wine served at the Passover meal represented the four expressions, or "I wills" of God's promised deliverance in Exodus 6:6–7. At this point in the meal, Christ poured the second cup of wine and narrated the story of Israel's exodus in response to the questions. Oh, friend, can you imagine? Christ, the Lamb of God, sat at their table and told the redemption story! He recounted the story as only He could have — and then, at the very next sundown — He fulfilled it! Oh, how I pray He will tell it again for all of us to hear when we take it together in the kingdom!

The One sent "to proclaim freedom for the prisoners" (Luke 4:18) told the story of captives set free, spared from death by the blood of the Lamb. Oh, the perfect plan of redemption, secured before God ever breathed a soul into man. Do you see, beloved? The creation of humankind would have been pointless without this awesome plan of redemption. Before we ever lived to see our first temptation, God procured a "way of escape" for all who would choose it. Indeed, God sealed the redemptive decision and named Christ the Lamb slain before the creation of the world (see Rev. 13:8). Hallelujah!

They ate the meal between the second and third cups. Note the time frame recorded in Luke 22:20: "After the supper he took the cup, saying, 'This cup is the new covenant in my blood, which is poured out for you.' "

Although all four cups would have been observed at the last supper, not all four cups are specified in Luke's Gospel. We know, however, exactly which cup is specified in Luke 22:20 because of its place of observance during the meal. The third cup was traditionally taken after the supper was eaten. It is represented by the third "I will" statement of God recorded in Exodus 6:6: "I will redeem you with an outstretched arm and with mighty acts of judgment."

This is the cup of redemption. I am convinced this cup is also the symbolic cup to which Christ referred only an hour or so later in the garden of Gethsemane when He asked God to "take this cup from me" (Luke 22:42). This was a cup of which He could partake only with outstretched arms upon the cross.

The imminent fulfillment of the cup of redemption signaled the release of the new covenant that would be written in blood. We know Christ did not literally drink this third cup because He stated in Luke 22:18 that He would not drink of another cup until the coming of the kingdom of God. Instead of drinking the cup, He would do something of sin-shattering significance. He would, in essence, become the cup and pour out His life for the redemption of man.

That most holy weekend, the Passover was completely fulfilled. "For Christ, our Passover lamb, has been sacrificed" (1 Cor.

5:7). God instructed the Hebrew people that they were to continue the Passover feast, celebrating it as an ordinance (see Exod. 12:14). As Gentile believers, we have much to learn and appreciate about the Passover, but we have been commanded to remember the death of Christ every time we observe the Lord's Supper (see 1 Cor. 11:26).

Christ never took anything more seriously than the cup of redemption He faced that last Passover supper. His body would soon be broken so that the Bread of life could be distributed to all who would sit at His table. The wine of His blood would be poured into the new wineskins of all who would partake. It was time's perfect night — a night when the last few stitches of a centuries-old Passover thread would be woven onto the canvas of earth in the shape of a cross. Sit and reflect.

> O perfect Lamb of Passover,
> Let me not quickly run.
> Recount to me the blessed plot,
> Tell how the plan was spun
> That I, a slave of Egypt's lusts,
> A prisoner of dark dread,
> Could be condemned unto a cross
> And find You nailed instead.

Chapter 46

Sifted like Wheat

Luke 22:14–38

"Simon, Simon, Satan has asked to sift you as wheat." (Luke 22:31)

Let's pull up our chairs to the Passover table. The meal has been eaten. The third cup of wine has been distributed among the disciples as a representation of His blood poured out for them. Rather than sip the cup of redemption, Christ soon will become the drink offering.

Once again I am caught off guard by the awesome love of Christ. He knows the battles we fight with our egos. He knows our every secret vulnerability. He knows the outcome of every conflict. At a time when His own imminent suffering could understandably have consumed His attentions, we find Christ still thinking of the others.

Let's climb the stairs to the upper room and once more sit down at His table.

I am intrigued by the fact that the disciples had no idea Judas was the betrayer. Luke 22:23 tells us the disciples questioned themselves about who the betrayer might be. Obviously, Christ treated Judas no differently than the others. Jesus fellowshipped with him, ate with him, prayed with him, laughed with him, and loved him as the rest . . . knowing all the while Judas would betray Him. Amazing.

I don't know about you, but if I worked every day with someone I knew had no affection for me and would betray me, I'd have a little trouble not differentiating. Oh, how I want to be like Jesus, but how I resist the painful conflicts that hasten the process!

Are you like me? Do you want to be made like Him — but more through His victories than His sufferings? Thankfully, we have a Savior who is willing to steadfastly walk with us even when we take three steps forward and two steps back. We'll see the colors of that willingness painted like a mural on the walls of the upper room.

If we often find ourselves in contrast to Jesus' perfect character, we're not so unlike His original disciples. Their inability at the Passover table to pinpoint who was the worst among them led to a dispute over who was the greatest. Had not Christ already dealt with them over this issue? Before we are too judgmental of the disciples, however, we'd better see if their sandals fit our feet. I ask this of you gently — but of myself a little less gently: how many lessons have we learned from Christ the first time He presented them?

I suppose if the disciples' sandals fit our feet, we'd better wear them. But, praise God, not for long. The remedy to our ego problems isn't found in simply admitting we're self-centered, ego-driven status seekers who, like the original disciples, are slow to learn and quick to judge. "Guilty as charged" only condemns us. Left alone, it does nothing to change us.

When we recognize that the disciples' sandals fit our feet, let's allow Christ to kneel in front of us, slip them off, and wash our feet. Oh, how we need Jesus to minister humility to us. Without it, He will vastly limit how much He ministers through us. John 13 tells us how Jesus laid aside His garments and washed the disciples' feet.

As effective as the lesson was, Christ still hadn't settled the issue of greatness. He knew that the matter was so critical that He would need to prove on a field trip what

He had taught in class. I could kick myself for forcing lessons into field trips instead of learning them in the classroom, but, I don't mind telling you, field trips are effective! I fear the lesson on greatness is rarely learned in the classroom alone.

Within hours, each of those disciples would encounter just how "great" they were. All would desert Christ and flee (see Matt. 26:56). However, the lesson taught and demonstrated in the upper (class)room, then confirmed during the field trip, would eventually "stick." Christ turned those eleven status seekers into humble servants.

Again I find myself so amazed at the character of Christ. Just when we wouldn't have blamed Him if He had thrown water all over them, He washed their feet. And just when they argued over who was the greatest, He paid them their greatest compliment. Luke 22:28 records His words, "You are those who have stood by me in my trials."

Then He continued, in essence, "you can kneel and wash a few feet now, because one day you're going to sit on thrones in my kingdom!" He really didn't owe them that kind of positive motivation, did He?

Please don't lose sight of the fact that as surely as Christ knew Judas would betray Him, He knew all those disciples would desert Him. He knew every move each disciple would make. Immediately following the conferral of the kingdom, He directed His attention to Peter and said, "Simon, Simon, Satan has asked to sift you as wheat" (v. 31).

The word *you* in verse 31 is the plural while the word *you* in verse 32 is singular. The implication is that Satan asked to sift the disciples as wheat in verse 31 and that Christ specified Peter's own encounter in verse 32. I tend to think the Scriptures imply Christ permitted Satan to attack Peter with greater force than the others. If so, we might want to ask ourselves why. I believe these few verses intimate several reasons.

1. Peter was the natural leader among the disciples. Christ seemed to be singling him out as a leader in Luke 22:31 as He directed the statement concerning all the disciples (plural "you") to Peter: " 'Simon, Simon, Satan has asked to sift [all of] you [disciples] as wheat.' " Very likely, Christ thought that Peter, as a leader among the disciples, could either take or needed the extra heat. I have a hunch both apply. Please be encouraged that Satan can't just presume to sift a believer like wheat. I believe this precedent suggests he must acquire permission from Christ. (Compare Job 1.) Christ will not grant the devil permission to do anything that can't be used for God's glory and our good — if we let it.

I'd also like to believe, based on the same precedent, that if Christ gives the enemy a little extra leash where we're concerned, He prays for us. The word for "prayed" in Luke 22:32 is *deomai,* meaning "to make one's need known." This particular word for prayer involves the petition for what one lacks. I don't think Christ's petition for Peter's need referred only to what he needed to be victorious in this sifting season. I believe Christ saw that this sifting season itself was something Peter needed.

Although I can think of many things someone in Peter's position might lack, humility as a servant of God and alertness as a target of the enemy most readily come to my mind. Peter was a natural leader and might have led in the flesh . . . if he were not taught its terrible weakness and danger. In about fifty-one days, Christ would transform him into a powerhouse among the disciples (see Acts 2). He needed a crash course only a fierce sifting could supply.

Those in critical positions aren't the only ones who can benefit from a good sifting. Please know if ever I put on a shoe that fits, it would be this one. I, too, as a servant, badly needed a sifting and, I assure you, God was faithful to permit it. Being sifted like wheat is not your regular brand of temptation. It's an all-out onslaught by the enemy to destroy you and cause you to quit. It surfaces what you detest most in yourself and reveals the ugliness of self. Not everyone has or needs such an experience.

The horror of my sifting season remains as real as yesterday, but, I pray, so is the grain left behind. The method of sifting wheat is to put it through a sieve and shake it until the chaff, little stones, and perhaps some tares, surface. The purpose is that the actual grain can be separated and ground into meal. You see, Satan's goal in sifting is to make us a mockery by showing us to be all chaff and no wheat. Christ, on the other hand, permits us to be sifted to shake out the real from the unreal, the trash from the true. The wheat that proves usable is authentic grain from which Christ can make bread.

Praise Christ's faithful name! Satan turned Peter's field trip into a field day, but he still couldn't get everything about Peter to come up chaff. Satan's plan backfired. He surfaced some serious chaff, but Christ let Peter have a good look at it. Then Christ blew the chaff away, took those remaining grains, and demonstrated His baking skills. Christ had a few other reasons for allowing Peter to be sifted like wheat.

2. Christ knew that Peter would turn back. "But I have prayed for you, Simon, that your faith may not fail. And when you have turned back . . ." (Luke 22:32). Not *if,* but *when.* We're somewhat like books Satan can read only from the outside. His book review is limited to assumptions he makes about what's inside, based on what he reads on our "book jackets." He cannot read the inside of us as Christ can.

Satan observed Peter's overconfidence and propensity toward pride. He surmised that, when the sifting came, every page would come up chaff. He was wrong. Christ knew Peter's heart. He knew that underneath Peter's puffed-up exterior was a man with a genuine heart for God. Jesus knew that Peter could deny Christ to others, but he could not deny Christ to himself. He would be back — a revised edition with a new jacket.

3. Christ knew how Peter's return and "revision" could be used for others. "And when you have turned back, strengthen your brothers"(v. 32). From falling, Peter was about to learn how to stand. Peter would indeed fall, but his faith would not fail. He would use everything Christ taught him to strengthen his brothers. You see, Christ didn't want to take the leader out of Simon Peter. He just wanted to take Simon Peter out of the leader. His goal was to let Satan sift out all the Simon-stuff so Christ could use what was left: a humble jar of clay with no confidence in his flesh.

Not everyone has to learn to stand by falling. Better ways to learn exist, but I'm afraid that I learned a similar way. I finally learned to stand on Christ's two feet because my feet of clay turned out to be so unstable.

I was not so unlike Peter. I was young when I surrendered my life to Christ and completely confident that nothing could shake my commitment. Excuse my bluntness, but I was an idiot. I cannot recall ever learning a more difficult lesson than that which my own sifting season taught me, but neither can I recall a lesson more deeply ingrained. Many years have passed, and I still do not live a day without remembering it and fearing another departure from Christ's authority more than I fear death.

I wouldn't wish a sifting on a single soul, but if that's what a life of harvest requires, may God use it so thoroughly that the enemy ends up being sorry he ever asked permission. Beloved, commitments can be shaken, but Christ cannot. When the shakedown comes, may the fresh winds of God's Spirit blow away the chaff until all that is left is the bread of life.

Chapter 47

The Kiss of Betrayal

Luke 22:39–46

Jesus asked him, "Judas, are you betraying the Son of Man with a kiss?" (Luke 22:48)

Tens of thousands of Jews celebrated the Passover that year in Jerusalem. For many, the year's observance was indistinct from the last. They had no idea that nearby the Lamb of God lifted the cup of redemption and offered it to all. In the upper room the disciples' stomachs were full, their recollections rekindled, and their feet washed by the Son of man. "Having loved his own who were in the world, he now showed them the full extent of his love" (John 13:1). The One who created time submitted Himself to it. In the same perfect order that the heavens and earth were created, salvation's story must unfold like a book already written . . . penned before the foundation of the world. The Spirit of God blew the next page open to the chapter called "Agony." The garden awaited.

"When they had sung a hymn, they went out to the Mount of Olives" (Matt. 26:30). Jesus singing! How I would love to hear that sound. When He sang, did the angels of heaven hush to His voice? Or did they cease their song and join in His? Did He sing tenor? bass? Did Christ and His disciples sing in harmony, or did they all sing the melody? Did Jesus sing often, or was this a moment of rarity?

How fitting that on this very night Christ, the coming King, would give voice to songs penned centuries earlier just for Him. Traditionally, every Seder or Passover celebration ended with the latter half of the Hallel, Psalms 115–118. Very likely Christ and His disciples sang from these psalms.

Imagine the Son of God singing these words as the seconds ticked toward the cross.

How can I repay the LORD
   for all his goodness to me?
I will lift up the cup of salvation
   and call on the name of the LORD.

I will fulfill my vows to the LORD
in the presence of all his people.
(Ps. 116:12–14)

The LORD is with me; I will not be afraid.
What can man do to me?
The LORD is with me; he is my helper.
I will look in triumph on my enemies.
(Ps. 118:6–7)

The stone the builders rejected
has become the capstone;
The LORD has done this,
and it is marvelous in our eyes.
This is the day the LORD has made;
let us rejoice and be glad in it.
(Ps. 118:22–24)

How many times have you sung "This is the day that the Lord has made"? Did you realize that in context the psalm speaks specifically of the day Christ was facing? The day "the stone the builders rejected" became "the capstone." Imagine Christ, fully aware of all that was coming, singing, "This is the day the Lord has made."

Whatever Christ sang as the Passover meal concluded that night, the words had significance for Him that the others could never have comprehended. I wonder if His voice quivered with emotion? Or did He sing with exultation? Perhaps He did both, just as you and I have done at terribly bitter-sweet moments when our faith exults while our sight weeps. One thing we know: Christ, above all others, knew that He was singing more than words. That night He sang the score of His destiny.

Now if you have your Bible with you, I'd like to ask you to read all three of the synoptic records of Christ's agony in the garden so you can focus your lens to the panoramic view. Matthew's Gospel probably offers the most detail. Read Matthew 26:36–46. Then compare Mark 14:32–42 and Luke 22:39–46.

Without Mark's Gospel, we would not know Christ cried out to His Father using the name, "Abba." I don't often give you an extensive quote, but this one captured my soul with rich meditation; I hope it will yours.

Abba is originally . . . a word derived from baby-language. When a child is weaned, "it learns to say 'abba (daddy) and 'imma (mummy)." . . . Also used by adult sons and daughters. . . . 'abba acquired the warm, familiar ring which we may feel in such an expression as "dear father." Nowhere in the entire wealth of devotional literature produced by ancient Judaism do we find 'abba being used as a way of addressing God. The pious Jew knew too much of the great gap between God and man to be free to address God with the familiar word used in everyday family life. . . . We find only one example of 'abba used in reference to God. It occurs in a story recorded in the Babylonian Talmud: "When the world had need of rain, our teachers used to send the schoolchildren to Rabbi Hanan ha Nehba [end of the 1st cent. B.C.], and they would seize the hem of his cloak and call out to him: 'Dear father ('abba), dear father ('abba), give us rain.' He said before God: 'Sovereign of the world, do it for the sake of these who cannot distinguish between an 'abba who can give rain and an 'abba who can give no rain.' "[1]

When Christ Jesus fell to His face and cried out, "Abba, Father," He cried out to the Abba who can give rain. The sovereign of the world was His Daddy. Everything was possible for Him . . . including removing the cup of dread.

Never minimize the moment by thinking

God couldn't have removed the cup. Do not subtract God's freedom of choice from this picture. God could have chosen to reject the way of the cross. After all, He is the sovereign of the universe.

That God could have stopped the process yet didn't is a matchless demonstration of love. Can you think of anyone for whom you'd watch your only child be tortured to death? " 'Abba, Father,' he said, 'everything is possible for you. Take this cup from me' " (Mark 14:36).

The request Christ placed before the Father ought to make us catch our breath. It ascended to heaven through wails of grief. God's beloved was overwhelmed with sorrow to the point of death. Luke's Gospel tells us His sweat dropped like blood, a condition almost unheard of except when the physical body is placed in more stress and grief than it was fashioned to handle. Do we think God sat upon His throne unmoved?

Our hearts ought to miss a beat. Christ could have walked past the cross. He could have — but He didn't. Luke 22:47 tells us, "While he was still speaking a crowd came up." Imagine the scene they walked into that night.

Please try to grasp Christ's physical condition just before the crowd headed up the

Mount of Olives to seize Him. Like a body that rejects a transplanted organ, the human body of Jesus Christ was practically tearing itself apart. The full throttle of divine impact and emotion was almost more than one human body could endure. The stress had nearly turned Him inside out. I do not make this point to emphasize His weakness. Quite the contrary. In fact I find the scene recorded in John 18:6 portrays His incredible power. When Jesus told the crowd, "I am he," even overwhelmed with sorrow to the point of death, the proclaimed presence of Jesus Christ knocked the mob to the ground.

Dear sweet Jesus. We really have no idea who You are, do we? Your God-ness could not be diminished for a moment, in or out of that prison of flesh. Lord, don't let us forget. You, who submitted Yourself to the hands of sinful men, were very God.

As we allow the Holy Spirit to escort us to a place of fresh insight and gratitude, we're considering not only what God has done that He didn't have to do, but also what He didn't do that He could have. God deserves our praise both for what He has done and what He hasn't done. Jesus clearly stated that He could have called twelve legions of angels (Matt. 26:53).

The reminder of Christ's immense power and complete God-ness makes Judas's betrayal even more despicable. Go back with me and capture the scene. Luke 22:47 tells us Judas "approached Jesus to kiss him." With the precision of a doctor, Luke shared his version of the events in the garden, but Matthew, the tax collector, collected evidence far more like that of a lawyer establishing premeditation. He tells us: "Going at once to Jesus, Judas said, 'Greetings, Rabbi!' and kissed him" (Matt. 26:49). Isn't it enough to make you nauseous? Betrayal is bad enough. Betrayal with a comrade's kiss on the cheek is almost too much to stomach.

Few things rend the heart like betrayal. Christ's knowing eyes ripped the smiling facade off Judas so fast his adrenaline probably plummeted. I would be interested to know just how long Satan hung around in Judas's body. The devil is such a user. He probably dumped the fraud the moment the betrayal was complete. Imagine Judas being on his own with the realization of what he had just done. It proved to be more than he could stand. The devil had not "made him do it," but he had certainly empowered him. Another inside job — Satan's favorite. In the most literal sense, Judas came near to Christ with his mouth that night, but his heart remained far from Him (see Isa. 29:13).

Our lesson concludes dramatically. Peter sliced off an ear before the rest of the disciples could even ask if they should draw swords. If Christ were not omniscient, I could almost picture Him thinking, *Remind me not to let Peter hold the sword next time.*

Luke never names the sword-wielding disciple, but Peter's friend John tattles on him. I can almost hear Peter: "I was going for his head!" The servant must have seen the sword coming and tilted his head to his left shoulder, leaving only his right ear exposed to the blade. I don't doubt he got a shave and a haircut too.

Dr. Luke is careful to tell us that Jesus "touched the man's ear and healed him" (22:51). Don't overlook this action. Reflect on the fact that the servant of the high priest knew without a doubt that Jesus was no ordinary man, let alone a vicious criminal. Do you realize how many people confronted the truth that this lynching was wrong as they came face-to-face with right? Only heaven knows how many people never slept peacefully again.

The hour had come — the one in which darkness would reign (see Luke 22:53).

Even in the dark, however, many knew that what they were doing was wrong. One thing about God: we can always depend on Him to turn the light back on. "He will bring to light what is hidden in darkness and will expose the motives of men's hearts. At that time each will receive his praise from God" (1 Cor. 4:5).

Chapter 48

A Serious Case of Denial

Luke 22:47–62

The Lord turned and looked straight at Peter. Then Peter remembered the word the Lord had spoken to him: "Before the rooster crows today, you will disown me three times." (Luke 22:61)

Our next scene doesn't "unfold" — it bursts with a moment so highly charged that our minds must work overtime to comprehend it. Like a film clip of frenzied activity, it must be viewed over and over to absorb the details. If God were to raise a video camera above the city of Jerusalem on this night of nights, we would see several scenes within a scene. We will attempt to capture some of those.

We know that Christ and His disciples dramatically encountered the entire detachment of soldiers, priests, and Pharisees somewhere on the Mount of Olives. While Luke's Gospel simply says they seized Him and led Him away, John's Gospel gets a little more specific. John 18:12–14 tells us that a detachment of soldiers arrested and bound Jesus. They took Him first to Annas, the father-in-law of Caiaphas, the high priest. Then John adds the note that "Caiaphas was the one who had advised the Jews that it would be good if one man died for the people" (v. 14).

Did you catch the terminology? This huge detachment of soldiers bound Jesus (see John 18:12). They couldn't know that all the ropes in Israel couldn't bind Him unless He chose to be bound. The time had come for Him to submit to a plan that included them. Jesus did not need to be bound. He resolutely set out for Jerusalem for such a time as this.

John's Gospel tells us they first took Christ to Annas. The trials can be very confusing, especially because they are not all recorded distinctively in each of the Gospels. Keep in mind that Christ was subjected to six trials — three religious and three civil. Perhaps the following list of trials in the order of their occurrence will help. You'll probably need to glance back at it several times before our focus on the hours leading up to Christ's crucifixion concludes.

Religious Trials

Before Annas:	John 18:12–14,19–23
Before Caiaphas, Sanhedrin:	Matthew 26:57–68; Mark 14:53–65; Luke 22:54, 63–65; John 18:24
Before the Sanhedrin alone:	Matthew 27:1–2; Mark 15:1; Luke 22:66–71

Civil Trials

Before Pilate:	Matthew 27:2, 11–14; Mark 15:1–5; Luke 23:1–7; John 18:28–38
Before Herod:	Luke 23:6–12
Before Pilate a second time:	Matthew 27:15–26; Mark 15:6–15; Luke 23:13–25

Annas was high priest when John the Baptist began his ministry (see Luke 3:2). By this time he had been deposed and succeeded by his five sons, one grandson, and

473

son-in-law, but still he was extremely influential. Christ was first taken to Annas, who then sent Him to Caiaphas, his son-in-law, the high priest who presided over these proceedings.

God obviously considered Peter's denial so significant that He inspired its record in all four Gospels. We will, therefore, give ample attention to this "scene within a scene." Luke's Gospel picks up in Luke 22:54 at the house of Caiaphas.

I am convinced that one reason God placed the account of Peter's denial in all four Gospels is so we'd sober to the reality that if Peter could deny Christ, any of us could. Never lose sight of the fact that Peter was certain he could not be "had." Take in these words with a fresh awareness: Peter denied he even knew Christ. Not once. Not twice. But three times. Denying Christ is huge.

At Christ's arrest the disciples scattered like scared rabbits. John 18:15–16 tells us Peter and John followed Christ to the high priest's house, but Peter had to wait outside. He was not known to the high priest as John was. Strangely, Peter's presence suggests a confession of sorts that he knew Christ, but he denied it with his mouth.

Notice the other nine were nowhere to be

found. Followers of Christ can deny they know Him in a variety of ways. Although I have never said, "I don't know Him," with my mouth, I've no doubt suggested something similar with my life and even at times with my silence.

Do you think the blows Christ later endured from the whip stung any more than Peter's denial? Don't minimize the sin in that courtyard. Peter adamantly and repeatedly denied even knowing Christ.

The following elements of the denial seem particularly significant to me. As we consider each one, I hope we'll recognize those factors that set Peter up for failure so we can avoid similar pitfalls.

1. Peter was willing to kill for Jesus, but he was reluctant to die for Him. Keep in mind the time element. Only an hour or so before Peter denied Christ to save his own skin, he had drawn a sword and cut off a man's ear. Maybe Peter's haste to use the sword was not just motivated by his desire to defend Jesus but by his concern to defend himself.

Nothing displays our self-love like a crisis. Christ's disciples, both then and now, are called to live above that human baseline of self-importance. Remember that Christ had called Peter and His disciples to deny themselves and take up the cross daily (Luke 9:23). If Peter had denied himself, he would not have denied Christ. God had a future mission for Peter, so He would not have allowed Peter's self-denial to have disastrous consequences. Peter, of course, had no way of knowing that confessing Christ would not lead to his capture or death, but Christ had unquestionably called him to follow at all costs.

We can "forget" about ourselves because Christ never forgets us. We can afford to be less important to ourselves because we are vastly important to God. We can willingly be crucified with Christ because we are raised to walk in resurrection life. Biblical self-denial will never fail to be *for* us rather than *against* us, whether here or in eternity. When Peter chose to deny Christ rather than himself, he really chose human limitations over divine intervention.

2. Peter followed Jesus, but at a distance. Obviously, if Peter had been holding onto Jesus' robe, he probably wouldn't have denied Christ. Even though Christ asked the soldiers to let His disciples go (see John 18:8), after all the miracles and proofs the Twelve had seen, why didn't even one insist upon staying? From a divine standpoint the answer is most likely God's sovereignty in fulfilling prophecy that Christ would be deserted and forsaken. From a human standpoint the answer is pure fear.

The scene reminds me of 2 Kings 2 when God was about to take His prophet, Elijah, up into a whirlwind. Elijah had several stops to make on his way to the Jordan River and continued his attempt to say farewell to his servant, Elisha. All three times, Elisha said, "As surely as the Lord lives and as you live, I will not leave you" (2 Kings 2:2, 4, 6). If Peter had been as insistent as Elisha, Satan would not have had the room to come between him and his master with a sieve to sift him like wheat. Elisha's actions showed sheer determination to follow his master to the ends of his earthly life.

Picture two sets of footprints in each scene: Elijah's and Elisha's in scene 1 and Christ's and Peter's in scene 2. In scene 1 the second set of footprints (Elisha's) was close and deliberate. Scene 2 depicts a second set of footprints (Peter's) at a much greater distance from the first. The prints appear tentative, almost as if they were cast on tiptoes. I believe we can safely say that we are far more likely to trip and fall from tiptoeing behind Christ than we are by stomping loudly and deliberately in a set of steel-toed boots. I can summarize the idea with two statements: A tentative (tiptoeing) walk leads to an almost certain detour, and distance creates room for denial. When we tiptoe to keep from being too obvious or to obscure ourselves in safe places and remain unidentifiable, we are already bounding toward denial.

3. Peter sat down with the opposition and warmed his hands by the same fire. John 18:18 tells us Peter joined "the servants and officials" at the fire in the middle of the courtyard.

I assure you the night was indeed cold; I've been in Jerusalem in the early spring. The semidesert climate may heat a spring day, but the temperature drops dramatically when the sun goes down. Since fear also has a way of quickening the senses, we're probably picturing him accurately as a young man who trembled nearly uncontrollably as he stood at that fire. I believe Peter made a very poor choice of company in the courtyard. However unintentionally, he ended up surrounding himself with others who, in effect, denied Christ. The risk of failure heightened dramatically at that moment. Can we ever note a point of application here! Being sent by God to be a witness to those who "deny" Christ is one thing. Warming our hands by the same fire is another.

In John 18:25–27 Peter's buddy John brings up the ear incident. He includes an interesting detail. A relative of the man whose ear Peter had cut off challenged Peter. Peter ended up doing the last thing he expected. He denied Christ. Satan most assuredly had sifted him like wheat. Needless to say, the enemy was hoping for "three strikes and you're out." Thankfully, he discounted Christ's mercy.

Peter's repetitive actions went beyond the realm of excuses. Rationalizing his choice to deny Christ and gaining sympathy from the others would have done nothing to help Peter become a man Christ could "crucify" and then use. Peter had to come face-to-face with the fact that in him no good thing dwelled. Only then would he be willing to deny himself and exist for the sole purpose of Jesus' renown.

I cannot help but relate some of my own seasons of defeat to Peter's. I will regret some of my choices every day of my life. Like Peter, I also made some choices in my past that went beyond rationalization. How thankful I am now that I couldn't just make excuses for my behavior! Any part of me I could have "excused" would still be "alive and kicking." Listen to my heart carefully: I want no part of myself. None. I want Jesus to so thoroughly consume me that *I* no longer exist. *I* am far too destructive. *I* would do far too much to deny His lordship. One regret I will never have is that God got me "over myself" by letting me confront the truth that in me dwells no good thing.

The scene ends in Luke 22:61–62 with an invisible sword piercing Peter's heart in a way no soldier's blade could have. The Lord turned and looked straight at Peter. In Peter's attempt to shield himself from the piercing sword, he fell to a far more piercing one: the look of Jesus into his eyes. Oh, I don't think the stab resulted from a look of condemnation. Rather, I imagine Peter's heart hemorrhaged from Christ's penetrating look of unveiled reality and love.

I do not doubt that Christ's face was painted with pain when their eyes met in the courtyard, but I think the conspicuous absence of condemnation tore through Peter's heart. I wonder if Christ's fixed gaze might have said something like this: "Remember, Peter, I am the Christ. You know that and I know that. I called you. I gave you a new name. I invited you to follow Me. Don't forget who I am. Don't forget what you are capable of doing. And, whatever you do, don't let this destroy you. When you have turned back, strengthen your brothers."

Surely nothing leads to repentance in those who are tender like the kindness of God (see Rom. 2:4). Peter was devastated. As we conclude this chapter, sit just a moment and listen to him cry. Is anything more painful to hear than the uncontrollable cries of a grown man? Peter went outside and wept bitterly. The original language suggests he took on every external form of grief. He wailed. He probably tore his robes. He may have grabbed a handful of sand and thrown it over his head. The conflict of his soul surged in a tidal wave of grief, betraying his true identity. His belief had not been a sham. His denial had.

Part 10

The Risen Hope

As I meditate on the final section of our study, the words of the apostle Paul consume my thoughts: "May I never boast except in the cross of our Lord Jesus Christ, through which the world has been crucified to me, and I to the world" (Gal. 6:14). The cost for each of us to be a new creation was far beyond anything we can fathom. Even though we will see only a glimpse, may a fresh wave of faith bring us face-to-the-floor. May a fresh look at the cross cause us to be more crucified to this world. A warning: there is nothing pretty about this immediate venture, but it was necessary to overcome the grave. Let's not be tempted to run from the cross as did Jesus' original disciples. Let's go with Him, step-by-step. Let's carry it for Him instead of letting Simon do it.

Let's hear the nails, the cries. Let's stand by until He draws His last breath. Then let's help Joseph take His body off the cross and carry it to the tomb. We'll then wait with the women. As sure as the earth will quake on Friday, a stone will roll on Sunday. Oh, beloved. Don't miss a moment of it.

Even if we have each walked to the cross to be saved, Galatians 2:20 invites us to walk to the cross and be crucified. Not so we can live like the dead — but so we can die to death and live in the power of Christ's resurrection. Let's not just read this part of the study, my friend. Let's live it with Him.

Chapter 49

The Ultimate Mock Court

Luke 22:63–23:25; Matthew 27:27–31

They all asked, "Are you then the Son of God?" He replied, "You are right in saying I am." (Luke 22:70)

We're about to have one of those chapters that causes us to hang our heads and whisper, "God, have mercy on humanity." Given over to our natural urges and instincts, we are more violent and dangerous than the beasts of the field.

I remember a childhood game I tried to avoid at all costs. It was called King of the Mountain. The players established a high place of some kind as the "mountain." The "king" was the one who could defend his territory by kicking or pushing anyone who came near him. It was a mean game. We play lots of mean games, though, don't we?

Not just when we're little. The games may appear more sophisticated and acceptable in adulthood, but they are also much meaner.

I wish we could skip this lesson, but we can't because Christ didn't skip it. Brace yourselves. We're going to see the inhuman side of humanity. Let's first consider the trials Jesus endured, and then we'll conclude with a look at the beatings He endured before and after. We'll analyze the scene by spotlighting the leaders of the opposition in each stage, but don't overlook the role of the crowd.

First notice Jesus' appearance before the council of elders. By the time Luke 22:66 unfolds, Christ had been kept awake all night long and subjected to illegal proceedings. The sun rose that morning over the Mount of Olives like a spotlight on the council of the elders — the chief priests and teachers of the law. Their robes of self-righteousness looked particularly ill fitted. They had a harder time than usual hiding their flint foreheads behind their phylacteries. They demanded in verse 67: "If you are the Christ, . . . tell us." Christ immediately pointed out three truths:

1. *"If I tell you, you will not believe me" (v. 67).* In other words, "My an-

swer would make no difference, would it?"

2. *"If I asked you, you would not answer" (v. 68).* I believe this statement referred to the messianic prophecies of healing and miracles. Christ was saying that if He asked if He had fulfilled those prophecies, they would refuse to answer.

3. *"The Son of Man will be seated at the right hand of the mighty God" (v. 69).* In other words, "What you think makes no difference anyway. The mission will be accomplished, and I will reign with my Father over the kingdom."

The council of the elders then asked the question they hoped would provoke the incriminating answer they needed: "Are you then the Son of God?" (v. 70).

As you picture every moment of the proceedings, don't lose sight of those words. Imagine every event unfolding on a large-screen TV. During the entire ordeal the words scroll boldly across the bottom of the scene: "the Son of God." The irony is this: the only reason Christ was standing in front of them was because He was exactly who they "tried" Him for being. Though His accusers couldn't see the truth for themselves,

Christ was found guilty of being the Son of God. They would end up releasing the insurrectionist and crucifying the Savior of the world.

I love Christ's answer: "You are right in saying I am" (v. 70). Christ repeated words to them not so unlike His Father's to Moses in Exodus 3:14: "I AM WHO I AM."

Aren't you thankful humanity can "try" Christ for being anything they choose, but He is who He is? No amount of disbelief can change Him or move Him. Why did the chief priests and teachers of the law disbelieve? Why couldn't they accept their Messiah? Because they wanted to be king of the mountain.

Their retort sends chills down my spine: "Why do we need any more testimony? We have heard it from his own lips" (v. 71). They were right. They needed no more testimony. Those who believe have all the proof we need; those set on disbelief had the evidence they needed to incriminate Him. Neither side needed more testimony. Heaven and hell were both armed for the showdown of all times.

Next notice Pilate. Luke 23 introduces us to Pilate, who was the fifth Roman prefect of Judea. He ruled from A.D. 26 to 36. John 18:31 tells us exactly why the religious leaders took Christ to Pilate. I hope you receive a bolt of fresh shock from it. When the Roman governor told the religious leaders to judge Jesus by their own law, they responded that they had "no right to execute anyone."

Don't let this get past you: Pilate offered several times simply to punish Jesus with a severe beating, but the *religious leaders* (read those two words over and over) would not have it. They wanted Him dead. That's pretty serious hatred. Jesus so greatly threatened their spot on the "mountain" that injuring Him wasn't enough. The only way to keep Him off their mountain was to kill Him. Pilate had the authority they needed.

In Pilate we see the consummate unprincipled politician. He simply wanted power. He wasn't driven by conviction or creed — just by need — that which he needed to stay in business. Pilate read the situation with amazing clarity. He recognized that he had encountered nothing less than a mob lynching, but he lacked the guts to challenge it. Mark 15:10 records something else he clearly recognized. He knew "it was out of envy that the chief priests had handed Jesus over to him."

The original word for "envy" in Mark 15:10 is *phthonos,* meaning "envy, jealousy, pain felt and malignity conceived at the sight of excellence or happiness." Compromising people can't stand the sight of excellence, and miserable people can't stand the sight of happiness. The definition proceeds to explain that *phthonos* is incapable of good and always is used with an evil meaning. Nothing is benign about envy. Like a cancer left untreated, it will consume us. Envy is deadly. It can kill anything from contentment to relationships to people.

Pilate not only discerned personally the malignancy in the religious leaders, but also he had several other sources that caused him to question the unfolding events. The first reason for Pilate to exercise caution came from his wife. She told him, "Don't have anything to do with that innocent man, for I have suffered a great deal today in a dream because of him" (Matt. 27:19).

I wonder what kind of conversation Pilate and the Mrs. had over dinner that night. Pilate resisted a word from his wife that confirmed his own sense of Christ's innocence. Then consider the interchange recorded in John 19:8–11. Pilate asked Jesus two questions, one He didn't answer and one He did. The first question was, "Where do you come from?" (v. 9). John 13:3 tells us that "Jesus knew that the Father had put all things under his power, and that he had come from God and was returning to God." The fact that Christ knew the answer gave Him the courage and motivation to stand before such a mock court.

Pilate's second question must have echoed irony through the heavenlies: "Don't you realize I have power either to free you or to crucify you?" (John 19:10). I can almost see the angels looking at one another in shock and hear them screaming in voices Pilate could not hear: "No, buddy. It's the other way around. Don't you realize He has the power to free or to crucify you?" Based on what he did "from then on" I believe Pilate's insides told him that Jesus was exactly who He said He was. "From then on, Pilate tried to set Jesus free, but the Jews kept shouting, 'If you let this man go, you are no friend of Caesar. Anyone who claims to be a king opposes Caesar' " (John 19:12).

So why did Pilate give in to the demands of the religious leaders and the crowds? He was afraid that if he didn't, he would no longer be king of the mountain on his little hill.

In our tour of characters, turn next to Herod. The Herod in Luke 23 was one of the sons of Herod the Great. His name was

Antipas, and he's the one who put John the Baptizer's head on a platter.

Herod absolutely epitomized human arrogance. His contributions to the kangaroo court appear in Luke 23:8–12. He plied Jesus with questions. Why didn't Jesus answer him? Probably for the same reason He didn't supply the miracles Herod wanted. Herod wanted a performance, not proof. He had no intention of believing Christ. Before Herod Jesus remained mute.

Christ's silence reminds me of Matthew 7:6: "Do not throw your pearls to pigs." The longer Christ stood silent, the more the chief priests and the teachers of the law accused Him (see Luke 23:10). Isn't their response typical of humans? If we have a lot banking on being right, we can't afford to be silent, and sometimes we feel we can't afford to be wrong. This passage reminds me of the evil that dwells in me apart from Christ.

Neither Pilate nor Herod could find a basis for the charges (see Luke 23:14–15). Herod sent Jesus right back to Pilate, but not until he did the unimaginable. He mocked the Son of God just to feel like the king of the mountain. For a few very difficult moments, please visit the scenes depicted in each of the following passages.

The men who were guarding Jesus began mocking and beating him. They blindfolded him and demanded, "Prophesy! Who hit you?" And they said many other insulting things to him. (Luke 22:63–65)

Then Pilate took Jesus and had him flogged. The soldiers twisted together a crown of thorns and put it on his head. They clothed him in a purple robe and went up to him again and again, saying, "Hail, king of the Jews!" And they struck him in the face. (John 19:1–3)

Then the governor's soldiers took Jesus into the Praetorium and gathered the whole company of soldiers around him. They stripped him and put a scarlet robe on him, and then twisted together a crown of thorns and set it on his head. They put a staff in his right hand and knelt in front of him and mocked him. "Hail, king of the Jews!" they said. They spit on him, and took the staff and struck him on the head again and again. After they had mocked him, they took off the robe and put his own clothes on him. Then they led him away to crucify him. (Matt. 27:27–31)

By the time these serial beatings were completed, do you see how Isaiah 52:14 perfectly describes our Savior? The prophet declared that many "were appalled at him — / his appearance was so disfigured beyond that of any man / and his form marred beyond human likeness." Those were no poetic descriptions. The words are a stark depiction of the reality of the most precious face ever to grace this planet.

Stripped. Mocked. Spat upon. Struck . . . again and again. Flogged. Beyond recognition. The fullness of the Godhead bodily. The bright and morning Star. The Alpha and Omega. The anointed of the Lord. The beloved Son of God. The radiance of His Father's glory. The Light of the world. The Hope of glory. The Lily of the valley. The Prince of peace. The Seed of David. The Son of righteousness. The blessed and only potentate, the King of kings, and Lord of lords. Emmanuel. The With of God.

The most terrifying truth a mocking humanity will ever confront is that no matter how Jesus is belittled, He cannot be made little. He is the King of the mountain.

On my holy mountain, the high mountain of Israel, declares the Sovereign

LORD, there in the land the entire house of Israel will serve me, and there I will accept them. (Ezek. 20:40)

Chapter 50

To the Cross

Luke 23:26–49

When they came to the place called the Skull, there they crucified him. (Luke 23:33)

The time had come when the seconds would not tick by but would pound to the rhythm of a hammer. Since a flaming sword flashed back and forth disbarring humanity from entrance to the garden of divine intimacy, God had crossed days off the kingdom calendar, preparing both heaven and earth for this one. The worst and the best day of all. Join me as we journey to the cross.

While they crucified Jesus, He cried, "Father, forgive them, for they do not know what they are doing" (Luke 23:34). From a human perspective we can hardly see the truth of His words. The religious leaders had been conspiring against Him and had simply been waiting for the perfect time to seize Him. Scripture is also clear that their goal was not His punishment but His death. Humanly speaking, they seemed to know exactly what they were doing.

As the story unfolds, we are told an innocent bystander on his way in from the country was forced to carry the cross. Luke 23:26 tells us they forced a man named Simon to carry the cross behind Jesus. Can you imagine the horror of walking behind a man whose back had been torn to shreds by whips laced with jagged metal? Christ had been beaten so badly that He could hardly stand under the weight of the cross. The severity of the beating administered prior to crucifixion often depended upon how long the officials wanted victims to live. They could live up to six days. Quite possibly, Christ's beating demonstrated the full extremity of severity, not to spare Him a lengthy death, but to allow the religious leaders to be home for supper. After all, it was a holiday weekend.

Throngs of people joined the procession as if part of a parade. The path twisted through the city and to Golgotha. Luke 23:32 tells us two other men also were led out with Him to be executed. Scripture's only description of these two men is that they were criminals, fulfilling Isaiah's prophecy that Christ "was numbered with the transgressors"(Isa. 53:12). Then, with startling brevity, Luke 23:33 records the most critical event of all: "When they came to the place called the Skull, there they crucified him."

According to ancient custom, the cross, or at least the crossbeam, was placed upon the ground, then Christ was stretched out upon it. I cannot imagine being the one who actually targeted the nail to the proper place in the skin and struck the blow. Do you think he at all costs avoided Christ's eyes? They probably secured His hands before His feet so that His arms would not flail when His feet were nailed. We often picture that the nail wounds were in the palms, but the delicate bones in the hands could not hold a victim to the cross. The nails were usually driven through the wrists. In Hebrew, the wrist was considered part of the hand rather than the arm.

Without becoming more graphic than necessary, crucifixion, almost always preceded by a near-to-death flogging, was unimaginably painful and inhumane. This kind of capital punishment was targeted as a deterrent for rebellious slaves and was forbidden to any Roman citizen no matter how serious his crime.

Crucifixion was a totally inhumane way for even the two criminals to die. But this was the King of glory! They took a hammer and nails to the "Word made flesh."

I want you to sit and "listen" to the sound of the hammer striking. I'm not trying to be melodramatic. I just want us to come as close as possible to being eyewitnesses. You don't have to open your eyes and "look," but I want you to open your spiritual ears and listen. Move close enough to hear the conversation of the marksman as he positions the nail at the wrist of Christ. You'll have to fight the crowd to get close enough. Then listen to the hammer hit the nail — several times at each hand and foot to make sure the nails are securely in place. I'm not trying to make you wince. I only want you to hear the sound as the nails are driven securely into the wood.

If you study the Old Testament prophecies of Jesus, you will find that they come in a dazzling variety of forms. In some places the predictions were clear. They obviously pointed to the coming Messiah. In other instances they were veiled. Join me now as we look at an absolutely fascinating passage —

these words that apply so beautifully to Christ at this moment. In their immediate sense, they were written about Eliakim, but you can see their ultimate significance in terms of the cross of our Christ. In the passage God said, "I will clothe him with your robe and fasten your sash around him and hand your authority over to him. He will be a father to those who live in Jerusalem and to the house of Judah. I will place on his shoulder the key to the house of David; what he opens no one can shut, and what he shuts no one can open. I will drive him like a peg into a firm place; he will be a seat of honor for the house of his father" (Isa. 22:21–23).

Note how God said He would give His servant the key to the house of David, opening a door no one can shut. He said He would "drive him like a peg into a firm place." As unfathomable as the process is to you and me, the cross was the means by which God chose to position Christ in the seat of honor for the house of His Father. The cross is the open door no man can shut.

Isaiah 22:23 says, "I will fasten him as a nail in a sure place" (KJV). The original word for "firm" in the NIV and "sure" in the kjv is *aman:* "in a transitive sense to make firm, to confirm . . . to stand firm; to be enduring; to trust."

Nothing was accidental about the cross of Christ. The Son of God was not suddenly overcome by the wickedness of man and nailed to a cross. Quite the contrary, the cross was the means by which the Son of God overcame the wickedness of man. To secure the keys to the house of David and open the door of salvation to all who would enter, God drove His Son like a nail in a sure place. A firm place. An enduring place.

As horrendous as the pounding hammer sounds to our spiritual ears, Colossians 2:13–14 says that while we were dead in our sins, God made us alive with Christ. He "canceled the written code, with its regulations, that was against us and that stood opposed to us; he took it away, nailing it to the cross."

My sin — oh, the bliss of this glorious tho't:
My sin not in part, but the whole
Is nailed to the cross and I bear it no more,
Praise the Lord, praise the Lord, O my soul![1]

I will never fully grasp how such human atrocities occurred at the free will of humanity, while God used them to unfold His perfect, divine, and redemptive plan. Christ was nailed to the cross as the one perfect human. He was the fulfillment of the law in every way. When God drove His Son like a nail in a firm place, He took the written code, finally fulfilled in His Son, and canceled our debt to it. With every pound of the hammer, God was nailing down redemption.

After the soldiers nailed Christ's body to the wood, either the crossbeam was hoisted to a timber prepared with an adjoining slot, or the entire cross was raised with ropes, then dropped with a thud into a socket, securing it upward. Imagine the cross raised over the heads of the people, placing Christ in full view.

Again with stunning meaning Christ had earlier told His disciples, "When I am lifted up from the earth, [I] will draw all men to myself" (John 12:32). Can you imagine how those words rang in the disciples' minds when they finally understood what Jesus had meant?

As if the physical wounds Christ suffered were not enough, they were not the killers in crucifixion. Death crept in slowly through exhaustion and asphyxiation from an increasing inability to hold oneself up to draw breath. If you've ever experienced anything close to "excruciating" pain, can you imagine how difficult talking would be?

Regardless of how many times you've heard sermons preached on Christ's next words, don't hear them casually. The moment words formed on His tongue and His voice found volume, He said, "Father, forgive them, for they do not know what they are doing" (Luke 23:34).

Not "Father, consume them," but "Father, forgive them." This may be the most perfect statement spoken at the most perfect time since God gave the gift of language. As unimaginable as His request was, it was so fitting! If the cross is about anything at all, it is about forgiveness. Forgiveness of the most incorrigible and least deserving.

I don't believe the timing of the statement was meaningless. It was the first thing He said after they nailed Him to the cross and hoisted it into view. His immediate request for the Father's forgiveness sanctified the cross for its enduring work through all of time. His request baptized the crude wood for its divine purpose.

Please understand, the cross itself had no power. Neither was it ever meant to be an idol, but it represents something so divine and powerful that the apostle Paul said, "May I never boast except in the cross of our Lord Jesus Christ, through which the world has been crucified to me, and I to the world" (Gal. 6:14).

Dr. Luke was the only one God inspired to record the forgiveness statement. How appropriate that a physician would be the one to pen such healing words. Surely, in the days to come, many involved were haunted by their consciences. No doubt many in the crowd at the crucifixion were saved on the Day of Pentecost, since both events occurred in Jerusalem only weeks apart and on major feast days. The main reason to believe these were the same people, however, is because God doesn't ordinarily refuse the request of His Son. Can you imagine how many of those sorrowing over their part in the crucifixion found healing in Christ's request for their forgiveness?

The curtain drops on our scene in the form of darkness, which lasted three hours. Christ said in Luke 22:53 that this would be the "hour — when darkness reigns." That Luke included the fact that the sun stopped shining is poignant. The Light of the world was about to be extinguished, if only for a brief time. Just before He breathed His last, Jesus cried out with a loud voice, "Father, into your hands I commit my spirit"

(23:46). How appropriate that He would use His last breaths to utter the trust upon which His entire life had rested. I'm not sure we can properly appreciate those words of faith unless we consider the ones spoken by Him only moments before.

In a moment of darkness David first prophesied the words in Psalm 22:1. Jesus gave ultimate expression to the phrase in Matthew 27:46. Do you know the agonizing words to which I refer now? "My God, my God, why have you forsaken me?"

I believe this cry marked the exact moment when the sins of all humanity — past, present, and future — were heaped upon Christ and the full cup of God's wrath poured forth. Somehow I believe that to bear the sin, Jesus also had to bear the separation. Though Christ had to suffer the incomparable agony of separation from the fellowship of His Father while sin was judged, I am moved that He breathed His last breath with full assurance of His Father's trustworthiness.

The human body of the life-giver hung lifeless. It was finished. He gave up His last human breath so He never had to give up on humanity. Try to absorb what had just happened. Jesus Christ, "being in very nature God, / did not consider equality with God something to be grasped, / but made himself nothing, / taking the very nature of a servant, / being made in human likeness. / And being found in appearance as a man, / he humbled himself / and became obedient to death — even death on a cross!" (Phil. 2:6–8).

Recently I had the privilege of participating in a solemn assembly of thirty thousand college students gathered on a huge field in Memphis, Tennessee. We heard a powerful message about the cross. As we responded with songs of worship, two young men began to walk down the hill carrying a large wooden cross. The two students, bent under the weight, carried the heavy cross through the crowd to a place just in front of the platform and then erected it as a visual aid. We couldn't possibly have planned what happened next.

Students began running to the cross with an urgency I can neither possibly describe nor recall without sobs. They sprinted from every direction through the crowd. Their sobs echoed in the open air. They lifted the cross out of the ground and began to pass it with their hands lifted high above their heads all over the crowd. They passed it from hands to hands all over the crowd and up the hill. I am covered with chills as I recall the scene when the repentant found refuge in the shadow of the cross.

In our sophistication and familiarity, have we been away too long? Run to the cross.

Chapter 51

He Has Risen!

Luke 23:50–24:12

"Why do you look for the living among the dead? He is not here; he has risen!" (Luke 24:5–6)

By the time I knew Jesus had been crucified, I also knew He had risen from the dead; yet, I am sitting here bawling like a baby. How I wish I could put my feelings into words. The underdog in me wants to stand up and cheer that the good guy wins. The romantic can't bear the man of my dreams being in that tomb another minute. The weakling in me longs desperately for resurrection power; the optimist fails without its hope.

The event we study next means everything to us! Pause and meditate. Try to picture it. Hear it. Feel it. Jesus has been crucified.

Joseph of Arimithea was a good and upright man, a member of the Sanhedrin. Luke 23:52 tells us he went to Pilate to ask for Jesus' body. Stop here for a minute. Allow your imagination to help you picture some of the dynamics in the room where they met. Two men of position faced one another: one a man of principle and the other a man of self-promotion. What do you think each was thinking about the other at that meeting?

Imagine the difficulty and courage of Joseph's task. Then let me ask you a purely practical question: How does one take down a body from a cross? Especially this One? I can hardly bear the thought. This broken human frame had housed the fullness of the Godhead, the radiance of the Father's glory. These fixed eyes had looked through everyone He met. These lips, cracked from fever, thirst, and death, had spoken nothing but truth. Hands, trained in carpentry, had rebuilt lives and raised the dead, then succumbed to a hammer and nails. Don't lose sight of it. This former "House" of the fullness of the Spirit was precious.

Imagine with what care Joseph tenderly took the body down into his arms. I wonder if he wept. Did he prick his fingers as he removed the crown of thorns embedded in that head? Did he brush hair out of that face? Did he speak to Jesus like I spoke to my mother as I stroked her lifeless hand? I have no idea what Joseph thought, felt, and experienced, but it could have been nothing less than profound. He wrapped the body of Jesus in linen cloth and placed it in a cleft of the rock as the Sabbath was about to begin.

How the Sabbath hours must have dragged for the women. They had prepared the spices and perfumes but were forced to rest on the Sabbath. They had come with Jesus from Galilee, so we can assume they were guests in others' homes. Surely the time seemed to be an eternity. Women two thousand years ago were not so unlike we are today. We want to do something. Feeling needed is sometimes the very thing that keeps a woman going. For months they "had followed him and cared for his needs" (Mark 15:41). Now all that was left to do was to serve Him in memorial. They needed to get to the tomb and do the one last thing they could for their Lord.

As the moments crawled by, I'm sure these women recounted with horror the last few days' events. Surely, at times, they sat in silence, each one weeping in painful solitude as she remembered every encounter with Him. Jesus had a way of making a person feel like the apple of His eye. He still does.

The women "rested" through a Sabbath dusk that frustratingly gave way to night. More waiting. They probably never slept a wink and were on their way to the tomb before a cock could crow. John 20:1, spotlighting Mary Magdalene, tells us "it was still dark."

Mark tells us that the women were hoping the officials would allow someone to roll away the stone so they could apply the spices and perfumes to the body. To their astonishment, they saw that the "very large" stone had been rolled away. The women had no way of knowing at that moment what Matthew 28:2–4 records. I love the wording in Matthew 28:2: "An angel of the Lord came down from heaven and, going to the tomb, rolled back the stone and sat on it." Can you fathom the angels' horror when humans mocked, spat on, beat, flogged, and crucified the Son of God?

Imagine the joy of the angel whose thunderous arrival caused the ground to shake. God chose him to be the one who rolled back the stone — not to free Jesus — but to reveal Him already missing! Can you picture the angel's gleaming face as he perched on that stone? The guards were so afraid that they shook and became like dead men. The graveyard needed a few folks acting like dead men since a number of the formerly dead were suddenly walking the streets (see Matt. 27:52–53). I'm about to have to shout hallelujah! The women entered the tomb, but they did not find the body.

Acts 2:24 tells us exactly why Christ was raised from the dead: "God raised him from the dead, freeing him from the agony of death, because it was impossible for death to keep its hold on him." Some things are simply impossible — and death keeping its hold on Jesus is one of them. Mind you, the women didn't yet understand. Luke 24:4 tells us "while they were wondering about this, suddenly two men in clothes that gleamed like lightning stood beside them." John's version hints at these two celestial ambassadors' assignment. He tells us the two angels were seated where Jesus' body had been, "one at the head and the other at the foot" (John 20:12).

Quite possibly, these angels also guarded the body of Jesus while it lay "in state" in the sepulcher. The Old Testament tabernacle contained a marvelous picture foreshadowing this moment. The ark of the covenant represented the very presence of God. In Exodus 25:17–22, the very specific instructions for the "mercy seat" (KJV) or "atonement cover" (NIV) on the ark of the covenant demanded the cherubim in exactly that position. Do you see the picture? No, I can't be dogmatic that the cherubim prefigured the angels at Christ's head and feet — but I am personally convinced. Jesus has always been the means by which God would "meet with" humanity (Exod. 25:22).

If the cherubim prefigured the angels in the tomb, can you imagine how they guarded the body through the wait? With their wings overshadowing Him, they faced each other, looking toward the cover. Picture their reactions when the glorified body of Jesus sat up from the death shroud and walked out of the tomb, right through the rock. Wouldn't you have loved to hear as Christ thanked them for their service?

Glory to God! Though the news echoed throughout the heavenlies at the moment of Christ's resurrection, the angels probably longed for God to turn on their volume in the earthly realm and announce it to the mortals. At the sight of the angels, the women fell on their faces. The celestial guards announced to them, "Why do you look for the living among the dead?" The what? The living! "He is not here; he has risen!" (Luke 24:5–6).

513

Oh, glorious, merciful, omnipotent God! He is risen indeed! I cherish the next five words of the angels: "Remember how he told you"(v. 6). Beloved, have you forgotten something He told you? Christ, our Lord, is faithful to His promises. If you're not presently "seeing" Him at work in your situation, do not live as if He's lifeless and you're hopeless. Believe Him and expect Him to reveal His resurrection power to you!

The angels reminded the women of three facts Jesus foretold, not just to His disciples, but obviously to them as well. "The Son of Man must be delivered into the hands of sinful men, be crucified and on the third day be raised again" (Luke 24:7).

All things had to go exactly according to the plan. No point was negotiable. After the heralds delivered their three-point sermon, "they remembered his words" (v. 8). Luke leapfrogs immediately to their departure and intent to tell the eleven, but Matthew shines a flashlight on something that happened en route. Jesus met them. They worshiped Him, and He gave them a message to deliver. "Do not be afraid. Go and tell my brothers to go to Galilee; there they will see me" (Matt. 28:10).

I hope God recorded that scene so we can watch the replay in heaven. As hard as pulling themselves away from the visible presence of Christ must have been, the women did as He commanded them. Luke 24:9 records one of my favorite reasons why I believe God might have chosen to reveal the empty tomb first to this group of women: "they told all these things to the Eleven and to all the others."

If I may say with a chuckle, one possible reason God chose to reveal the resurrection first to women is because He can trust us to get the word out! Telling what we've been told is our specialty! However, nothing can deflate the spirits of an enthusiastic woman like an apprehensive audience. Luke 24:11 records that the apostles "did not believe the women, because their words seemed to them like nonsense."

Sisters, don't be insulted by this scene in Luke 24:11. Rather, be blessed that God was up to something awesome even in this seemingly insignificant detail. You see, "the witness of women was not [even] acceptable in that day."[1] They couldn't testify as witnesses.

Now isn't this just like my Jesus! He threatened the status quo in countless ways, not the least of which concerned women. He invited them into Bible class (see Luke 10:39) after they had spent centuries learning what little Scripture they could from their husbands. He honored their service during a time in which men were the only ones who ministered publicly (see Mark 15:41). He healed, forgave, delivered, and made whole the very ones society shunned. Women of ill repute.

Appointing these women as the first to share the news of Jesus' resurrection was a definite "custom shaker." Jesus knew the apostles wouldn't believe them, but perhaps He felt that the pending discovery of their authenticity would breed a fresh respect. After all, at the first roll call in the post-ascension New Testament church you'll see women listed as part of the first New Testament cell group (see Acts 1:13–14).

For centuries the synagogue had kept men and women separate. Suddenly they would be working, praying, and worshiping shoulder-to-shoulder. Christ built His church on a foundation of mutual respect. Don't misunderstand. Christ wasn't prioritizing women over men. He simply took the ladder down to the basement where society had lowered women. With His nail-scarred hands, He lifted them to a place of respect and credibility.

The last thing we women should want to do in the body of Christ is to take men's places. They have far too much responsibility for my taste! But by all means, let's take our places! We have also been called to be credible witnesses of the Lord Jesus Christ.

Oh, how I have enjoyed this chapter! I could almost see Him. I could feel the hair stand up on the back of my neck as Mary gazed into the tomb and saw two angels. I could smell the earth as the women fell on their faces at the sight of the angels. I could race down the streets this minute and proclaim to every doubter, "He is risen!" And, if I should run into Him on the way, my knees would buckle involuntarily. I would drop to the ground, clasp His feet, and wash them in my tears. I would grab Him, worship Him, and never want to let Him go. Someday, my dear friends, we will get our chance.

Until then, "Don't be afraid. Go and tell."

Chapter 52

A Burning Heart

Luke 24:13–35

They asked each other, "Were not our hearts burning within us while he talked with us on the road and opened the Scriptures to us?" (Luke 24:32)

Reading the Bible is like taking a wild ride through a vast land, but instead of wondering about the stories of those you pass, you get to stop off and see them face-to-face. I've tended sheep in the desert with Moses. I've laughed my head off with Sarai in Abraham's tent. I've shouted with Joshua at the walls of Jericho. I've danced with David down the streets of Jerusalem, and I've been shipwrecked with Paul. What a ride! Now we get to travel the road to Emmaus where we'll hop off the roller coaster and walk for a while.

I love this story! Let's get a little sand in our shoes and walk with Cleopas and his companion on the very Sunday of Christ's resurrection. I can't help but wonder if Christ had the time of His life that day surprising people. Apparently the two men we're joining were followers of Christ. They described the women who discovered the empty tomb as "some of our women" (24:22). We can also assume they were members of the same group Christ told about His capture, crucifixion, and even His resurrection.

The scene unfolds with a pair of mouths traveling faster than their feet. Luke 24:15–16 tells us that Jesus joined them on the road but kept them from recognizing Him. Christ may not make a habit of walking up to us in human form, but I think He sometimes "joins us" in our circumstances in ways we don't recognize.

The next scene is mind-boggling. Christ asked what they were discussing. With downcast faces they answered Him. Freeze the frame for a moment. Trade places with Cleopas and paste his expression on your face. Can you imagine how ridiculous we look with hopeless, downcast faces while the immortal Son of God stands right beside us?

Imagine that God has decorated your mansion in glory with a number of framed pictures of two of His very favorites: you and Christ. The pictures capture the two of you during momentous earthly occasions. You could not see Him with your eyes, but He was there every moment in living color. Hopefully, we've each walked with Him long enough to have a few treasured photos with expressions suggesting we chose to see with the eyes of faith rather than the eyes of humanity.

I can almost imagine Christ sitting around heaven with small groups of us, pulling out the photo album, pointing out a few sour expressions. Picture us covering our faces with good-humored embarrassment, turning as red as beets. No doubt the still shot of Cleopas in Luke 24:17 is one that would spur a little good-natured, heavenly ribbing. Christ, however, didn't find it nearly so amusing this side of heaven. Note that the events surrounding Christ's crucifixion were so well publicized that Cleopas implied Christ would have to be a visitor to be unaware of the recent happenings. He then proceeded to tell Christ . . . about Himself. Can you imagine being in Cleopas's sandals? Wouldn't you hope you got the facts straight? If Christ had been a teacher grading Cleopas on his oral report, what grade do you think He would've given him?

If I were grading Cleopas's oral report, I wouldn't have subtracted points until the "kicker" in Luke 24:21: "But we had hoped that he was the one." Picture the downcast face, the sagging posture. Listen to the tone in his voice. For a clue, see Christ's indignant response in Luke 24:25: "He said to them, 'How foolish you are, and how slow of heart to believe all that the prophets have spoken!'" Cleopas seemed to be saying, "We had hoped . . . but He let us down." Cleopas needed a good dose of Psalm 43.

I love how the psalms reveal the thought processes of a writer. The psalmist, while feeling rejected by God, sank into mourning. In Psalm 43:5 the psalmist wrote his own prescription for a downcast soul: "Put your hope in God, / for I will yet praise him, / my Savior and my God." The Word of God often couples a downcast soul with feelings of hopelessness. In Greek the word for "hope" encompasses far more than wishful thinking. It means "confident expectation." Christ told His followers what to "expect" and reminded them that a victorious ending would follow the tragic means. When Christ gives us His Word, He wants us to live in absolute expectation of it, trusting that whether it happens sooner or later, it will happen.

Cleopas and his friend had allowed the very evidence that could have ignited them instead with hope to make them hopeless. Remember now — the women had shared the testimony that Christ was alive. I realize I'm taking the next statement out of context, but I get a kick out of Cleopas's words in Luke 24:22: "In addition, some of our women amazed us." There you have it. Women are amazing. It's absolutely scriptural. Of course, *amazing* can mean many things. The most common colloquialism we have that matches the word for *amazing* is to say something has "blown our minds." I blow Keith's mind all the time — but it's not always a good blow. Sometimes he just stands there and gives me that, "She's blonder than she pays to be" look.

Christ clearly showed His displeasure over the men's disbelief. He rebuked them but followed the rebuke with some of the most amazing moments in Scripture: "Beginning with Moses and all the Prophets, he explained to them what was said in all the Scriptures concerning himself" (v. 27). What I would give to hear that comprehensive dissertation! Christ began with the books of Moses, went straight through the prophets, and explained what was said in all the Scriptures concerning Himself. Part of heaven for me will be hearing a replay of this sermon! The entire Old Testament was written about or toward Christ. Imagine Jesus Himself explaining the hundreds of ways the Scriptures predict and prepare for His coming. I could teach on this subject for hours, and I don't know even a fraction of the ways Christ is taught in the Old Testament.

Luke's use of "explained" (v. 27) in reference to Christ's teaching approach means "to interpret, translate. To explain clearly and exactly." I can't wait to know exactly what some Scriptures mean. Unlike me, Christ never had to say, "I think . . ." or "I believe this means . . ." He knew. What a Bible lesson those two men heard! A lesson that would have taken forty years of wilderness wanderings for me, Christ delivered with glorious precision over a few Emmaus miles.

No wonder the two men hated to part with Jesus! "Jesus acted as if he were going farther. But they urged him strongly, 'Stay with us' "(vv. 28–29).

Don't you love the part in a movie when the surprise is revealed? We have now arrived at that climactic moment. Allow me to set the stage for you. The men invited Jesus into one of their homes. A simple meal was prepared. They reclined at the table. Christ took the role as server. He broke the bread and called down divine favor through a benediction. He handed each of them a portion of the small loaf. As if the veil of the holy of holies was torn again before their very eyes, they recognized Him! Then He disappeared. Talk about a photo I want to see in a heavenly album! Can you imagine those expressions? I have a feeling "downcast" wouldn't be an adequate description.

I relish few things more than witnessing someone's fresh reaction to Jesus Christ. How blessed we are that God chose to tell us what the men said after they picked up their chins off the floor. "Were not our hearts burning within us while he talked with us on the road and opened the Scriptures to us?" (Luke 24:32). Oh, this question is so chockfull of riches, I'm almost too excited to teach it! First, did you notice that spiritual heartburn is scriptural? You bet it is! "Did not our heart burn?" (KJV).

The word *burn* means exactly what you think it does: "to make to burn, . . . flaming . . . to consume with fire." Beloved, if you have ever paid any attention to anything I've ever written about the key to a passionate relationship with Christ, pay attention now. Your heart means far more to Christ than anything. That your heart is utterly taken with Christ is more important than any amount of service you could render or rules you could keep. If Christ has your heart, He will have your obedience (see John 14:21). God wants to completely captivate your heart and cause it to burn with passion for Him. It is His absolute priority for you according to Mark 12:30; joy and satisfaction will elude you in its absence. Two immutable keys exist that turn our spiritual ignition and inflame godly passion. Both are tucked like rubies in the embers of Luke 24:32. " 'Were not our hearts burning within us while he [1] talked with us on the road and [2] opened the Scriptures to us?' "

To me, "talked with us on the road" is a wonderfully personal and tender representation of prayer and "opened the Scriptures to us" is a perfect representation of Bible study. Beloved, we may do many other things to fan the flame of our spiritual passion for Christ, but all other efforts are in vain without the two sticks of prayer and Bible study rubbed together to ignite a fire.

In our final chapter we will conclude our present adventure, and our paths may not cross again this side of heaven. Our hearts have burned together like a raging fire, and I will miss you terribly, but you certainly don't need me. You can always know what causes a heart to burn in the presence of Jesus Christ.

Some may say, "But I've said prayers before and attended Sunday school many times, and my heart didn't burn." I'm not referring to popcorn prayers and drive-thru lessons. I'm talking about entering into a love affair of prayer with Jesus Christ, where you talk to Him throughout the day recognizing that He, the unseen One, is a far greater reality than those within your vision. I'm talking about opening up the Word, throwing back your head, face toward heaven, and saying, "Thrill me with Your Word!" (see Ps. 119:18). Evolving into this kind of intimacy with God takes time, but the road trip is half the excitement!

Don't confuse a passionate relationship with God with an unrealistic state of perpetual chill bumps. I'm talking about the meshing of two lives, yours and Christ's, increasingly engulfing and igniting the whole of heart, soul, mind, and strength. God is more than eager to give you a heart full of fire for His Son. Tell Him you want it more than blessing or your daily bread. Beloved, promise me you will not settle for mediocrity! When Jesus, the Alpha and the Omega, the Author and Finisher of our faith, takes the wheel, you won't lack excitement, amusement, or a seat with a view. He has nothing less in mind for you than a great adventure. A wild ride awaits you. All aboard?

Chapter 53

Jesus Himself

Luke 24:36–53

"Look at my hands and my feet. It is I myself! Touch me and see." (Luke 24:39)

Our last chapter? How can this be? The months seem to blow off the calendar faster and faster these days. In a flash, our lives on earth will evaporate like a cloud, but every moment we've spent in the Word is an eternal investment in the treasury of heaven. Stay in God's Word! Study under biblically sound teachers so you develop into a follower of Christ and not a follower of the world. Worship Christ alone. Stay connected to a local body of believers, and serve God with contagious joy. I commit to you that I will do the same. If we never meet here on earth, I cannot wait to get to know you in heaven. Please drop by my house and share a heavenly cup of java with me. Come tell me how you love Him and what you felt when you saw Him face-to-face.

I am at a loss for words to express my gratitude to you. That a person of your character would choose to walk through the Word of God with someone like me — a former pit dweller with so much left to learn — is so humbling I cannot assimilate it. I simply cast the privilege like a perfect rose at the feet of my Savior. As always, my eyes sting with tears as we meet on a well-worn page of God's Word for our final steps together.

Let's set the stage for the events described in Luke 24:36. After Christ revealed Himself at their table and then disappeared, Cleopas and his companion walked what was perhaps the fastest seven miles of their lives, right back to Jerusalem. By the time they reached the Eleven, the disciples were swept up in the excitement of Christ's appearance to Peter. Finally, they were proclaiming, "It is true! The Lord has risen" (v. 34).

I love Christ's dramatic timing. "While they were still talking . . ." (v. 36). Who? The chaps from Emmaus! They kept getting caught giving their testimony about Jesus, but I think they received a much better grade on this one. Jesus Himself stood among them. Oh, glorious day! After all the conjecture, all the doubt. Not Gabriel. Not the heavenly hosts. Not a vision. No apparition. Jesus. Beloved, when our eyes are unveiled to heavenly sight, we will see Jesus Himself. "For the Lord himself will come down from heaven. . . . And so we will be with the Lord forever!" (1 Thess. 4:16–17). Be still, my heart!

The first words out of Christ's mouth when He interrupted the scene in Luke 24:36 were "Peace be with you." *Peace* or *Shalom* is the most common greeting among the Hebrew people, but nothing was common about this greeting that resurrection night.

Does your heart thrill to those words as mine does? Ephesians 2:14 amplifies the significance of Jesus' greeting: "For he himself is our peace." He didn't just say "shalom" — He is shalom.

I have to laugh out loud from the delightful irony that Christ's greeting of peace nearly scared the disciples to death (see Luke 24:37). John 20:19 helps explain why Christ's surprise visit incited such fear. The disciples were locked in for fear of the Jews.

Luke 24:37 translates two very strong

original words to describe the terror of the disciples. Suffice it to say, they could not have been more frightened. I think they would have run for their lives if they could have moved. Notice that just minutes earlier they were cheering, "It is true!" But somehow when they came face-to-face with Jesus, the sight was almost more than they could bear. I delight in knowing our future will be somewhat similar. You and I have banked our entire Christian lives on the fact that Jesus is very much alive, yet I have a feeling when we actually behold Him, it will only be eternal life that keeps us from dropping like dead men. Christ responded to the fright of His disciples by asking, "Why are you troubled, and why do doubts rise in your minds?" The original word for "troubled" implies a sudden disturbance of all sorts of emotions.

The original word for "doubts" in Luke 24:38 is *dialogismos.* You see in it the word *dialogue.* The Greek word means "thoughts and directions" and can also mean "debate." I think the disciples' minds went on instant overload, dialoguing all sorts of debates between what their eyes suddenly saw and what their brains could not rationalize. I can almost hear Christ saying, "Boys, you don't have a mental file already prepared to stick this information in. This one won't compute intellectually. Quit trying. Just behold and believe." Christ's willingness to continue to draw us to belief totally astounds me. At no time did He say, "You bunch of idiots! I'm sick of trying to talk you into believing me!" When the sight of Him wasn't enough, Jesus said, "Look at my hands and my feet. It is I myself! Touch me and see; a ghost does not have flesh and bones, as you see I have" (v. 39).

Christ did not have to retain the scars in His resurrected body. I wear a bracelet on my wrist as a visible reminder that I am the Lord's. In such a poignant way, I believe the nail scars represent something precious to Christ. The scars are ways you and I have been engraved on His very hands and feet (see Isa. 49:16).

The nail scars weren't the only ones He retained. In John 20:27 Christ also referred to the spear wound in His side. Many believe the spear wound in Jesus' side pierced His heart. The wound suggests a picture of the bride of Christ. His betrothed has come from His side like the first woman came from Adam's. Not from His rib, however — from His heart.

Unlike His first disciples, you and I have never looked upon Christ's touchable hands and feet. At first, it may seem the disciples had such an advantage over us. After all, they saw the risen Christ with their own eyes. Christ, however, announced that we are the ones with a special advantage. Of us, Jesus proclaimed, "Blessed are those who have not seen and yet have believed" (John 20:29).

Oh, sister or brother! We who believe, yet have never seen, are blessed because it is faith that pleases Him so (see Heb. 11:6)! We have often seen His hands through constant provision and glorious intervention. We have often seen His feet as He's gone before us. Surely we have beheld the hands and feet of Christ with eyes of faith!

Luke 24:41 paints an almost disturbing picture of the disciples until we grasp what I believe God is implying. After the disciples saw His hands and feet, we are told "they still did not believe." But I don't think the implication is that they were stiff-necked and obstinate, demanding further proof.

Have you ever been so excited over a piece of news that it didn't seem real until later? That's how the disciples felt! They were thinking something like, *Is this too good to be true?* Christ's response marvelously implies what was going through their minds. He immediately asked for something to eat, demonstrating that He was real. This was no ghost! Can you imagine the resurrected body of Christ? He walked through walls yet ate real food. His resurrected body had complete form and firmness yet was unrestrained by earthly boundaries. For the most incredible part, read 1 John 3:2: "But we know that when he appears, we shall be like him, for we shall see him as he is."

This incredible verse suggests that while we don't yet know what we will be in our glorified state, we know what we will be like. We shall be like Him. I believe this Scripture implies that the physical properties of our glorified bodies will be much like His. How thrilling! Among many other more spiritual things, I am delighted we will be able to eat! But, if it's all the same to Jesus, I think I'd rather have the fried fish instead of broiled since I'll have a heavenly body.

Someone might be thinking, *This is no time for fun and games!* But I think Jesus had a bunch of fun with His disciples when He saw their joyous disbelief and asked for a piece of fish to prove the point! No one can tell me that behind those closed doors there wasn't hilarity, replete with unreligious laughter and unsophisticated jumps for joy. We have been created in the image of our God. Ecstatic joy is His gift, and what better time to share it than dancing in the moon-light on resurrection night? I am convinced that the brief moments between Luke 24:43 and 44 were filled with celebration. Some-where between those lines, the disciples saw and believed!

Christ then reminded the disciples in verse 44: "Everything must be fulfilled that is written about me in the Law of Moses, the Prophets and the Psalms." That includes His return. The Old Testament is perfectly clear that the Messiah will return to earth and occupy the throne of David. He entered Jerusalem before as a humble servant on a donkey. Revelation 19:11 declares how He will next make His entrance — on a white horse in victorious splendor.

Hallelujah! My dear sibling in Christ, as surely as Jesus died and rose again, He will return. Everything must be fulfilled. After Christ's adamant reassurance, Luke 24:45 records something magnificent: "Then he opened their minds so they could under-stand the Scriptures." I'm not sure original definitions get much better than the one for *understand* in Luke 24:45. Meditate on this definition: "The comprehending activity of the mind denoted by *suniemi* entails the as-sembling of individual facts into an orga-nized whole, as collecting the pieces of a puzzle and putting them together. The mind grasps concepts and sees the proper relationship between them." Beloved, I believe Christ can do the same thing for you and me! No, we will never be infallible in our understanding, but again and again the Holy Spirit urges us to pray for spiritual wisdom and understanding. (See Col. 1:9–10; 2:2–3; Eph. 1:17–18)

That's plenty to ignite our excitement! For the rest of our days, let's ask Him to open our minds, putting one puzzle piece after another in our hands, causing the unspeakable joy of seeing how they fit together. May we shout for joy at times! Weep with wonder at others! May we spend the days of our lives fitting together one piece after another until all we lack is the vivid picture of His perfect face. Oh, happy day!

As the curtain drops on resurrection night, the disciples finally saw the puzzle pieces coming together. They began to comprehend why the plan necessitated Christ's suffering and His resurrection from the dead. Like a small battalion of soldiers, they received their marching orders. Preach "repentance and forgiveness of sins . . . in [My] name to all nations, beginning at Jerusalem." I love the next statement: "You are witnesses of these things" (Luke 24:47–48).

And so are we. What they saw with their eyes, we have seen with our hearts. I pray that nothing can keep us from telling.

Luke's account of the evening concludes with the promise of the power and presence of the Holy Spirit. "I will ask the Father, and he will give you another Counselor to be with you forever — the Spirit of truth. . . . I will not leave you as orphans; I will come to you" (John 14:16–18). Very soon Christ's words would be fulfilled. With their minds freshly opened, perhaps they wondered *when,* but I think they no longer wondered *if.*

Luke's Gospel pen, filled by the ink of the Spirit for 24 glorious chapters, appropriately runs dry on a priceless scene. A small band of motley men, whose lives had been turned every which way but loose by Jesus of Nazareth, strained for their last earthly glimpse of Him. From the first page to the last, Luke's entire Gospel has been about glory interrupting the ordinary. They never asked for Jesus. He asked for them — and their lives would never be the same. The last thing they saw was the scars on His feet.

Thirty-three years earlier, the feet of God toddled their first visible prints on earth, a young mother's footprints chasing close behind. The walk grew rough, the path strewn with stones and thorns. Now God incarnate stepped off this planet with feet scarred and bruised. As God predicted at the fall, the ancient serpent struck Christ's heel, but on the day He ascended, all things were under Christ's feet. Jesus Christ walked the way of humanity so humanity could walk the way of God. How beautiful the feet that brought good news.

Not one of those disciples was sorry He had come their way. Their losses were incalculable. Most of their friends. Much of their family. Their jobs. The blessings of their fathers. Physical safety. And now, a leader they could see. Yet they left the Mount of Olives with great joy, continually praising God, for their ordinary lives had been interrupted by glory.

The words of Romans 8:18 became their reality long before each disciple fell prostrate on heaven's floor. The sufferings of this world simply could not compare to the glory He had revealed to them. They, like no others, could say, "The Word became flesh and made his dwelling among us. We have seen his glory, the glory of the One and Only, who came from the Father, full of grace and truth" (John 1:14). It sustained and swelled them long after the visible became invisible. You and I are the spiritual descendants of Peter, James, John, and all the others who offered their lives, not for what they thought or what they hoped, but for what they knew. Whom they knew. Our faith is based on fact, beloved. Never let anyone convince you otherwise.

Jesus the One and Only — the title is His forever. He was the One and Only long before He breathed a soul into humanity, and He will continue to be the One and Only long after the last soul has been judged. He is changeless. But you and I were destined for change. So determined is God to transform us, we cannot draw near Him and remain the same.

As we conclude our journey through Galilee, Jerusalem, and Judea, the question is not, "Is Jesus the One and Only?" Our vote cannot elect Him to a position He already occupies. The question is this: Has Jesus become your One and Only? Is He transcending all else in your life? Is He beyond compare? Your one and only Savior? Your one and only Deliverer? The one and only Lover of your soul? If so, my dear friend, you are being transformed from glory unto glory like Moses who descended the mount of God with face radiant. You may not see it, but others do. That's God's way. May our lives be obscured by the glory of Christ, hidden in the shadow of His cross. And when all is said and done, may our tenure on this planet be characterized by one simple word — Jesus.

There is a Name above all names
Let mine be lost in His
Hide me in His crimson heart
O, way of secret bliss!
One life alone is worth the find
Nail mine onto the tree
Till Jesus ever shining here
Is all beheld in me.
Bring Him forth each day I live
And leave me in the tomb
I seek no other glory here
Make not the smallest room.
Blessed anonymity!
Count my life but loss.
— Jesus the One and Only —
Tread over me, Dear Cross.

Endnotes

Chapter 2
1. Ronald F. Youngblood, ed., *Nelson's New Illustrated Bible Dictionary* (Nashville: Thomas Nelson, 1995), 883.

Chapter 3
1. Beth Moore, *Things Pondered* (Nashville: Broadman & Holman, 1997), 7.

Chapter 4
1. Youngblood, *Bible Dictionary*, 687.

Chapter 9
1. Ray Vander Laan, *Faith Lessons on the Life and Ministry of the Messiah*, prod. and dir. Bob Garner and Stephen Stiles, vol. 3, video one, "In the Shadow of Herod," 77 min., Focus on the Family, 1996, videocassette.

Chapter 11
1. Robert H. Stein, *Jesus the Messiah: A Survey of the Life of Christ* (Downers Grove, Ill.: InterVarsity Press, 1996), 106.

Chapter 16
1. Dr. Chuck Lynch, *I Should Forgive, But . . .* (Nashville: Word, 1998), 33–34.

Chapter 17
1. Matthew Henry, *Matthew Henry's Commentary on the Whole Bible* (New York: Fleming H. Revell, n.d.), 634.
2. Francis Frangipane, *Exposing the Accuser of the Brethren* (Cedar Rapids, Iowa: Arrow Publications, 1991), 37.

Chapter 20
1. Spiros Zodhiates, ed., *The Hebrew-Greek Key Study Bible* (Chattanooga, Tenn.: AMG Publishers, 1996), 1647.

Chapter 21
1. Zodhiates, ed. *The Hebrew-Greek Key Study Bible*, 1583.

Chapter 24
1. Jim Cymbala, *Fresh Wind, Fresh Fire* (Grand Rapids, Mich.: Zondervan Publishing House, 1997), 19.

Chapter 32
1. Herbert Lockyer, *All the Parables of the Bible* (Grand Rapids, Mich.: Zondervan, 1963), 261–62.
2. Ibid., 262.

Chapter 40

1. Youngblood, *Bible Dictionary*, 759-60.

Chapter 43

1. See www.persecution.net.

Chapter 45

1. Frank E. Gaebelein, ed., *The Expositor's Bible Commentary* (Grand Rapids, Mich.: Zondervan, 1984), 1026.
2. Kevin Howard and Marvin Rosenthal, *The Feasts of the Lord* (Orlando, Fla.: Zion's Hope, Inc., 1997), 55.
3. Ibid., 57.

Chapter 47

1. Colin Brown, *The New International Dictionary of New Testament Theology* (Grand Rapids, Mich.: Zondervan, 1986), 614.

Chapter 50

1. Horatio G. Spafford, "It Is Well with My Soul," public domain.

Chapter 51

1. Gaebelein, *Bible Commentary*, 1049.